"十三五"职业教育国家规划教材

21世纪高职高专规划教材

酒店管理系列

餐饮服务

（双语）

主　编　郭贵荣　方　敏　王　昭

副主编　杨轶哲　杨月其

FOOD AND BEVERAGE SERVICE

中国人民大学出版社

·北京·

图书在版编目（CIP）数据

餐饮服务：汉文、英文 / 郭贵荣，方敏，王昭主编 .—北京：中国人民大学出版社，2019.8
21 世纪高职高专规划教材 . 酒店管理系列
ISBN 978-7-300-27403-4

Ⅰ. ①餐… Ⅱ. ①郭… ②方… ③王… Ⅲ. ①饮食业 – 商业服务 – 高等职业教育 – 教材 – 汉、英
Ⅳ. ① F719.3

中国版本图书馆 CIP 数据核字（2019）第 190967 号

"十三五"职业教育国家规划教材
21 世纪高职高专规划教材 · 酒店管理系列
餐饮服务（双语）
主　编　郭贵荣　方　敏　王　昭
副主编　杨轶哲　杨月其
Canyin Fuwu (Shuangyu)

出版发行	中国人民大学出版社		
社　址	北京中关村大街 31 号	邮政编码	100080
电　话	010–62511242（总编室）		010–62511770（质管部）
	010–82501766（邮购部）		010–62514148（门市部）
	010–62515195（发行公司）		010–62515275（盗版举报）
网　址	http://www.crup.com.cn		
经　销	新华书店		
印　刷	唐山玺诚印务有限公司		
开　本	787 mm × 1092 mm　1/16	版　次	2019 年 8 月第 1 版
印　张	13 插页 1	印　次	2024 年 12 月第 6 次印刷
字　数	256 000	定　价	35.00 元

前言
PREFACE

旅游市场的全面国际化给餐饮服务行业带来了巨大的机遇与挑战，这就要求餐饮行业经营管理与提供的各项服务日益规范化与国际化，尤其是餐饮服务工作人员要能够熟练地运用双语为客人提供标准化与个性化服务。

随着教学改革的不断深入，餐饮服务教学在课程体系、教学内容、教学手段和教学模式等方面都发生了许多新的变化。党的二十大报告明确指出，要培养造就大批德才兼备的高素质人才，加快建设世界重要人才中心和创新高地。为顺应餐饮服务人才专业化、时代化、国际化培养的需求，我们着手编写一本既能涵盖中高职餐饮服务实践教学需要的基础理论与技能，又能反映时代特色和行业需要的双语教材。本书根据餐饮企业岗位设置，基于岗位工作过程，对于与客人有着直接接触的一线岗位的服务语言、服务流程用双语进行了分析和描述，并根据工作岗位会遇到的很多普遍问题设置了较多的情景模拟，让学习者能够在真实的环境中锻炼各方面的技能，提高服务质量与水平。

依据教育部在 2020 年 5 月 28 日印发的《高等学校课程思政建设指导纲要》，本书在编写时以立德树人为目标，梳理相关课程思政内容、元素等信息，把正确的价值观融入知识的传授和能力、素养的培养中，全面推进课程思政建设。

本书共分为 8 个项目，包括：认识餐饮服务（Cognition of Catering Services），预订、问候及领位服务（Reservation, Greeting, Hostess Service），餐前准备（Preparation），摆台（Table Setting），点餐服务（Order Service），酒水服务（Beverage Service），席间服务（Table Service），结账和送客服务（Handling Payment and Seeing off Guests）。每个项目下又分为若干个任务，大部分任务都包括任务评价（Task Evaluation）和拓展阅读（Extended Reading）等内容。本书重视培养学习者的学习能力，训练学习者的服务技能。任务评价环节中的任务设置能够使学习者通过特定情景的模拟训练，解决工作中可能会遇到的问题，灵活运用相应流程的服务技巧。本书清晰地展示了餐饮服务中各岗位的工作和服务技能，供学习者模仿和练习。

本书项目一、项目三、项目六由方敏、王昭老师完成，项目二、项目四、项目五由郭贵荣、杨轶哲老师完成；项目七、项目八由郭贵荣、王昭、杨月其老师完成。

目前，针对餐饮服务与管理方面的中文教材有很多，但关于餐饮服务的双语教材却寥寥无几，本书正是顺应餐饮服务人才国际化培养的需求而专门编写的，具有较大的实用性。本书既可以作为餐饮服务教学的学生指导用书，也可以作为餐饮企业人员的培训和学习资料。

对于本书的疏漏和不足之处，敬请各位专家和广大读者批评指正。

编者

目 录
CONTENTS

项目一　认识餐饮服务 / 1

Project 1　Cognition of Catering Service / 1

项目二　预订、问候及领位服务 / 33

Project 2　Reservation, Greeting, Hostess Service / 33

项目三　餐前准备 / 55

Project 3　Preparation / 55

项目四　摆台 / 79

Project 4　Table Setting / 79

项目五　点餐服务 / 111

Project 5　Order Service / 111

项目六　酒水服务 / 133

Project 6　Beverage Service / 133

项目七　席间服务 / 155

Project 7　Table Service / 155

项目八　结账和送客服务 / 181

Project 8　Handling Payment and Seeing off Guests / 181

参考文献 References / 202

Project 1

Cognition of Catering Service

项目一

认识餐饮服务

项目概述 PROJECT SUMMARY

众所周知，餐饮业属于消费性服务业，与其他行业相比有着很大的差异。因此，在学习并从事餐饮服务业之前，我们有必要了解餐饮服务的基本概念、基础知识，只有这样我们才能为客人提供优质的服务。

餐饮服务需要亲切热忱的态度，服务人员要时时刻刻为客人着想，使客人有宾至如归的感觉。餐饮服务质量是餐厅的灵魂，更是餐厅所销售的主要产品。作为餐饮从业者，我们要了解餐饮服务的真谛，了解服务对餐厅经营的重要性。

餐饮服务从业者要想将自己的工作做到完美，就必须具备餐饮服务的专业知识和基本素质。从开始提供服务到服务结束的每一个阶段都是环环相扣的，这关系到餐厅服务品质的制定和实施。

目前，常见的餐饮服务方式可统分为中餐服务方式和西餐服务方式，每种服务方式各有详细的分类和特点。

项目目标 PROJECT OBJECTS

知识目标：了解餐饮服务的概念及特性；了解餐饮服务品质的内涵；掌握从事餐饮服务应具备的基本技能；掌握中、西餐的服务方式。

技能目标：能够根据餐厅的规模设计餐厅的组织架构。

素养目标：坚定文化自信、民族自信；树立自我提高、爱岗敬业意识；激发对餐饮行业的热爱，树立餐饮服务意识。

任务一：餐饮服务概述
Task 1: An Overview of Catering Services

案例导入

王先生第一次入住泰国东方饭店时感觉很不错，所以，他第二次到泰国出差时仍选择了东方饭店。

当他走进餐厅时，餐厅服务人员向他微笑致意并问道："王先生还要坐在靠窗的老位子吗？"王先生感到十分吃惊，心想尽管他不是第一次在这里吃饭，但最近一次也有一年多了，难道这里的服务员记忆力这么好？

看到他惊讶的样子，服务员主动解释说："我刚刚查过电脑记录，您在去年的6月8日，在靠近第二个窗口的位子上用过早餐。"

王先生听后兴奋地说道："老位子！老位子！"

服务员接着问道："老菜单，一个三明治、一杯咖啡、一个鸡蛋？"

王先生已不再惊讶了："老菜单，就要老菜单！"

上餐时餐厅赠送给王先生一碟小菜，他是第一次看到，就问："这是什么？"

服务员马上后退两步说："这是我们的特色小菜，赠送给您品尝，希望您喜欢。"

服务员为什么要先后退两步呢？他是怕自己说话时口水不小心落在客人的食物上。这种注意细节的服务不要说在一般酒店，就是在顶级饭店，对于常住酒店的王先生来说都很少遇到。

后来，王先生有两年没有再到泰国去。在他生日时，收到一封东方饭店发来的生日贺卡，并附上一封信，表示东方饭店全体员工十分想念他，希望能再次见到他。王先生当时激动得热泪盈眶，发誓再到泰国去，一定要住在东方饭店，并且要说服所有的朋友像他一样选择东方饭店。

从这个案例中我们可以得到什么启示？

知识准备

一、餐饮服务的概念及特性 The concept and characteristics of catering services

餐饮业所销售的不仅是餐食和饮料，同时包括餐厅的空间、装潢、设备以及服务。

Restaurants sell not only meals and drinks, but also restaurant space, decorations, equipments and services.

服务是一种态度，是在特定的时间和地点及时去了解并提供客人所需，让客人有宾至如归的感觉。服务必须是发自内心、表现于外的具体呈现。

Service is an attitude of knowing and providing what guests need at a specific time and place to make them feel at home. The service impulsion must be from the heart, manifests in the outside concrete appearance.

服务对客人而言是一种感觉。客人置身于餐厅中，对服务的需求是十分广泛且抽象的，对服务的评价也会随环境、心境的变化而有所不同。对于服务的特性，各专家给出了不同的说法，在这里我们总结为以下 4 点：

Service is a kind of feeling to the customer. When the customer is in the restaurant, the demand for the service is very extensive and abstract, and the evaluation of the service will be different with the change of the environment and mood. Experts have given different accounts of the nature of the service. Here we summarize the following four points:

（一）无形性 Intangibility

服务的无形性是指服务不是具象的。

The intangible service refers to the service that is not specific.

（二）异质性 Heterogeneity

服务的异质性是指不同服务人员对客人提供的服务会有所不同，同一服务人员对不同客人提供的服务也会有所不同。

The heterogeneity of service means that the service provided to the guests by different service personnel will be different, and the service provided by the same waiter to different customers also will be different.

（三）不可分割性 Indivisibility

提供服务的人和设备必须与客人的需求同时出现，服务有着不可分割的特性。

Service providers and equipment must come together with the customers' demand, with its indivisible characteristics.

（四）易逝性 Perishability

服务是稍纵即逝的，是无法储存的。

Service is fleeting and cannot be stored.

二、餐饮服务的品质 The quality of catering services

餐饮服务的品质包括：服务效率、适时服务、与客人沟通良好、服务一致性、良好的服务态度、具备专业知识、服务具有弹性、建立顾客反馈系统。

The quality of catering services includes: service efficiency, timely service, good communication with guests, consistency of service, good service attitude, professional knowledge of service personnel, flexibility of service, and establishment of customer feedback system.

（一）服务效率 Service efficiency

对餐厅服务人员而言，在工作中表现快速而顺畅，能够使客人感到舒适自在。在餐厅营业前做好相应的准备工作，团队成员配合良好，能使工作效率提高，从而顺利完成服务接待工作。

For restaurant service personnel, the performance of a rapid and smooth rhythm in the work can make guests feel comfortable. That the service personnel make the corresponding preparation work before the restaurant is open and the team members cooperate well, can make the working efficiency improve, thus smoothly completing the service reception work.

（二）适时服务 Timely service

一名优秀的服务人员要能够随时观察并预知客人的潜在需求，主动并适时地提供适当的服务。

A good service personnel should be able to observe and predict the potential needs of guests, to deliver appropriate services initiatively at proper time.

（三）与客人沟通良好 Good communication with guests

服务人员与客人的沟通方式会因为餐厅类型不同而有所差异，同时，服务人员应针对不同类型的客人适时调整自己的沟通方式。若客人刻意保持与服务人员的距离，不愿多沟通，那么服务人员就尽量不要打扰客人。

The ways of communication between service personnel and guests will vary according to the types of restaurant. At the same time, the service personnel should adjust their communication methods according to different types of guests. If guests deliberately maintain a distance from service personnel and do not want to do more communication, then service personnel should not disturb guests as far as possible.

（四）服务一致性 Consistency of service

若客人喜欢餐厅的食物、环境、服务，就会再度光临餐厅。如果餐厅无法提供一致性、高水准的食物和服务，客源就会逐渐流失。服务的一致性是指针对每一位客人在每一个时刻，均能提供一致的高品质服务。

If guests like the restaurant’s food, environment and service, then they will come to the restaurant again. If the restaurant can not provide a consistent standard of food and service, the guests will gradually leave. Consistency of service means that every guest can be provided with consistent high quality services at every moment.

（五）良好的服务态度 Good service attitude

良好的服务态度包括服务人员态度主动积极、服务殷勤周到、服务技巧熟练等。

Good service attitude includes active attitude, courteous service, proficient service skills and so on.

（六）具备专业知识 Professional knowledge of service personnel

服务人员必须对餐厅所提供的产品进行充分了解，才能介绍或回答客人提出的问题。

The service personnel must have a good understanding of the products provided in the restaurant in order to introduce or answer guests' questions.

（七）服务具有弹性 Flexibility of service

虽然餐厅各岗位均有各自的标准作业流程（SOP），但有时候服务规则必须根据实际情况做出调整。服务人员应根据实际情况来调整服务策略。

Although restaurant positions have their own standard operating procedures(SOP), sometimes service rules must be adjusted to the actual situation. The service personnel should adjust the service strategy according to the actual situation.

（八）建立顾客反馈系统 Establishment of customer feedback system

餐厅应建立顾客反馈机制和系统，对于顾客反馈的问题进行积极调查并做出回应，以此作为改进服务的依据。

Restaurant should establish customer feedback mechanism and system, and actively investigate and respond to customer's feedback which should be the basis for service improvement.

三、餐饮部组织架构 Organizational structure of food and beverage department

表 1.1　　餐饮部组织架构表

Organization Form of Food and Beverage Department

岗位名称 Position	上下级隶属 Subordinate	岗位职责简述 Job Description
餐饮部经理 Manager of F&B Department	直接上级：餐饮总监 Immediate Superior: F&B Director 直接下级：餐饮部副经理 Direct Subordinate: Vice Manager of F&B Department	制定并实施本餐厅工作计划和经营预算；督导餐厅的日常运转和管理；确保为客人提供优质、高效的服务并进行成本控制 To formulate and implement the restaurant's work plan and operating budget; Supervise the daily operation and management of the restaurant; Ensure to provide high quality and efficient service to guests and control cost

续前表

岗位名称 Position	上下级隶属 Subordinate	岗位职责简述 Job Description
餐饮部副经理 Vice Manager of F&B Department	直接上级：餐饮部经理 Immediate Superior:Manager of F&B Department 直接下级：餐厅主管 Direct Subordinate: Restaurant Supervisor	负责餐厅人力、物品管理；负责和重要客人沟通；及时反馈客人投诉的信息 Responsible for the management of restaurant staff and items; Responsible for communicating with VIP guests; To give feedback to guest's complaints timely
餐厅主管 Restaurant Supervisor	直接上级：餐饮部副经理 Immediate Superior: Vice Manager of F&B Department 直接下级：餐厅领班 Direct Subordinate: Headwaiter	协助餐饮部副经理做好各项工作；做好员工培训工作 Assist the vice manager of F&B department to do the job well; Do a good job in staff training
餐厅领班 Headwaiter	直接上级：餐厅主管 Immediate Superior: Restaurant Supervisor 直接下级：餐厅服务员 Direct Subordinates: Waiter	协助餐厅主管做好服务工作，确保餐厅服务质量 Assist restaurant supervisor to ensure the quality of restaurant service
餐饮部文员 F&B Clerk	直接上级：餐饮部经理 Immediate Superior: Manager of F&B Department	完善餐饮部经理交代的各项工作 Improve the work assigned by the manager of F&B department
餐厅服务员 Waiter	直接上级：餐厅领班 Immediate Superior: Headwaiter	负责向客人提供高质量服务 Responsible for providing high quality service to guests
吧员 Bar Attendant	直接上级：餐厅领班 Immediate Superior: Headwaiter	负责酒水的领用、发放；负责酒水、饮料的台账 Responsible for the reception and distribution of drinks; Responsible for beverage ledger
传菜员 Pantry Helper	直接上级：餐厅领班 Immediate Superior: Headwaiter	负责餐厅菜肴传递工作；做好餐饮服务后勤工作 Responsible for the restaurant dishes accessories transfer work; Do a good job in catering services logistics
保洁 House Keeper	直接上级：餐厅领班 Immediate Superior: Headwaiter	负责餐厅公共区域的环境卫生 Responsible for the environmental sanitation of the public area of the restaurant

任务实施

第一步：教师介绍什么是餐饮服务、餐饮服务的特性及餐饮服务的品质。

Step 1: The teacher introduces the concept，characteristics and qualities of the catering services.

第二步：教师介绍不同类型餐厅的组织架构及相应的岗位职责。

Step 2: The teacher introduces the organizational structure of different types of restaurants and the corresponding job responsibilities.

第三步：以小组（5 人 1 组）为单位，根据教师给定的餐厅规模及性质，规划该餐厅的组织架构。

Step 3: According to the size and nature of the restaurant given by the teacher, the organizational structure of the restaurant should be changed according to the group (5 people in 1 group).

任务评价

表 1.2　　××餐厅组织架构评价表

The Evaluation Form of ××Restaurant Organizational Structure

评价事项 Evaluation Items	评价结果 Evaluation Result			备注 Notes
	达成 Achieve	部分达成 Partly Achieve	未达成 Fail	
岗位设置合理 Reasonable post setting				
岗位职责明确 Clear job responsibilities				
组织结构明晰 Clear organizational structure				

拓展阅读

微笑服务在酒店中的作用

微笑，它同眼神一样是无声的语言，是人际交往中的“润滑剂”，是人们表达愉快之情的感情外露，是善良、友好、赞美的象征。一种有分寸的微笑，再配上优雅的举止，往往比有声语言更有魅力，在特定场合可以收到“此时无声胜有声”的效果。

“今天你对客人微笑了吗？”这是美国希尔顿酒店集团董事长康拉德·希尔顿在50多年里，不断地在各地希尔顿酒店视察业务时经常问员工的一句话。他说：“酒店里第一流的设备很重要，而第一流的服务员的微笑更重要。缺少了服务员的美好微笑，就好比花园里失去了春日的太阳和暖风。假如我是顾客，我宁愿住进那些虽然只有残旧地毯，却处处可见到微笑的旅馆，而不愿走进一家只有一流设备而没有微笑的饭店。”正是微笑的魅力，帮助希尔顿酒店渡过了20世纪30年代美国经济大萧条时期，获得了快速大发展。

泰国曼谷的东方饭店曾数次摘取“世界十佳饭店”的桂冠，其成功的秘诀之一就是把“笑容可掬”列入迎宾接待的规范。

微笑是一门学问，又是一门艺术，是优质服务的重要内容之一，对提高酒店的声誉和获得最佳的经济及社会效益，起着十分重要的作用。

（1）微笑是自信的象征。一个人要充分尊重自己，展现自己存在的价值，必须重视强化自我形象，自信在微笑中得到了全面的体现。

（2）微笑是礼仪修养的充分展现。一个有知识、重礼仪、懂礼貌的人必然十分尊重别人。即使是陌路相逢的人，他也不会吝啬把微笑当作礼物，慷慨地奉献给别人。

（3）微笑是和睦相处的反映。现实生活是多姿多彩的，既有风和日丽也有雨雪交加，但是只要我们脸上充满微笑，就会使人们感到愉快、融洽、平和。

（4）微笑是心理健康的标志。一个心理健康的人，定能将美好的情操、愉快的心境、温暖的情谊变成微笑传递给他人。

任务二：餐饮服务人员职业素养要求

Task 2: The Quality Requirements of Food and Beverage Service Staff

案例导入

王经理从事酒店工作20年，从服务员开始一步一步做起，现在担任某五星级酒店总经理。在20年的工作经历中，他不断提高自己的学历层次和综合素质，从只有初中学历到自考本科文凭，并且还熟练掌握英语、日语，对人热情、周到、细致，受到客人、同事、上司的一致好评。

思考讨论：如果你是客人，你希望看到餐厅服务员具备什么形象？

知识准备

一、仪容仪表 Grooming

餐饮服务一经开始就无法退换，这就要求每位服务人员注意自己的形象举止，要拥有仪容端庄、仪表得体的服务礼仪。

The catering service cannot be replaced once it is started. It requires every service staff to pay attention to their image behavior, which include decent appearance and behavior in service etiquette.

（一）仪容规范标准 Facial expression requirements

（1）在岗时应精神饱满，表情自然，面带微笑。

Employees should be full of energy, natural expression and smile.

（2）眼睛应有神，体现出热情、礼貌、友善、诚恳。

The eyes should show enthusiasm, courtesy, kindness and sincerity.

（3）说话时应语气平和，语调亲切，不可过分夸张。

When you speak, you should have a peaceful and friendly tone which is not over-exaggerated.

（4）与客人交谈时，目光应自然平视，不应上下打量客人。

When you talk with guests, you should look naturally and do not look up and down.

（5）遇事从容大方、不卑不亢。

Neither overbearing nor servile and be easy to deal with troubles.

（二）仪表规范标准 Standard behavior requirements

1. 服装 Clothes

（1）酒店全体员工按规定统一着制服，并穿戴整齐。

All the restaurant staff should wear clean, ironed and fully accessorized uniform.

（2）制服应得体挺括，不应有褶皱、破损、污渍，领子、袖口、裤脚要保持清洁，不应挽袖子或裤腿。

The uniform should be clean, ironed, no wrinkles, damages and stains, and do not roll up your sleeve or trouser legs.

（3）工号牌要佩戴在上衣的左胸上方，工号牌水平，不得歪斜。

The name tag should be in the left of the top uniform, and should not be skewed.

（4）制服扣子应齐全、无松动。

The uniform buttons should be complete and free of loose.

（5）男员工着深色（黑色或深蓝色）袜子、女员工着肉色丝袜，袜子不应有破洞或抽丝，应每天换洗。

Male staff should wear dark（black or dark blue）socks, and the female staff should wear flesh-colored silk stockings. Socks should not be torn, and should be changed every day.

（6）鞋子应保持干净、不变形、无破损，不得有污点、灰尘；鞋带要系好，不可拖拉于地面。

The shoes should be clean, indeformable and without breakage, stain or dust. The shoelace should be well knoted, and should not be loosed on the ground.

（7）男员工头发分缝要齐，不得留大鬓角，前发不盖额、侧发不盖耳、后发不盖领。

Male staff's hair should be short and combed. Sideburns is not allowed. The hair should not cover neck, ears or shoulders.

（8）女员工长发应盘起，发髻不宜过高或过低，以不过衣领为标准。短发不能过领，虚发应用发胶定型。额前头发不可挡住视线，头发颜色应自然，不要另类。

For female staff, long hair should be coiled up. And the bun should not be too high or too low (should higher than the collar). Short hair should not below the collar. If the hair is massy, the staff should use hair spray to control the appearance. At last, the hair color should be natural and not weird.

2. 仪态 Manners & etiquette

仪态是人在行为中的姿势和风度，对酒店的员工来说，仪态和仪容仪表一样重要。

Manners & etiquette is the posture and presence of a person in action, which is as important to a hotel employee as grooming.

3. 站姿 Standing posture

（1）应自然挺拔，不可僵硬呆板，两眼平视前方。

The standing posture should be natural and upright, not stiff, looking straight ahead.

（2）身体直立，应把重心放在两脚中间，男员工双脚自然分开，基本与肩同宽，女员工则双脚自然并拢。

The body should be upright. Male staff's feet are naturally separated to keep the shoulder-width apart. Female staff close their feet naturally.

（3）挺胸收腹，两肩放平。

Keep your shoulders flat, chest slightly out and abdomen in.

（4）餐饮服务员双手应自然交叉在前，右手轻握左手的手腕。

The restaurant service personnel should cross hands naturally, with the right hand holding the left hand's wrist.

（5）站立时双手不可抱在胸前、叉腰，双手不可插在口袋中。

Never cross your arms on your chest or stand akimbo, and also do not put the hands in your pockets.

4. 走姿 Walking posture

（1）行走时上体要保持正直，身体重心可稍向前倾，头部要端正，双目平视，肩部放松。

While walking, keep your body upright and lean slightly forward. Keep the head upright, look straight ahead and relax your shoulders.

（2）两臂自然摆动，行走时步伐要轻稳。

Wiggle two arms naturally, and walk with a gentle pace.

（3）步幅不要过大，步速不要过快。

Don't step too far, and don't walk too fast.

二、餐厅服务人员基本素质 Service qualities of restaurant staff

随着竞争的日趋激烈，客人对餐饮服务质量的要求越来越高，而餐饮服务质量的提高有赖于高素质的员工。在餐饮业工作，不仅需要具备菜肴与饮料知识，还需要具备一定的素质和能力。

With the fierce competition, guests pay more attention on F&B service quality. The improvement of the quality of catering services depends on the high quality staff. The high quality staff not only need to know well about food and beverage knowledge, but also need to have professional quality and ability.

（一）服务态度要求 Requirements of attitudes

服务态度取决于员工的主动性、创造性、积极性、责任感和素质。

Service attitudes depend on staff's initiativity, creativity, positivity, responsibility and quality.

1. 主动 Initiativity

餐饮服务人员应牢固树立“宾客至上、服务第一”的专业意识。凡是客人需要的，要发现后立即主动、及时地予以解决，做到眼勤、口勤、手勤、脚勤、心勤，把服务工作做在客人开口之前。

Catering service personnel should firmly establish the “guest first, service first” professional awareness. Whether it's your job or not, when guests need,each staff should take the initiative to solve the problem immediately after finding it. Each service should be done before guests ask for.

2. 热情 Enthusiasm

餐饮服务人员在服务工作中应热爱本职工作，热爱自己的服务对象，像对待亲友一样为客人服务，做到面带微笑、精神饱满、诚恳待人、助人为乐。

F&B service staff should love the job and love the guests, and treat the guests as their relatives and friends. They should always smile, full of spirit and energy and be kindly and helpful.

3. 耐心 Patience

餐饮服务人员在为各种不同类型的客人服务时，应有耐心。服务人员应善于揣摩客人的消费心理，对于他们提出的所有问题，都应耐心解答，百问不厌；并能虚心听取客人的意见和建议，对事情不推诿。与客人发生矛盾时，应尊重客人，并有较强的自律能力，做到心平气和、耐心解释。

F&B service staff should have patience when serving the guests. Service staff should try to figure out the guests' consumption psychology, and be able to listen to the guests' opinions and suggestions. When conflicting with the guests, the staff should respect the guests, and have strong self-discipline, be calm and be patient.

4. 周到 Consideration

在服务前，服务人员应做好充分的准备工作，对服务工作制定细致、周到的计划；在服务时，应仔细观察，及时发现并满足客人的需求；在服务结束时，应认真征求客人的意见或建议，并及时给予反馈，以将服务工作做得更好。

Before work, F&B service staff should make full preparations, work out the detailed and thorough plan. When serving guests, the staff should observe and try to meet the needs of guests. At the end of the service, they should conscientiously solicit the opinions, suggestions of guests in order to provide better service.

（二）服务知识要求 Requirements of service knowledge

餐饮服务人员应具有较广的知识面。

F&B service staff should have a broad scope of knowledge.

1. 基础知识 Basic knowledge

主要有员工守则、服务意识、礼貌礼节、职业道德、食品安全与卫生、服务心理学、外语知识等。

The basic knowledge includes staff regulations, service consciousness, etiquette, professional morality, food safety, service psychology and foreign language.

2. 专业知识 Professional knowledge

主要有岗位职责、工作程序、运转表单、管理制度、设施设备的使用与保养、饭店的服务项目及营业时间、沟通技巧等。

The staff should be familiar with duty responsibilities, work procedures, rotating forms, management regulations, facility operation and protection, restaurant's services & operation time, communication skills.

3. 相关知识 Relating knowledge

主要有宗教知识、哲学、美学、文学、艺术、法律，各国的历史地理、习俗和礼仪、民俗与旅游景点及交通等。

It includes religion knowledge, philosophy, aesthetic, literature, art, law, history and geography, custom and etiquette, folk culture, tourist attractions and traffic etc.

（三）服务能力要求 Requirements of skills

1. 语言能力 Language skills

餐饮服务人员在工作中要做到：语言要文明、礼貌、简明、清晰；提倡讲普通话。此外，服务人员还应掌握一定的外语，如英语、日语。

The staff's language should be civilized, polite, clear and simple in their work; the staff should grasp the Mandarin and should master some foreign languages such as English and Japanese if necessary.

2. 沟通能力 Communication skills

餐饮服务人员必须具备良好的沟通能力，减少因沟通不畅而导致的投诉和问题。注意的是：沟通因人而异，语言要得当。

The service staff should have great communication skills which could reduce the complaints and problems from the guests, and pay attention to serving different people with different and properly words.

3. 反应能力 Reaction capabilities

餐饮服务人员必须具备灵活的应变能力，遇事冷静，及时应变，妥善处理。注意：客人性别、年龄、国籍、兴趣爱好等的不同，会导致不同的服务要求和期望。

F&B department staff should be flexible and calm. They should have the ability of settling the crisis and guests' complaint. Pay attention that the guests' different gender, age, nationality and habits will result different service needs and expectation.

4. 推销能力 Promotion skills

餐饮服务人员必须根据客人的爱好、习惯及消费能力灵活推销，以尽力提高客人的消费水平，从而提高餐饮部的经济效益。

The restaurant staff should have good promotion skills to increase the consumption level of guests according to the guests' interest, habits and consumption abilities. In doing so, the F&B department's economic benefits could be enhanced.

5. 技术能力 Technical skills

技术能力是指餐厅服务员在提供服务时显现出的技巧和能力，它不仅能提高工作效率，保证餐厅服务的规格标准，更可给客人带来赏心悦目的感受。

Technical ability refers to the restaurant staff's skills and abilities when providing the service, which could not only improve the work efficiency, guarantee the specification of the restaurant service standards, but also bring cheerness and pleasance to the guests.

6. 观察能力 Observation ability

餐厅服务质量的好坏取决于客人在享受服务后的生理、心理感受，即客人需求的满足程度。这就要求服务人员在为客人提供服务时具备敏锐的观察能力，随时关注客人的需求并给予及时满足。

Restaurant service quality depends on the physiological and psychological feelings of the guests after receiving the service, which is how satisfied the guests are. It requires that the service staff should have the observation ability, pay more attention to the demands of the guests and meet guests' request timely.

7. 记忆能力 Memorizing ability

餐厅服务人员通过观察了解到的客人需求信息，除了应及时给予满足之外，还应加以记忆，当这位客人下次光临时，服务人员即可提供有针对性的个性化服务，这无疑会提高客人的满意度。

Restaurant staff should have excellent memorizing ability to remember the information about guests' needs. When the guests come again, the service staff could provide targeted personalized service, which will undoubtedly improve the satisfaction of the guests.

8. 自律能力 Self-discipline ability

自律能力是指餐厅服务人员在工作过程中的自我控制能力。服务人员应遵守餐厅的员工守则等管理制度，明确知道在何时、何地能够做什么，不能够做什么。

Self-discipline refers to the restaurant staff's self-controlling ability during the working process. Service personnel should abide by the management system, such as knowing clearly what things should be done or not be done anytime and anywhere.

9. 服从与协调能力 Obeying and coordinating ability

餐厅服务人员对直接上级的指令应无条件服从并切实执行。与此同时，服务人员还必须对客人提出的要求予以满足，但应服从有度，即满足客人符合传统道德观念和社会主义精神文明的合理需求。

Restaurant staff should obey the orders of direct supervisor. At the same time, they also must satisfy the guests' request. However, they should obey moderately, which meets the guests' reasonable requests of traditional moral concepts and socialist spiritual civilization.

（四）身体素质要求 Physical quality

1. 身体健康 Be healthy

餐饮从业人员必须身体健康，定期体检，取得卫生防疫部门核发的健康证。如患有不适宜从事餐厅服务工作的疾病，应调离岗位。

Catering service staff must be in good health, do the regular physical examination, and obtain health certificate issued by the health and epidemic prevention department. If someone is not suitable for the work, then another job should be provided for him.

2. 体格健壮 Be strong

餐饮服务工作的劳动强度较大，餐厅服务人员的站立、行走及餐厅服务等必须具有一定的腿力、臂力和腰力等，因此，餐饮从业人员必须拥有健壮的体格才能胜任工作。

The labor intensity of catering service work is relatively large. Restaurant service staff must have certain leg strength, arm strength and waist strength when standing, walking and serving in the restaurant. Therefore, catering service staff must have a robust physique to be competent for the work.

任务实施

第一步：课前教师给学生 8～10 个案例，学生被分为 8 个小组，每个案例对应一项“餐饮从业人员的服务能力要求”内容，要求学生以小组形式讨论分析，各组总结出各个案例对应的能力要求。

Step 1: The teacher will give students 8–10 cases before class, and the students are divided into 8 groups. Each case expresses one requirement of ability of F&B department staff. The teacher should ask students to discuss and analyze in groups, and summarize the corresponding ability requirement of each case.

第二步：教师导入本节内容，并抽取 1 个小组（每个小组选其中 1 个案例）进行现场模拟表演。

Step 2: The teacher introduces this section and selects one group(each group should choose one case) to do the simulation exercise.

第三步：教师讲授本节内容，并带领学生分析案例，给出正确答案。各小组进行对照检查。

Step 3: The teacher gives the lecture and leads the students to analyze the cases and gives the correct answers. Each group carries on the comparison inspection.

任务评价

表 1.3　　餐饮从业人员素质要求评价表

The Evaluation Form of the Quality Requirements of Food and Beverage Service Staff

评价事项 Evaluation Items	评价结果 Evaluation Result			备注 Notes
	达成 Achieve	部分达成 Partly Achieve	未达成 Fail	
情节还原完整 The content is authentic and the plot is complete				
服务礼仪符合情景，用语规范、表述正确 The service etiquette conforms to the situation, and the expression is normative and correct				
案例分析方法得当，逻辑性强 The case analysis method is appropriate and logical				
案例分析简述清晰，分析正确 The case analysis is clear and correct				
分工明确，团队协作 The division of labor is clear, and the teamwork operates well				

拓展阅读

团队建设的有效途径

1. 设定目标

这里旨在强调个人和团队清晰目标的重要性。团队成员参与行动计划去识别成功和失败的方法并实现目标，是为了增强团队成员的积极性并培养其主人翁精神。通过确定具体的结果，整个团队可以据此来考量进度。

2. 角色阐述

这里重点强调提高团队成员对自身或他人角色的理解，旨在减少歧义并在定义和调整角色的过程中培养他们对组织结构重要性的理解。同时，也强调团队成员的独立性和在每个小组中，每位成员专注于自己的角色对整个团体成功的重要性。

3. 解决问题

这里强调团队成员确定团队中的主要问题，并共同寻找解决方案，从而提升成员的批判性思维能力。

4. 人际关系

这里旨在强调提升团队成员的合作能力，如给予支持、接受帮助、沟通和分享能力。人际关系冲突较少的团队通常比其他团队更能有效地发挥作用。团队通常会有一个引导者，帮助团队成员建立相互信任和开放交流的氛围。

任务三：中餐服务的形式与特点

Task 3: The Forms and Characteristics of Chinese F&B Service

案例导入

《史记·项羽本纪》中描写的“鸿门宴”，虽然充满刀光剑影，但也透露出当时实际的就餐情况。在这次历史上著名的宴会上，项羽、项伯东向坐，范增南向坐，刘邦北向坐，张良西向侍，这五人便是一人一案。如果他们围坐一张食床的话，项庄的剑对项羽也会产生危险。而且，项庄要越过范增才能刺向刘邦。聪明的范增绝不会做如此决定。这说明当时的场景就是他们每人一张食案，分坐于不同的方向，实行分餐制。在他们之间有一片足够的空间让项庄、项伯舞剑。

然而现在，中国人全家吃年夜饭的习俗渐渐形成，在每年的除夕，这个一年一度的中国人最重要的节日中，大江南北的人们，无论是吃饺子还是年糕，都会阖家团圆围坐在一起，菜肴全部放在一个桌上，全家人共同吃上一顿其乐融融的年夜饭。

进餐方式的变化是根据不同时期的地理、文化、政治因素的相互交错影响而形成的。那么，现代中餐服务还有其他的形式吗？

知识准备

一、中餐服务的形式 The forms of Chinese F&B service

中餐在其长期的发展过程中，逐步形成了一定的服务方式，并使之和菜肴的特点相适应。同时，随着人们就餐方式的多样化，中餐的服务方式也经历了一定程度的变革，出现了许多新的方式。目前，中餐服务中常见的服务方式有以下几种：

In its long-term development, Chinese food has gradually formed a certain way of service and adapted itself to the characteristics of dishes. At the same time, with the diversification of people's dining needs, Chinese F&B service has also undergone a certain degree of change, and have new changes. At present, the common service forms of Chinese food and beverage service are as follows:

（一）共餐式服务 Shared meal service

共餐式服务方式是目前团队餐、会议餐以及非正式宴请中常用的一种服务方式。但现有的服务方式改变了传统服务方式的做法，不再由各人自己用筷子去夹菜，而是用公筷，公用勺、匙取菜，或由主人用公用餐具为客人取菜，以示好客。

Shared meal service is a common service method in team meals, conference meals and informal banquets at present. However, the existing service mode has changed the traditional service mode. Instead of using their own chopsticks to pick up dishes, each person will use public chopsticks, public spoon to pick up dishes. Or the host will pick up food for the guests with the communal tableware to show their hospitality.

共餐式服务的优点是客人用餐时比较自由。主人可以为其他客人分菜，其他客人也可以各取所需，用餐气氛比较融洽。用餐过程中所需的服务人员较少，一个服务员可以同时为多桌客人服务。同时，这对服务人员的技术要求不高。但是，共餐式服务也会使客人得到的服务较少。另外，由于所有菜肴一起上，到用餐后半程容易出现杯盘狼藉的现象。

The advantage of the shared meal service is that the guests have more freedom when having a meal. The host can serve the dishes to other guests, or the guests can take what they need, so the dining atmosphere is harmonious. Fewer service personnel are needed during the meal. At the same time, the technical requirements for service personnel are not high. However, the shared meal service will also make the guests get less service. In addition, since all dishes are served together, it is easy to have a mess in the second half of the meal.

（二）转盘式服务 Turntable service

转盘式服务是中餐服务中比较普遍的一种服务方式，适用于直径 1.5m 以上的大圆桌的就餐服务，既可用于便餐服务，也可用于宴会服务。转盘式服务中转盘的配置很有讲究，一般直径 1.5m 的圆桌配备直径 0.8m～0.9m 的转盘，直径 1.8m 的圆桌配备直径 1m～1.2m 的转盘。不管选择多大直径的转盘，每个餐座都至少需要保证离转盘边 0.3m～0.4m 的用餐距离。

Turntable service is a common service mode in Chinese food service, which is applicable to the dining service of large round tables with a diameter of more than 1.5m. It can be used for both light meal service and banquet service. The configuration of the turntable in the turntable service is very particular. In general, a round table with a diameter of 1.5m is equipped with a rotary table with a diameter of 0.8m-0.9m, and a round table with a diameter of 1.8m is equipped with a rotary table with a diameter of 1m-1.2m. Regardless of the diameter of the rotary table, each seat should be at least 0.3m-0.4m away from the rotary table.

转盘式服务的优点是非常适合于团体用餐和中高档宴会用餐，就餐时客人既可以自己取菜，也可以由服务员分菜。传统的分菜服务还具有一定的表演性，但这对服务员的技术要求较高，服务员分菜时不但要一次分完，而且每份菜的菜量要基本相等。另外，分菜时容易弄脏转盘，尤其是在分羹汤和带汁较多的菜肴时。

The advantage of turntable service is very suitable for group dining and upscale banquet dining.

During the meal, guests can either take the food by themselves or have it served by the waiter. Traditional splitting entrees service is also a kind of performance, but it requires the highly skilled staff. The server should not only divide the dishes at one time, but also serve the same amount of dish per person. In addition, it is easy to dirty the turntable, especially when serving soup and dishes with more juice.

（三）分餐式服务 Individual dining service

分餐式服务是近几年发展起来的一种比较流行和受欢迎的服务方式。它是吸收了西餐服务方式的优点并使之与中餐服务相结合的一种服务方式，人们将这种服务方式称为“中餐西吃”，它比较适用于较正规的高档宴会服务。

Individual dining service is a relatively popular service mode developed in recent years. It is a service mode that absorbs the advantages of western food service mode and combines it with Chinese food and beverage service. People call this service as “eat Chinese food in the western way”, which is more suitable for the formal high-end banquet service.

分餐式服务又可分为“边桌服务”和“派菜服务”两种。边桌服务是在宴会餐桌旁设一个固定的或可手推的流动餐桌，在边桌上放一些干净盘碟和其他餐具，进行宴会的分菜服务。派菜服务是由服务员将菜肴放到小圆托盘上，左手托盘，右手用服务匙、服务叉分菜。分派的次序按照主宾、主人，然后按顺时针方向绕桌进行，分菜时一律从客人的左侧进行，这样可以避免托盘与匙、叉的交错。

Individual dining service can be divided into “side table service” and “distributing food service”. The “side table service” is to set a fixed or movable table beside the banquet table, and place some clean plates and other utensils on the side table for serving dishes. The “distributing food service” is served by placing dishes on a small round tray. The server should hold the tray by the left hand and use right hand to serve with service spoon and service fork. The order of distribution is as follows: guest of honor, host, and then move clockwise around the table. When distributing a dish, the server should stand at the left side of the guest which can avoid staggering the tray with the spoon or fork.

分餐式服务适用于中餐宴会服务，它不但能给客人以较多的服务，而且对客人的干扰较少，不至于太多影响客人的谈话。另外，分餐式服务比较卫生，非常适合现代人的消费习惯。但是，这种服务方式的不足之处在于比较费人工，对服务员的操作技能的要求也较高。

Individual dining service is applicable to Chinese banquet service. It can not only provide more service to the guests, but also less interference to the guests, which will not influence the guests' conversation. Additional, individual dining service is more wholesome. It is very suitable for modern consumption habits. However, the disadvantage of this service is that it costs labor and requires higher skilled waiters.

二、中餐服务的特点 The characteristics of Chinese F&B service

现代中餐服务的形式及其发展是适应社会进步和文明需求的产物，它与传统的中餐服务有着很大的区别。这些区别主要体现在下述几方面。

Modern Chinese food and beverage service's form and its development are the products of social progress and civilization demand, which is very different from traditional Chinese food and beverage service. These differences are mainly reflected in the following aspects:

（一）现代中餐服务开始使用托盘Modern Chinese F&B service begins using the tray

西餐服务中使用托盘的技巧是最先影响中餐服务的。在西餐服务中，在传递比托盘小的餐碟时，如果不使用托盘会被认为是不规范的服务。现在，无论是在国际化大酒店的中餐厅中，还是在一般餐饮场所，服务员无不使用托盘。

The technique of using tray in western service is the first aspect to affect Chinese service. In western food and beverage service, if the waiter or waitress doesn't use tray when serving guests, it will be considered as non-standard service. Today, whether in the Chinese restaurant of the international hotel, or in the general dining places, the service must use the tray.

（二）餐巾的使用改变用餐礼仪The use of napkins changes the dining etiquette

餐巾是舶来品，传统的中餐服务并不提供餐巾。从西方传入的餐巾在用来擦嘴时，只能用餐巾的一个角，轻轻地碰一下嘴角，将可能留在嘴边的一点汤汁沾到餐巾上，有些时候擦拭只是一种优雅的礼仪而已。这跟中餐的用餐氛围是完全不同的。应该说，西餐服务在很大程度上是一种对宫廷和贵族餐饮文化的普及，而中餐则由于贵族餐饮文化的断层，延续下来的都是大众化的社会餐饮文化。这种文化的江湖味比较浓，大碗喝酒、大口吃肉的社会酒肆文化传统主导着传统的中餐饮食文化，这也是中餐厅和中餐酒家在20世纪70年代前一直未能进入国际性酒店行业的原因。餐巾的使用改变了人们用餐的文明礼仪。虽然很多人还是愿意接受将餐巾铺在膝盖上这样的西方用餐礼仪，但在中餐服务中，人们似乎更愿意将纸巾压在餐碟底下。这是中餐的一大特色。

The traditional Chinese F&B service does not offer napkins, which are are the imported goods from the west. When using a napkin to wipe the mouth, you could use only one corner of the napkin and touch the mouth gently. Sometimes wiping mouth gently is just an elegant etiquette. It should be said that western F&B service is a largely popularity of the court and aristocratic dining culture. The dining atmosphere is completely different from Chinese F&B service. Chinese F&B is a mainly popular social catering culture due to the fault of aristocratic dining culture. That's why the Chinese restaurant failed to enter the international hotel industry until the 1970s. Although many people have accepted the western etiquette of eating with napkins on their knees, the Chinese people seem more willing to put the napkins under the plates. This is also the characteristic of Chinese F&B service.

（三）上菜程序的重新规划 The reprogramming of the serving procedure

传统的中餐服务对上菜程序并没有明确规定，而现代中餐服务，大多是按照冷菜、汤、热菜到甜品这样的顺序来上菜的，这完全是套用西餐的上菜顺序。可见，西餐对中餐的影响不仅在于餐饮文化和礼仪方面，还在于饮食科学方面。

The traditional Chinese F&B service has no clear rules on the procedure of serving dishes. However, in the modern Chinese F&B service, it has a normal sequence from cold dish, soup, hot dish to dessert, which follows the sequence of western F&B service. It is visible that the influence of western F&B service on Chinese F&B service is not only in catering culture and etiquette, but also in dietary science.

（四）各种服务形式的结合 The combination of service forms

现代的中餐服务已经彻底吸收了英、美、法三种经典西餐服务形式，并将它们融合在中餐的传统饮食文化中。需要特别强调的是，现代中餐服务既有单一的英式服务（整个用餐过程只采用英式服务，即通常所说的“围餐”）、单一的美式服务（整个用餐过程只采用美式服务，即通常所说的“位上”或“各客”）以及单一的法式服务（整个用餐过程只采用法式服务，即通常所说的“堂做”），也有综合三种服务形式的宴会服务，但这在现代西餐服务中颇为少见。

Modern Chinese F&B service has thoroughly absorbed the three classical western F&B service forms. It integrates British, American and French service forms into Chinese traditional F&B culture. Which should be emphasized is that, there are not only a single English service(Family service), a single American service(Plate service) or a single French service(Cart service), but also a banquet service that combines those three western services. However, the integrated service is unusual in the modern western F&B service.

（五）分餐叉和转盘的使用 The usage of split fork and turntable

使用分餐叉分菜也是现代中餐服务的特点。分餐叉同样是从西餐服务中传入的，这是接纳不同民族的餐饮文化最好的例子。转盘本来只是在用餐时方便用餐者拿取餐桌上的菜，现在转盘已经成为中餐服务和中餐圆桌摆台的特色了。

The usage of split forks is also a feature of modern Chinese F&B service. Split forks are also introduced from western food service. It is the best example of accepting different cultures. At first, the turntable was just a convenience for diners to pick up the dishes at the table. However, today it has become the feature of Chinese F&B service and the table set-up.

任务实施

第一步：成立学习小组，每组6～8人，各组深入酒店中餐厅，观摩中餐厅服务流程，了解中餐厅服务的方式和特点。

Step 1: Form a study group of 6–8 people. Each group goes to a Chinese restaurant of the hotel to observe the service process of the Chinese restaurant, and understands the service mode and characteristics of the Chinese restaurant.

第二步：各小组代表课堂上分享观摩结果，教师点评、分析并引入本节内容，讲授本节内容并安排课堂模拟演练。

Step 2: Representatives of each group share what they have learned from the observation in class. The teacher makes comments, analyzes and introduces the content of this section, and then arranges the class simulation exercise.

第三步：将餐饮实训室布置成拥有两种规格餐桌（10人标准圆桌）的餐厅：一种无转盘，另一种有转盘。提前准备好各种规格的餐盘（由学生自带食品或零食放在盘中模拟菜肴）。根据本节内容，各小组轮流扮演客人和中餐厅服务员，进行共餐式服务、转盘式服务、分餐式服务三种服务的模拟练习。

Step 3: Arrange the catering training room into a restaurant with two types of tables (standard round table for 10 people): one with turntable and the other without. Prepare plates of various sizes in advance (students bring their own food or snacks and place them on the plates to simulate dishes). According to this section, each group takes turns to act as guest and Chinese restaurant waiter, and practices the simulation exercise of three kinds of service: shared meal service, turntable service and individual dining service.

任务评价

表 1.4　中餐服务方式模拟评价表

The Evaluation Form of Chinese F&B Service

评价事项 Evaluation Items	评价结果 Evaluation Result			备注 Notes
	达成 Achieve	部分达成 Partly Achieve	未达成 Fail	
共餐式服务：操作规范，流程完整、顺畅 Shared meal service: the service conforms to the specification; the service process is complete and smooth				

续前表

评价事项 Evaluation Items	评价结果 Evaluation Result			备注 Notes
	达成 Achieve	部分达成 Partly Achieve	未达成 Fail	
转盘式服务：操作规范，流程完整、顺畅 Turntable service: the service conforms to the specification; the service process is complete and smooth				
分餐式服务：操作规范，流程完整、顺畅 Individual dining service: the service conforms to the specification; the service process is complete and smooth				
服务礼仪规范，语言得当 The service etiquette conforms to the standard, and the expression is suitable				
分工明确，团队协作 The division of labor is clear, and the teamwork operates well				

拓展阅读

中国人的就餐礼仪

用餐这件事尽管极其平常，却又十分重要。尤其在有“美食王国”美誉的中国，若用餐时举止失当，违反有关禁忌，将失礼于人。

中国的用餐礼仪主要体现在就餐的位次、方式、环境以及菜肴的选定等方面。中国人在宴会或宴席上非常讲究座位的排列，根据宴会的目的和性质不同，客人入座的顺序与位置也有所不同。这一点无明确的规定，多按照约定俗成，既能尊重主宾，又能合理安排其他宾客，营造欢乐和谐的就餐气氛。中国历来“尚左”“尊东”。现在的宴会通常以圆桌为主，以面向大门为尊。另外，贵宾和主宾的席位应当首先安排，以示尊重。

在用餐时，中国人多用筷子，因此产生了许多有关用筷的讲究和禁忌。例如，不能在上菜之前用筷子敲击碗碟；用餐时不可将筷子久含于口中，更不能吮筷子或用筷子当牙签；夹带有汤汁的菜肴时，不要让菜汤滴入别的菜肴中；不能用筷子在菜肴中随意翻拣等。关于用餐的方式，在宴席上，一定要注意其他客人的进餐速度，绝对不能只顾自己而大口狂吃。一般来说，中国人在一起就餐时，更注重的是交流。

关于就餐的环境，过去中国人不太注意外在的环境，只注重热闹的就餐气氛。如今，大众会去一些就餐环境幽雅、菜肴种类丰富和服务质量高的饭店就餐。

关于点菜的讲究比较少，一般以长者、女士或客人为先，轮到主人点菜时，应注意客人的禁忌和偏好。

任务四：西餐服务方式
Task 4: Western F&B Service

案例导入

据传有一年夏天，大臣李鸿章出国访问。到了国外后，外国使臣邀请李鸿章到大使馆就餐。按照该国的饮食习惯，餐前要喝开胃汤，餐后要吃甜品。饭后，一杯杯冒着烟的乳白色东西被端了上来，李鸿章不知道这是冰激凌，舀了一勺后习惯性地用嘴吹了一阵子，放到嘴里才发现是冰的。旁边的洋人哈哈大笑，李鸿章知道自己被嘲笑了，不动声色地对洋人说："感谢贵国的厚宴款待，改天我也回请各位大人。"

第二天，洋人应邀来到李鸿章设宴的地方。按照洋人的惯例，先上开胃汤，汤上面是一层厚厚的油，洋人以为是温热的汤，随即就喝了一大口，滚烫的汤这么被喝下去后，洋人被烫得哇哇大叫，说不出话来。

思考讨论：西方各个国家的餐饮习惯不同，饮食及服务方式又有哪些区别呢？

知识准备

西餐服务方式主要有法式服务、美式服务、英式服务、俄式服务和自助式服务 5 种。这 5 种西餐服务方式因起源国别不同而有所差异，在时代变迁中相互影响。

Western food service mainly includes French service, American service, British service, Russian service and Buffet service. These five kinds of western food service are different from country to country, and influence each other through the change of times.

没有哪一种服务方式是最好的，每一种服务方式的存在，都是为了迎合客人的需求及应对不同状况的要求。

There isn't a best service mode. Each service mode is designed to satisfy the needs of customers and to meet the requirements of different conditions.

一、法式服务 French service

法式服务是指餐厅所使用餐具均以银器为主，由受过专业训练的两名服务人员在手推车或服务桌上现场烹饪，再将烹制好的食物分盛于热餐盘服侍客人。法式服务的基本原则如下：

French service means that the dishes used in the restaurant are mainly silverware, which are cooked by two trained service personnel on a cart or service table in front of the guests, and the cooked food is served to the guests on the hot plate. The basic principles of French service are as follows:

（1）服务人员将菜肴盛于银盘中端出厨房，置于服务桌或手推车上再加热。

Dishes are served out of the kitchen on silverware and reheated on service tables or carts.

（2）服务人员手持服务叉匙，视客人需要从银盘上夹取其所需菜肴。

The server holds the service fork and spoon, then picks up the dishes as the guest required from the silverware.

（3）当餐盘分盛好后，助理服务员从客人右侧呈递给客人。

When the plate is served, the assistant waiter presents it to the guest from the right side.

（4）除面包、黄油、沙拉及特殊盘碟需要由客人左侧服务外，其余服务一律由客人右侧进行。

Except bread, butter, salad and other special dishes, all the services should be carried out from the right side of the guest.

（5）餐后也是在客人右侧收拾餐碟。

The clear-up work after the meal is also from the right side of the guest.

法式服务的另一个特点就是洗手盅的提供，凡是需要客人用手取食的菜肴，都需要同时为客人提供洗手盅。

Another feature of French service is the provision of finger bowl. Any dishes that guests need to pick up with their hands should be provided with finger bowl at the same time.

二、美式服务 American service

美式服务是西餐厅最常见的服务形式，又称为餐盘式服务。美式服务是西式服务中最简单、便捷、快速且成本低廉的服务方式。在美式服务餐厅，所有的菜肴在上菜前都已在厨房盛放妥当，直接由服务人员端到客人的餐桌上。客人除享受一道主菜外，还会有面包、沙拉及咖啡饮品的供应。美式服务的基本原则如下：

American service is the most common form of service in western restaurants, which is also known as plate service. American service is the simplest, most convenient, fastest and low-cost service in western service. In the American service restaurant, all dishes are ready in the kitchen and served directly to the guests' table. In addition to the main course, the guest will be served with bread, salad and coffee or other drinks. The basic principles of American service are as follows:

（1）在客人左侧服务菜肴，在客人右侧服务饮品。

Dishes are served on the left side of the guest and drinks on the right side.

（2）收拾餐具时一律在客人右侧进行。

All dishes are cleared up at the right side of the guest.

（3）一名熟练的服务员一次可同时服务 3～4 位客人。

A skilled waiter can serve 3-4 guests at a time.

三、英式服务 British service

英式服务源自英国传统的饮食习惯，由主人做切割、配量、分菜的工作。而在餐厅则由服务人员来完成主人的角色。英式服务的基本原则如下：

British service originated from the traditional British dietary habits, during which the host took responsibilities of cutting, proportioning and serving. In the restaurant, the service personnel will take the role of the host. The basic principles of British service are as follows:

（1）服务人员将银盘、餐盘端出厨房，按顺时针方向，从客人右侧给客人上餐盘。

The staff takes the silverware or plate out of the kitchen, then serves the guest clockwise and on the right side.

（2）用左手先向客人展示菜品。

Show the dishes to the guests with left hand.

（3）使用服务叉匙从左侧向客人呈递菜肴。

Use the service fork and spoon to present the dishes to the guest from the left side.

英式服务与法式服务比较类似。唯一不同的是法式服务中，客人可以自取菜品，而英式服务中，服务人员由女主宾开始在其左侧，以逆时针方向用服务叉匙将银盘上的菜肴分至客人餐盘中，故英式服务又被称为“银盘服务”。

The British service is similar to the French service. The only difference is that guests can pick up their own dishes during French service. The British service is served by the service personnel counterclockwise starting from the female guest of honour on her left side, and using service forks and spoons to divide the dishes on the silver platters into the guests' plates. Therefore, the British service is also known as "silver plate service".

四、俄式服务 Russian service

俄式服务起源于俄罗斯，拿破仑战争时，在欧洲大陆初次出现。当时欧洲以英式服务和法式服务为主，俄式服务因其简单快速，彰显出了优越性，立即成为皇宫中最受欢迎的服务方式。俄式服务的基本原则如下：

Russian service originated in Russia and first appeared in Europe during the Napoleon War. At that time, Europe was dominated by British and French services. Russian service, because of its simplicity and speed, immediately showed its superiority and became the most popular service mode in the palace. The basic principles of Russian service are as follows:

（1）出菜前，服务员先用右手从客人右侧顺时针送上空盘，冷菜用冷盘子，热菜用加温过的餐盘。

Before serving the dishes, the waiter delivers the plate from the guests' right hand clockwise, cold dish with cold plate, hot dish with heated plate.

（2）从厨房中将装好菜肴的大银盘托到餐桌旁，站立于客人左侧，用右手从客人左侧逆时针分菜。

Hold the large silver plate from the kitchen to the guest table, stand on the left side of the guest, use the right hand to serve the dishes counterclockwise from the left side of the guest.

（3）服务酒水和撤盘都在客人右侧操作。

The services of drinks and clear-up are on the right side of the guest.

五、自助式服务 Buffet service

自助式服务最大的特点就是客人可以随意挑选自己喜爱的食物，另外一个特点是餐厅没有固定的菜单。自助式服务依照餐厅的供餐方式又可以分为瑞典式自助餐服务和速简式自助餐服务。

The biggest feature of self-service is that guests can choose their favorite food at will. Another feature is that restaurants do not have a fixed menu. The buffet service can be divided into Swedish buffet service and Luncheonette buffet service.

（一）瑞典式自助餐服务 Swedish buffet service

瑞典式自助餐服务又称"欧式自助餐服务"，是以用餐人数作为计价单位。餐厅供应餐食丰富多样，包括汤类、沙拉类、肉类、甜点、水果及各类饮品。

The Swedish buffet service is also known as "the European buffet service", which is based on the number of guests as the unit of account. The restaurant offers a wide range of meals, including soups, salads, meats, desserts, fruits and drinks.

由于是自助式服务，因此除了大型肉类食物需要厨师负责切割供应外，其他食物都是由客人自取。餐厅服务人员的主要工作不同于一般餐厅，需要随时注意餐台上餐食的取用情况，避免发生食物短缺的情况；注意食物的加热及保温设备是否正常运作；随时收取客人餐桌上的空盘，保持桌面的卫生。

Since it is a self-service, the food is taken by the guest except for the large meats, which the cook is responsible for cutting and serving. Therefore, the main work of the restaurant service staff is different from that of the general restaurant. It is necessary to pay attention to the amount of food on the table at any time in order to avoid food shortages, to pay attention to the normal operation of the heating and insulation equipment for food, and to clear up the empty plate on the guest table.

（二）速简式自助餐服务 Luncheonette buffet service

速简式自助餐主要是让客人沿着餐食陈列区前进，由服务人员供应客人所挑选的食物，并在餐食陈列区出口处结账，然后由客人自行端到就餐区用餐。与瑞典式自助餐服务不同的是，速简式自助餐的餐盘一般由客人自行收拾。这种方式通常以学校餐厅最为常见。

The Luncheonette buffet mainly lets the guest walk along the food display area. The service personnel supplies the food which the guest chooses, and checks at the dining area exit. Then the guests take the meal to the dining area by themselves. Unlike the Swedish buffet service, dishes of the luncheonette buffet are usually cleared up by guests themselves. The luncheorette buffet service is common in school dining room.

任务实施

第一步：教师讲解西餐服务方式的相关内容。

Step 1: The teacher explains the related content about western food service method.

第二步：以小组（5 人 1 组）为单位，其中，1 位学生扮演餐厅服务员，另外 4 位学生扮演客人，分别模拟进行法式服务、英式服务、美式服务及俄式服务。（5 位学生轮流进行情景模拟）

Step 2: Form a study group of 5 students, in which one student acts as the restaurant attendant, the other four students play the guest. Take turns in simulation exercise on the French service, British service, American service and Russian service.

第三步：各小组随机抽取所要考核的西餐服务方式，进行模拟测试。

Step 3: Each group selects the western F&B service randomly to be evaluated, and conducts the simulation test.

任务评价

表 1.5　西餐服务方式模拟评价表

The Evaluation Form of Western F&B Service

评价事项 Evaluation Items	评价结果 Evaluation Result			备注 Notes
	达成 Achieve	部分达成 Partly Achieve	未达成 Fail	
上菜顺序正确 The serving order is correct				

续前表

评价事项 Evaluation Items	评价结果 Evaluation Result			备注 Notes
	达成 Achieve	部分达成 Partly Achieve	未达成 Fail	
上菜位置正确 The serving position is correct				
服务工具使用正确 The service tool is used correctly				
服务顺畅 The service is smooth				
与客人积极互动 Interact actively with guests				
服务面带微笑、服务用语恰当 Service with smile and appropriate expression				

拓展阅读

西餐发展史

西餐，泛指根据西方国家饮食习惯烹制出的菜点。在西餐烹饪史中，有文字记载和实物作证的西餐烹饪最早出现在古埃及，在公元前2000年古埃及的城市遗址中发现了厨房和餐厅。罗马帝国受到古埃及文化和古希腊文化的熏陶，厨师的烹饪技术和社会地位得到提高，使西餐菜肴制作得以发展。经过了漫长的发展时期，直至1533年，法国国王亨利二世娶了酷爱烹调艺术的意大利豪门闺秀凯瑟琳·德·梅第奇，法国人将传统的法国烹饪与意大利烹饪有机融合，创办了烹饪学校，开创了法国烹饪的新时代。因此，西餐菜肴和服务尤以法式为代表。

17世纪末，法国烹饪已闻名于世。法国国王路易十四经常举办的烹饪大赛，也推动了法国烹饪业的发展，涌现出很多著名的厨师，创造了许多美味佳肴。

近代西餐烹饪发展的重要特征，就是西餐对世界各地的影响越来越大。这一现象出现的原因是新大陆的发展和英国的殖民扩张等，使西餐在全球范围发展。到了19世纪，欧洲各国的菜肴特色和饮食风格已经基本形成。

西餐传入中国是在1840年鸦片战争之后。当时帝国主义国家蜂拥而入，西方各国菜点也随之传入中国，并形成一个新型行业。随后，陆续出现了中国人自己开设的以营利为目的的西餐馆，在当时又称为“番菜馆”。除西餐馆外，还有咖啡厅和面包房等。据清末史料记载，最早的番菜馆是上海福州路的“一品香”。北京的西餐行业始于光绪年间，以“醉琼林”和“裕珍园”为代表。1900年，法国人创办了北京饭店，专营西餐。1903年，法国人又创建了“得利面包房”，专制西式面包。另外，当时的宫廷和王府等都设有番菜房。

辛亥革命以后，我国处于军阀混战的半殖民地半封建社会，军政头目、洋人、买办和豪门贵族把大饭店、酒楼和西餐馆作为自己交际享乐的场所。西餐业在这种形势的推动下很快发展起来，较有名的是北京的“北京饭店”“六国饭店”，上海的“礼查饭店”，南京的“福昌饭店”等。

新中国成立后，我国与世界各国的友好往来日益增多，又陆续建起一些新饭店。如北京在20世纪50年代建成的“北京饭店西楼”“和平宾馆”等都设有西餐厅。由于当时我国与以苏联为首的东欧国家交往密切，因此20世纪50年代和60年代我国的俄式西餐厅发展较快，而西餐行业却无大进展。

党的十一届三中全会后，我国实行对外开放政策，旅游业也迅速发展起来。全国各地相继建了许多星级涉外饭店，其中不少饭店是中外合资或外商独资企业，聘用了大量的外国厨师，并引进了不少新设备和新技术。与此同时，很多饭店派厨师去国外学习，使我国的西餐业又有了新的发展。

Project 2

Reservation, Greeting, Hostess Service

项目二

预订、问候及领位服务

项目概述 PROJECT SUMMARY

作为餐厅经营者，希望餐厅每天都能客满，客人先到先坐，无须提前预订。或者客人在用餐前会体贴地给餐厅打电话，询问什么时候方便前来用餐，以免给厨师和服务人员造成压力和负担。但是，这只能是设想，现实中几乎所有的客人都想在上午 11:30-12:30、晚上 6:00-7:00 用餐。因此，餐厅必须解决预订的问题。

目前，许多餐厅的预订是通过电话来完成的，当然也有部分预订是客人亲自到餐厅完成的。无论是电话还是当面完成的预订，这都是餐厅为客人提供一流服务的机会。作为餐厅经营者，要确保每一个可能被要求预订的服务人员都经过专业培训，不仅表现在熟练使用餐饮预订系统，而且具有恰当的语言沟通和电话礼仪。

客人到餐厅用餐，除了享受美味的菜肴、轻松惬意的用餐环境，对服务人员提供的服务也抱有极大的期望。客人走到餐厅门口，服务人员一声亲切的问候会迅速拉近与客人的距离。

服务人员可以用不同的方式来问候客人，最常见的便是“早上好 / 中午好 / 晚上好，先生 / 女士，欢迎光临 XX 餐厅。”如果是比较熟悉的客人，服务人员的第一声问候应该是包含客人姓氏的。

问候完毕，询问客人是否有预订后，服务人员微笑着将客人带到餐位上。在领位的过程中，服务人员要保持与客人的交流。

看似在几分钟内完成的动作，实则体现了餐厅服务人员精准到位的服务流程，这将会使客人还未开始用餐，就已经体验到餐厅宾至如归的服务。

项目目标 PROJECT OBJECTS

知识目标：了解餐饮预订系统相关知识；掌握餐饮预订服务基本流程；掌握问候、领位的原则。

技能目标：能够准确地处理客人电话预订的需求并给予安排，以确保客人满意；能够依照不同客人的实际情况灵活进行迎宾问候、带客入座，满足客人的需求。

素养目标：具备大局观意识；爱岗敬业、谦和有礼，有较强的服务意识；具备信息安全意识。

任务一：认知预订服务
Task 1: A Cognition of Reservation Service

案例导入

马上要到圣诞节了，某酒店自助餐厅推出了圣诞促销活动，促销广告一经推出，餐厅预订咨询电话络绎不绝。餐饮预订员埃玛刚开始对于客人的各种询问会耐心解答，但随着咨询量的增加及客人对相同问题的反复询问，埃玛的语气越来越冷淡，态度也不再热情了。

圣诞节到了，餐厅并没有预想中那么爆满，许多咨询预订的客人并没有到餐厅来。这是为什么呢?

知识准备

预订是指客人提前告知餐厅为其提供餐位、餐标、酒水、菜品等的服务。预订是餐厅对订餐客人的一种服务承诺，确保能够为客人在约定的时间保留餐位。

Reservation is to inform guests' requirements, including table, dishes, wine and other services. Reservation is a kind of service commitment of the restaurant to the guests to ensure that the table can be reserved for the guests at the appointed time.

预订通常是客人与餐厅的第一次接触，预订人员的态度、用语直接影响客人对餐厅的第一印象。每个客人都希望得到礼貌、热情和高效的服务。如果在预订过程中客人不满意，他们很可能会选择其他餐厅。

Reservation is usually the first contact between the guests and the restaurant. The attitude of the reservation staff directly affects the guests' first impression of the restaurant. Every guest wants courteous, warm and efficient service. If guests are not satisfied during the reservation process, they are likely to choose another restaurant.

一、预订的方式 The way of reservation

目前，餐饮预订的方式主要有电话预订与当面预订两种。

At present, the way of restaurant reservation mainly includes telephone reservation and walk-in reservation.

二、预订的内容 The contents of reservation

预订的内容一般包括预订人的姓名、预订人的电话、就餐人数、抵达时间以及客人的特殊要求等。

The contents of reservation generally include the name of the reservation person, telephone number, number of meals, arrival time and other special requirements of the guest.

三、预订系统 Reservation system

目前，酒店餐饮预订系统主要使用 TMS 和 ResPAK。

Currently,TMS（Table Management System）and ResPAK（Reservation PAK）are most popular in the hotels' food and beverage reservation system.

四、受理预订的程序 Procedures for making a reservation

问候客人→聆听客人预订需求→接受预订→记录客人特殊需求→确认预订信息

Greeting → getting guests' reservation information → making a reservation → Recording guests' special requirement → Confirming reservation's information.

任务实施

第一步：由指导教师介绍什么是餐厅预订服务，以及预订服务在餐饮服务中的重要作用。

Step 1: The instructor introduces what the restaurant reservation service is and the importance of reservation.

第二步：由指导教师介绍要完成一个完整的预订包括哪些内容。

Step 2: The instructor introduces what is included in a complete reservation.

第三步：由指导教师介绍受理预订程序的步骤。

Step 3: The instructor introduces the steps of making a reservation.

第四步：以小组（5 人 1 组）为单位，以案例导入为切入点，查找餐厅预订的相关资料，了解影响餐厅预订的相关因素。

Step 4: Take the group (5 people) as the unit, take the case introduction as the starting point, look up the relevant information of the restaurant reservation, and understand the relevant factors that affect the restaurant reservation.

第五步：在前一步的基础上，分析预订服务对餐厅运营的影响。

Step 5: Based on the previous step, analyze the influence of reservation service on restaurant operation.

任务评价

表 2.1 预订服务模拟评价表
The Evaluation Form of Reservation Service

评价事项 Evaluation Items	评价结果 Evaluation Result			备注 Notes
	达成 Achieve	部分达成 Partly Achieve	未达成 Fail	
寻找影响餐厅预订量的因素 Look for the factors that affect restaurant reservation				
分析预订服务对于餐厅运营的影响 Analyze the influence of reservation service on the restaurant				
掌握餐厅预订的相关知识 Get the related knowledge of reservation				

拓展阅读

餐饮预订管理系统简介

如何合理地安排餐厅的座位从而使利益最大化，是每位餐厅经营者最关心并迫切希望解决的问题。利用 TMS（Table Management System）和 ResPAK（Reservation PAK）管理系统，不仅能帮助餐厅管理餐桌的运转情况，还能提供一系列的分析报告。餐饮预订管理系统采用灵活的系统模块和公共硬件平台，有效提升了餐厅的预订效率，提高了顾客的满意度，给餐厅无形中带来了更多的利润。

餐饮预订管理系统的功能特征包括：

1. 准确的预订处理

餐厅采用预订管理系统后，所有的顾客来电预订、所有的预订信息都会集中处理，避免了采用人工而造成的错订、重复预订等现象，在提高效率的同时也确保了座位预订的准确性。餐饮预订管理系统能实现交互预订，预订中心能支持一天 24 小时的电话预订，不间断的电话预订服务特别适合各类餐厅的预约需求。

2. 有效的等候管理

餐饮预订管理系统对上门顾客座位的管理以及来电预订顾客都能进行有效的处理。对于上门顾客，操作者能对餐桌使用情况进行快速地浏览，并很快安排座位。对于来电订座的顾客，会及时安排其座位，预订客满时可将顾客添加到等候列表中。等候列表与上门顾客的等候管理有助于缩短顾客的排队等候时间。

3. 客户资料的共享

通过接口与其他系统（宾馆系统、Gourmate、iGourmate 等）共享顾客资料，只需在餐饮预订系统上浏览顾客资料，操作者立即能知道顾客的个人资料并按照其爱好为其安排座位。

任务二：掌握预订服务流程
Task 2: Master the Reservation Service Process

案例导入

杭州城中香格里拉大酒店的中餐厅自开业以来，就以得天独厚的地段优势、亲民的价格以及五星级酒店的服务品质受到了市民的青睐。一般的五星级酒店中餐厅动辄人均两三百元，还要加收服务费，杭州城中香格里拉大酒店中餐厅不仅不收服务费，而且人均只要150元就能吃得很满意，相较于其他酒店，性价比很高。自开业以后，不少客人用餐后就会顺带把之后的用餐时间和餐位都预订了。中餐厅厨师长俞师傅认为，预订火爆还归结于餐厅尚不接受二轮就餐预订，就是俗称的“翻桌”。“为了保证客人用餐的品质，二轮很难预订，一般客人就餐都在两小时左右，但是要是坐下来喝喝茶、聊聊天，翻桌时间很难估计，所以我们不接受二轮预订。”俞师傅说。这样也使得很多客人翘首以盼，吃上了还会特地发朋友圈。

川味观、名人名家、杭州酒家、味庄这些餐厅的预订情况也同样火爆。川味观的运营负责人说：“国庆节前三天，包厢基本已经订满了，大厅尚有余位。为了提高服务质量，我们还把接受预订的最晚到店时间从6点提前到了5点半。”热门餐厅以前经常发生客人在店门口排长队，包厢大桌子却还是空着的情况，不少客人甚至会投诉。为了提升餐厅的整体品牌，不给客人带来一种饥饿营销的感觉，也让更多的客人可以尽早吃上饭，不少餐厅都把预订时间往前挪了半个小时。

但新白鹿、外婆家、老头儿油爆虾这些不接受预订的餐厅，在国庆期间想吃上估计就要花上点儿时间早点去取号了。

思考讨论：数字时代，预定如何实现高效、快捷智能化？

知识准备

一、预订服务流程 Reservation service process

表 2.2 预订服务流程表

The Process Form of Reservation Service

<table>
<tr><th>服务流程
Service Process</th><th colspan="2">服务标准
Service Standard</th></tr>
<tr><td rowspan="2">问候客人
Greeting</td><td>电话预订
Phone Reservation</td><td>电话铃响三声之内接听电话；
Answer the phone within three rings;
主动地向客人礼貌问好，并准确报出餐厅名称及自己姓名；
Greeting and tell the guest restaurant's name and your name;
及时表示愿意为客人提供服务，如“有什么事情可以帮您”或“很高兴为您服务”等。
Express willingness to provide services to the guest, like “What can I do for you? ” “I am glad to help you”, etc.</td></tr>
<tr><td>当面预订
Walk-in Reservation</td><td>当客人来到餐厅，迎宾员首先要礼貌地问候客人；
When the guest walks in, the server needs to do the greeting first;
知道客人是来订餐时，要主动向客人介绍自己，并表示愿意为客人服务；
When knowing that the guest is coming to make a reservation, the server needs to introduce herself/himself and express willingness to do the service;
如果餐厅设有专职订餐员，迎宾员要及时引领并做好交接工作。
If there is a reservation clerk in the restaurant, the server needs to lead the guest to find the clerk and make the reservation.</td></tr>
<tr><td>了解需求
Investigating the Requires</td><td colspan="2">礼貌地问清客人姓名，对报出姓名的客人应称呼其姓氏，以示对客人的尊重；
Ask the name of guest politely, and then call his or her last name to show the respect;
仔细聆听客人介绍，了解客人的身份、用餐日期及时间、宴请对象、人数、台数及其他要求；
Listen to the guest's introduction to get the status, dining date and time,the guests' information and numbers, table numbers and other special requirements;
征得客人的同意后，为其安排相应的包间或餐台，并告知客人房号或台号。
After getting the agreement, arrange the appropriate tables or rooms for the guest and tell him the room number or table number.</td></tr>
<tr><td>接受预订
Making the Reservation</td><td colspan="2">复述客人预订的内容，并请客人确认；
Repeat the reservation information, and let the guest confirm;
留下客人的电话、姓名及其他联系方式；
Leave the guest's name, telephone number and other contact information;
告知客人预订餐位的最后保留时间；
Let the guest know the reservation deadline;
若已订满，让客人知晓并致歉。
If the reservation is already full, let the guest know and apologize.</td></tr>
</table>

续前表

服务流程 Service Process	服务标准 Service Standard
预订通知 Reservation Notice	填好预订单； Fill the reservation form; 已订菜单的预订，立即通知餐厅经理和厨师长； If the menu is already set up, let the manager and chef know immediately; 未订菜单的预订，只通知前台即可； If the reservation information does not include the menu, just let the front desk know. 有特殊要求的预订，要及时通知餐厅总领班和厨师长。 If there are some special requirements in the reservation, inform the headwaiter and the chef.
预订记录 Reservation Record	将预订的详细内容记录在预订登记本上或录入预订系统； Put the reservation detail into the reservation notes or the system; 零点餐厅预订登记本一般每月一本，用后存档。 The reservation notebook of a-la-carte restaurant is normally one per month and kept in the archives after finish.

二、服务操作注意事项 Service operation announcements

（一）预订登记要素 Reservation registration elements

（1）客人基本信息：客人姓名或团队名称、联系电话、联系地址；就餐人数、就餐时间、就餐目的（会议或旅游包餐）等。

Basic information of the guest: name of the guest or the team, contact number and address; number of the guests, dinner time, purpose(conference or travel package meal), etc.

（2）客人要求：所需餐位或包房的种类及数量；价格标准；其他特殊要求，如餐厅布置、菜式要求等。

Guests' requirements: the type and number of seats or private rooms required; price standard; other special requirements, such as restaurant layout, dish requirements and etc.

（二）餐厅政策说明 Description of restaurant policy

折扣优惠及付款方式；餐位保留时间；对客人的预订变更、取消预订的政策规定。

Discounts and payment; reservation time; policy for guests of changing and cancelling the reservation.

（三）跟踪预订 Tracking the reservation

较重要的、时间较远的预订都要跟踪。跟踪是指要主动联系客人，确认预订或者更改预订，争取尽早发现可能发生的意外。对大型的预订尤其需要再次进行确认。

The more important or long-time-interval reservations should be tracked. Tracking is to actively contact guests, confirm or change the reservation, and try to realize the change as early as possible. In particular, group reservations need to be reconfirmed.

（四）为客人保留餐位 Reserving seats for the guests

预订是对订餐客人的一种承诺，因此在约定时间内必须为客人保留餐位。在实际接待服务中，常常出现客人预订后未按约定时间到达，或不来就餐的现象。所以，在为客人预订餐位时，应强调时间的重要性，主动告诉客人为其保留座位的时间期限，超过保留期限的餐位会让给其他客人使用。

Reservation is a commitment to the guests, so the seats must be reserved for the guests within the appointed time. In the actual reception service, there is often a phenomenon that the guests do not arrive or do not come to dinner at the appointed time after booking. Therefore, the importance of time should be stressed when reserving seats for guests, and the time limit of reserved seats should be told voluntarily. The seats beyond the reserved deadline will be given to other guests.

（五）更改客人预订 Changing reservation

餐厅如有特殊情况需要更改客人预订的时间和地点，要事先征得客人同意。标准和条件应对客人有利，并达到客人的要求。

If the restaurant needs to change the time or place of reservation on special occasion, the server should obtain the guest's consent in advance. The standard and conditions should be favorable and meet the requirements of the guest.

（六）提升预订服务质量 Improving reservation service

预订人员既要精通预订业务，又要具备良好的服务素质和道德意识。预订服务应注意服务的主动性，展现良好的服务态度，尽量满足客人的需求。避免接听电话不及时、不使用礼貌用语、对客人的预订没有进一步确认、对客人的具体要求不做详细记录等情况发生。如果无法满足客人要求，不可没有提出替代性建议便立即回绝。

Reservation clerk must be proficient in booking business, and have a good quality in service and moral awareness. During the reservation service, the server should be initiative, take a good service attitude to meet the needs of guests. Make sure to answer the phone in time, use polite expression, confirm the guests' reservation, make detailed records of the requirements. When we can not match the guests' request, we can not immediately reject without making an alternative advice.

任务实施

第一步：教师导入本节情景设定，露西女士想预订晚上 7 点在较安静的区域就餐，共 4 人，但预订员埃玛查阅后发现只有晚上 8 点半才有位置。假设你是这个餐厅的预订员，你会怎样为露西女士做预订？请考虑多种结果，并使用中英双语为露西女士做预订。

Step 1: The teacher introduces the settings of this section. Ms. Lucy wants to book a table for 4 people at 7:00 p.m. in a quiet area, but the reservation clerk Emma checked the system and found that only 8:30 p.m. is available. Suppose you were a reservation clerk of this restaurant, how would you make a reservation for Ms. Lucy? Please consider a variety of results and make a reservation for Ms. Lucy in both Chinese and English.

第二步：教师列出餐饮预订用到的相关英文词汇、短语或句型，以供学生参考。

Step 2: The teacher lists the relevant English vocabulary, phrases or sentence patterns for students' reference.

- 您更喜欢坐在哪里？

Where do you prefer to sit?

- 有空。

Free/Available.

- 五人桌。

Table for five.

- 安静的区域。

A quiet area.

第三步：教师给出示范案例，并予以示范。

Step 3: The teacher gives the demonstration case, and sets an example.

埃玛：早上好，这里是悦玺餐厅。我是埃玛，请问有什么可以帮您的吗？

Emma: Good morning, Yuexi Restaurant. This is Emma speaking. How may I help you?

露西：我想预订今晚 7 点的餐位，4 个人，能帮我们安排一下吗？

Lucy: I'd like to reserve a table for four at 7:00 p.m. Could you please arrange it for us?

埃玛：请稍等，我先查看一下是否有合适的位子。（过了一会儿……）十分抱歉，女士，7 点没有合适的位子了，8 点 30 分有空位，您看需要帮您预订吗？

Emma: Just a moment, let me see if there are any suitable seats available. I'm very sorry, Ms, there are no available seats at 7:00 p.m. but we do have some seats available at 8:30 p.m. Would you like to make a reservation?

露西：让我想想，时间有点晚了。

Lucy: Let me see, it's a little late.

埃玛：女士，通常那个时间餐厅会十分的安静。

Emma: Yes, but usually, the restaurant is very quiet at that time.

露西：这倒是，事实上我的确需要一个安静的地方。

Lucy: That's true. In fact, I really need a quiet place.

埃玛：如果可以，我给您推荐王子包间。那是一个安静且空间舒适的包间，餐厅在 8 点 30 分后会提供免费的果汁。

Emma: If so, I'd like to recommend the Prince's Room, which is a quiet and comfortable private room. And free juice will be provided for free after 8:30 p.m.

露西：听起来很不错，我预订 8 点 30 分的吧。

Lucy: Sounds great. I'll make a reservation at 8:30 p.m.

埃玛：好的，女士。再帮您确认一下，今晚 8 点 30 分王子包间 4 人用餐。请问，我可以知道如何称呼您吗？

Emma: All right, Ms. Let me confirm again. There will be four people in the Prince's Room for dinner at 8:30 p.m. this evening. Excuse me, may I know how to address you?

露西：我是露西。

Lucy: I'm Lucy.

埃玛：十分感谢，露西女士。再见！

Emma: Thanks a lot, Ms. Lucy. Goodbye.

第四步：以小组（5 人 1 组）为单位，其中，1 位学生扮演预订员，另外 4 位学生扮演订餐客人，分别模拟进行中英文电话预订和当面预订（5 位学生轮流进行情景模拟）。

Step 4: Take the group (5 people per group) as an unit, in which one student plays the role of the reservation clerk and the other 4 students act as the guests of the reservation. Make telephone reservation and walk-in reservation in both English and Chinese (5 student take turns to simulate).

☑ 任务评价

表 2.3　　预订服务操作模拟评价表

The Evaluation Form of Reservation Service Operation

评价事项 Evaluation Items	评价结果 Evaluation Result			备注 Notes
	达成 Achieve	部分达成 Partly Achieve	未达成 Fail	
当面预订服务 Walk-in reservation				

续前表

评价事项 Evaluation Items	评价结果 Evaluation Result			备注 Notes
	达成 Achieve	部分达成 Partly Achieve	未达成 Fail	
电话预订服务 Telephone reservation				
中英文表述能力 Language skill				
应急处理能力 Ability of emergency management				
团队精神 Teamwork				

拓展阅读

国外餐厅预订的习惯表达

当你在国外餐厅订餐时，餐厅服务员接起来的第一句话会是介绍其姓名和餐厅名，然后礼貌地问你是否需要帮助。作为客人，不要被服务员飞快的语速吓到，或者觉得没有听清她的名字是苏珊还是玛丽，你只需要打个招呼，然后开始陈述目的即可。

中国人崇尚礼节，而西方人亦如此。例如，中文的“我想订个餐 / 点个菜”，在英文里不可以对应成“I want to...”，而必须用礼貌的问句“Can I/May I ...”。又如，服务员会非常客气地说：“How may I help you?”等，此时顾客应答时也要讲究礼貌，同时应在对话中加入一些其他的回答，如“Perfect”“No problem”“Have a good day”等。这些都是非常必要的交际用语，一定要对这些用语及其回答非常熟悉，做到脱口而出。

当服务员问你多少人的时候，作为客人不能直接回答“Two”等直白的数字，而应说“A party of ...”，这里的“party”不是“聚会”或者“政党”的意思，而是“同伴、一群人”的意思。所以“A party of...”其实就是“一共……人（为伴）”的意思。其实在预订机票时，若是你帮自己和朋友一起预订的话，确认信上就会写“×××Party”，前面的×××是姓氏。例如，周先生预订机票的话，确认信上就会显示“Zhou Party”，就表示这个预订是周先生和他的同行者的。

预订时，服务员会问客人到达的时间，要记得说上午还是下午。如果客人想订的时间，服务回答“not available”（没有空位），客人可以提出希望的第二时间，如“How about 8:00 p.m.?”，如果服务员查后还是没有空位，则客人可以问：“Would you please tell me what time is available?”（你可否告诉我有空档的时间），然后客人可以在服务员给的时间里选定一个合适时间：“××× a.m./p.m. is okay.”

任务三：迎宾及领位服务
Task 3: Welcome and Hostess Service

案例导入

某天晚上，中餐厅门口来了一位外宾，门口领位员有礼貌地用英语问候：“先生，您好，请问您有预订吗？”

客人回答道：“我是住店客人，刚才已经打电话预订过了。”领位员没有听明白客人的回答，继续询问客人是否有预订，客人有点不耐烦地告诉领位员，刚才电话预订时，前台告诉他可以直接到这个餐厅来用餐，并出示房卡。领位员看到客人房卡后，立刻将客人带进了餐厅。

领位员把客人带到靠近走廊的餐桌前，说“请坐”，可是客人不肯落座，并说了一串领位员听不懂的英文。领位员尝试着与客人沟通，还是没有明白客人到底在说什么。

此时，餐厅经理走过来，经过询问才知道，客人预订的是酒店西餐厅靠窗的位子，领位员在没有充分沟通的情况下就直接将客人带进了中餐厅。经理连声致歉，并亲自将客人带到了西餐厅。

餐厅领位员在问候与领位时出现了哪些错误？如果你是餐厅的领位员，你会如何做呢？

知识准备

餐厅服务员在开餐前例会时，会了解到当日预订的客人信息，特别是 VIP 客人信息。对于餐厅领位员来讲，在开餐前查阅并熟悉预订客人的相关预订信息是工作的重点。

In the regular pre-meal meeting, the waiters and waitresses will get the reservation guests' information of today, especially the VIP guests' information. For the restaurant hostess, it is the most important work to check and get familiar with the reservation information of the guests before opening.

一、迎宾问候 Welcome greetings

餐厅开始营业后，领位员站在餐厅门口等候宾客的到来。当客人走向餐厅门口时，领位员要面带微笑，主动与客人打招呼，对客人的到来致以诚挚的欢迎。若客人为常客，则可直接称呼客人的姓氏加职位头衔，并可适当与客人寒暄，但要注意语言分寸。

When the restaurant opens, the hostess stands at the door of the restaurant waiting for guests. When the guests walk to the restaurant, the hostess should greet the guests with a smile, and extend a sincere welcome to the guests. If meeting with a frequent guest, the hostess can directly address the guest's last name and title, and communicate with the guest appropriately, but pay attention to the appropriate expression.

对于不熟悉的客人，领位员要询问客人是否有预订。如果客人有预订，查询预订系统相关记录，再将客人引导至所预订的桌位。

For unfamiliar guests, the hostess needs to ask if the guest has a reservation. When there is a reservation records in the system, guide the guest to the reserved table.

如果客人没有预订，则需要询问客人有几位，根据客人人数来安排座位，并将客人引领至桌位。

If the guests do not have a reservation, it is necessary to ask the amount of the guests, then arrange seats according to the guests' number and lead the guests to the table.

表 2.4　迎宾服务的流程及标准

The Process and Standard of Welcome Service

	服务流程 Service Process	服务标准 Service Standard
1	注意步入餐厅的客人。 Pay attention to the guests who enter the restaurant.	时刻注意入口是否有客人走进来。 Keep an eye on the guests at the entrance.
2	在距离客人 3 米处微笑着迎上，并有目光接触。 At a distance of 3 meters, greet the guest with a smile and eye contact.	在客人步入餐厅 1 分钟内，有人上前招呼。 Within a minute of the guest entering the restaurant, someone needs to come forward to greet him.
3	向客人问候，鞠躬 15 度说："× × 先生 / 女士，早上 / 下午 / 晚上好！有什么需要帮助的吗？" Greet guests, make a 15-degree bow and say: "Good morning/afternoon/evening, Mr./Ms. × ×! Is there anything I can do for you?"	语调必须轻柔、友好，建立起目光联系。手放两侧，上身保持挺直。 The tone must be soft and friendly. Keep eye contact with guests. Keep hands on sides and body straight.
4	面带微笑地询问客人："××先生 / 女士，请问有预订吗？"或"请问您预订的是哪个包间，××先生 / 女士？" Ask the guest,"do you have a reservation, Mr./Ms. × ×?"or"which private room did you book, Mr./Ms. × ×?"with a smile.	
5	如无预订，先问："× 位吗？"然后等待答复。"让我看一下是否还有空余的桌位。" If there is no reservation, ask first, "Table for ×?" Then wait for an answer. "Let me check if there is any table available."	
6	如有桌位，说："请问怎么称呼您？"记下来，微笑着说："× × 先生 / 女士，很高兴我们还有空余的桌位。" If there is a table available, ask the guest,"may I have your name, please?"Write it down and say with a smile,"Mr./Ms. × ×, I'm glad we have a table available."	

续前表

<table>
<tr><th></th><th>服务流程
Service Process</th><th>服务标准
Service Standard</th></tr>
<tr><td>7</td><td>如无空位，向客人表示歉意，并提出其他建议，如“非常抱歉，××先生/女士，餐厅现在已经客满。半小时以后会有空位，您介意等候片刻吗？”或“这儿今晚已经订满了。您愿意去我们的中餐厅用餐吗？”
If there is no vacancy, apologize to the guest and make other suggestions, such as “I’m so sorry, Mr./Ms.××, the restaurant is full now.Would you mind waiting for a moment?”or“we’re fully booked tonight. Would you like to have dinner in our Chinese restaurant?”</td><td rowspan="3">永远不要向客人说“不”，总是能够提出其他建议。
Never say “no” to the guest and always be able to give other suggestions.</td></tr>
<tr><td>8</td><td>若客人接受你提议的用餐地点，微笑着说：“您稍等，我给您看一下那边是否有空位。”
If the guest accepts your offer, smile and say, “Just a moment, please. I’ll check if there is a table available for you.”</td></tr>
<tr><td>9</td><td>如果那个餐厅确认有位，感谢客人的耐心等候，并带客人去。
If the table is available, thank the guest for their patience and guide them there.</td></tr>
<tr><td>10</td><td>如果客人仍然选择在这儿用餐，询问客人是否愿意被列在等候名单上，并估计需要等候的时间。
If the guest still chooses to have dinner here, ask him/her if he/she would like to be put on the waiting list and estimate how long he/she will have to wait.</td><td rowspan="2">如果等候的时间较长，建议客人先去大堂吧或其他较近的地方喝一杯。留下客人的联系方式，当有位时，你会通知他/她。
If the waiting time is long, suggest the guest go to the lobby bar or other nearby places for a drink.Leave the guest’s contact information and inform him/her when the table is available.</td></tr>
<tr><td>11</td><td>向客人解释情况，并让他们不断了解最新的进度。
Explain the situation to guests and keep them to be informed of the latest situation.</td></tr>
</table>

二、领位（引客入座）Hostess (Guide guests to their seats)

对于没有预订的客人，若餐厅上座率不高，领位员要仔细观察客人的人数、身份、年龄、性别、喜好来选择适当的餐位，同时还要考虑餐厅空间的平衡。

For guests without reservation, if the restaurant attendance is not high, the hostess should carefully observe the number, identity, age, gender, preferences of guests to choose the appropriate table, and also consider the balance of restaurant space.

引导客人时，领位员要配合客人走路的速度，以适度的步伐在客人侧前方带领，不时以目光关注客人是否紧随其后。遇到台阶或转弯时，应提醒客人并以手势加强，请客人注意安全。引导客人至桌位后，应先询问客人对桌位的安排是否满意。对于常客或 VIP 客人，要尽量将其安排到其习惯的区域与桌位。

When guiding the guest, the hostess should match up with the guest's walking speed, guide in the front of the guest with moderate pace, keep an eye on the guest to make sure he/she is not far behind, remind the guest when meeting step or turn, and use gesture to emphasize the safety. After leading the guest to the table, ask if the guest is satisfied with the table arrangement first. For frequent guests or VIP guests, try to place them in their customary area and table.

领位员引客入座时，区域服务员要主动上前问候，领位员要及时将区域服务员介绍给客人认识，并协助客人入座。具体操作是：用双手帮客人轻轻拉开椅子，请客人入座，当客人将要坐下时，将椅子轻轻往前推送。拉椅顺序以主宾优先，若无法判断，则以女士及年长者优先。

When the hostess guides guests to the table, the area server should take an initiative greet to the guests. The hostess should introduce the area server to the guests in time and assist the guests to take the seats. The specific operation is to gently pull the chair with both hands, ask the guest to sit down, gently push the chair forward when the guest is about to sit down. The principal guest should be priority. If it's unable to judge who is the principal guest, serve the lady and the elderly first.

表 2.5 领位服务的流程及标准

The Process and Standard of Guiding Service

	服务流程 Service Process	服务标准 Service Standard
1	走向客人，及时问候。 Walk to the guest and greet in time.	服务人员必须在 10 秒钟内向客人致意；不要站在迎宾台的后面。 Greet to the guest first within 10 seconds; do not stay behind the front desk.
2	主动对客人说："下午好，× × 先生 / 女士，欢迎您来……" Talk to the guest: "Good afternoon, Mr./Ms. × ×, welcome to..."	如果知道姓名，应响亮、清晰地称呼客人的名字。 If the hostess knows the guest's name, speak it out loudly and clearly.
3	询问客人的要求，如"有什么需要帮忙的吗？" Ask for the guest's requirements, like"Is there anything I can help?"	微笑，建立目光交流，要表现得自然而真诚。 Smile with eye contact; act naturally and sincerely.
4	如果客人想在餐厅用餐，询问是否已订座。 Ask the guest if he/she already has the reservation or not.	有预订的客人应在到达后 1 分钟内被引导至桌位。 The guest who has reservation needs to be guided to the table in 1 minute.
5	如得到肯定的答复，口头致意。查询 TMS 上的预订情况，然后把客人带到指定的桌位。 If a positive reply is received, feedback a verbal compliment.Check the reservation status on the TMS and take the guest to the assigned table.	再次确认客人的信息。 Confirm the guest's information again.

续前表

	服务流程 Service Process	服务标准 Service Standard
6	如未订位，询问客人用餐的人数以及对餐桌位置的选择。根据预订系位，查看是否已有人预订。 Ask the guest about the number of diners and preferred table, then check the system to make sure the table isn't under reservation.	未预订的客人应在到达后 2 分钟内引导至桌位。 The guest who does not have reservation needs to be guided to the table in 2 minutes.
7	请客人跟随自己，说："× × 先生 / 女士，请随我来。" Make sure the guest is following and say "Mr./Ms. × ×, this way please."	在客人前面，保持 3～4 步的距离。不要走得太快。不时回头，确认客人跟在身后。 Keep 3 or 4 steps in front of the guest; Do not walk too fast; Look back to make sure the guest is following.
8	引导时，走在客人右侧前方。 When guiding the guest, remember walk in front of the guest on the right side.	
9	在桌边停下，微笑并征询客人是否满意这个桌位，然后为客人拉出椅子。 Stop at the table, smile and ask if the guest is satisfied with the table, then pull out the chair for the guest.	参照注意事项列出的基本礼仪礼节。 Refer to the basic etiquette listed by the precautions.
10	站在椅子的正后方，右手五指并拢，示意客人入座，同时说"× × 先生 / 夫人，请坐。" Stand behind the chair, keep five fingers of right hand together to guide the guest to have a seat, and say "Mr/Ms. × ×, please have a seat."	动作要慢，要小心。 Move slowly and be careful.
11	当客人要坐下时，双手把扶椅子两侧，用右膝把椅子往里送。 When the guest is ready to sit down, put both hands on the sides of the chair and push the chair in with your right knee.	
12	祝客人用餐愉快。 Wish the guest enjoy the food.	

任务实施

第一步：教师导入本节情景设定。

Step 1: The teacher introduces the settings of this section.

［情景 1］露西女士一行 4 人在晚上 8 点 30 分到达餐厅门口，领位员珍在餐厅门口迎接，询问客人信息后，将客人引领到王子包间，并向客人介绍包间的服务人员。

Scenario 1: Ms. Lucy and her party of 4 people arrive at the restaurant at 8:30 p.m. Jen, the restaurant hostess, greets the guests at the door of the restaurant. After asking the information of the guests, she leads the guests to the Prince's Room and introduces the service staff to the guests.

［情景 2］王先生一行 4 人在没有预订的情况下到餐厅用餐，餐厅领位员在餐厅有空位的情况下应该如何做？在餐厅没有空位、需要客人等位的情况下又该如何做？

Scenario 2: Mr. Wang and his party of 4 people come to the restaurant without reservation. What should the restaurant hostess do when the restaurant has vacancy? What should the restaurant hostess do when the restaurant does not have vacancy and the guests need to wait?

第二步：教师列出迎宾问候、领位用到的相关短语或句型，以供学生参考。

Step 2: The teacher lists the relevant phrases or sentence patterns used in greeting and guiding for the students' reference.

– 先生 / 女士，请问有预订吗？

· Do you have a reservation, sir / ma'am?

– 让我看一下是否还有空余的桌位。

· Let me see if there is any table available.

– 请问怎么称呼您？

· May I have your name, please?

– 很高兴我们还有空余的桌位。

· I'm glad we have a table available.

– 非常抱歉，×× 先生 / 女士，餐厅现在已经满了。×× 分钟以后会有空位，您介意等候片刻吗？

· I'm very sorry, the restaurant is full now, Mr./Ms ××. There will be a table available in ×× minutes. Would you mind waiting for a moment?

– 这儿今晚已经订满了。您乐意去我们的中餐厅用餐吗？

· We're fully booked tonight. Would you like to go to our Chinese restaurant?

– 您稍等，我给您看一下那边是否有空位。

· Just a moment, please. I'll show you if there is a vacant seat over there.

– 请随我来。

· Please follow me.

– 祝您用餐愉快！

· Hope you enjoy the meal!

第三步：教师给出示范案例，并予以示范。

Step 3: The teacher gives a demonstration case, and sets an example.

第四步：以小组（5 人 1 组）为单位，其中，1 位学生扮演领位员，另外 4 位学生扮演客人，分别模拟进行迎宾问候与带客入座（5 位学生轮流进行情景模拟）。

Step 4: Take the group (5 people per group) as the unit, in which one student acts as the hostess and the other four students act as the guests. Respectively simulating greeting the guests and guiding them to the seats (5 students take turns to do scene simulation).

任务评价

表 2.6 迎宾、领位服务操作模拟评价表

The Evaluation Form of Greeting and Guiding Service

评价事项 Evaluation Items	标准评分 Evaluation Standards	评价结果 Evaluation Result			备注 Notes
		达成 Achieve	部分达成 Partly Achieve	未达成 Fail	
迎宾问候 Greeting	集中注意力 Intense concentration				
	及时问候 Greeting in time				
	笑容亲切 Friendly smile				
	音量适中 Moderate volume				
	语言亲和 Amiable expression				
	服装得体 Appropriate dressing				
	礼仪规范 Appropriate etiquette				
	准确快速查看预订信息 Get the reservation information accurately and quickly				
	询问是否吸烟 Ask the guests if they smoke				
带位入座 Guiding	引领客人入座 Guide the guests to the table				
	引领过程中关注客人 Pay attention to the guests while guiding				
	至少为一位客人拉椅且动作规范 Pull the chair for at least one guest with proper behavior				
	向客人介绍区域服务人员 Introduce the area server to the guests				

拓展阅读

如何解决餐厅排队等位的问题

各大火爆餐厅在吃饭时间都会有客人排队等位的情况。如何对排队进行管理，是餐厅

经营者面对的一个挑战。在餐厅的经营中，排队现象令经营者喜忧参半。喜的是客人对餐厅的认可，忧的是现有客人或未来就餐选择机会的失去，也许下次客人将选择另一家餐厅。

有调查者选择了北京工体附近的两家餐厅，对排队现象进行研究，最后得出结论：有一定规模的连锁店铺对排队都有管理，客人的流失率在20%左右；规模较小但同样有特色的餐厅对排队没有管理，客人的流失率超过50%。

1. 排队产生的原因

服务的生产和消费是同时进行的，需求波动性的存在是必然的。客人的特点是随机到达，并且想立即得到服务。如果客人到达时，所有的服务资源都已经被占用，那么客人就需要耐心地排队等待。

客人需求的自然波动，如同时性波动，造成了在某些时间段，餐厅处于闲置状态，而在某一特定的时间段，客人不得不为接受服务而等待，此时排队现象就出现了。由于文化、习惯以及工作时间等原因，人们养成了固定时间就餐的习惯，如12点吃午饭、18点吃晚饭。因此，在11:30—12:30、18:30—19:40这两个时段形成了集中的就餐高峰期。调查发现，一家火爆餐厅在11:30之前就餐客人还寥寥无几，但半点一过，尤其是11:40—12:00仅20分钟内，可容纳170人就餐的大厅已座无虚席，门厅处甚至排起了长队。

服务能力的有限性。服务不像其他的产品那样能够贮存在仓库中以待未来消费。一家餐厅在初期投资中就确定了其服务能力，如餐位数量、餐台设计、服务流程等，经营者每天都要面对动态变化的环境，协调供给和客人需求之间的矛盾。

店铺之间的同质性或差异性。消费者对价格的敏感度、口味的偏好、就餐环境和品味的要求，以及在距离、方便性、以前就餐的感受等方面的综合心理影响其餐厅的选择。前文提到的位于工体附近的两家餐厅经营各有特色，一家是湖北菜，另一家是四川菜，装修设计风格虽不同，但装修水平相近。两家餐厅面积相当，都是以融合北京风味的地方特色菜肴为主。但由于四川菜馆的价格略低，餐厅10米之外就飘着川菜特有的香味，因此排队人数常常比湖北菜馆多。经营的差异化——价格机制、诱人菜香发挥了作用。有趣的现象发生了，我们经常会发现来就餐的客人分别在两家餐厅领号，哪家先排到就先到哪家就餐。经营的同质性也很明显，对客人来说，选择哪一家餐厅就餐都没有太大的区别，只是看哪一家更快。

2. 客人等待的心理

对于消费者来说，等待的成本是放弃了在这段时间里可以做的其他事情，此外还有厌烦、焦急和其他心理反应的成本。客人在等待中首先感到的是焦虑，不知道自己是否被遗忘了？不知道什么时候能轮到自己？不知道能否被公平地对待？……无论这些担心是否合乎逻辑，都会影响其心情。其次，客人会感到无聊。在排队期间人们无法做自己喜欢的事，这种空闲或者无所事事会让人感觉很难受。通常排队时，客人感觉只能任凭服务员摆布，这也令人感觉不舒服。不公平的待遇会使客人不满。当一位客人看到后来的人比自己更早接受服务，而自己还不知道会等多久时，常常会很恼火，甚至暴跳如雷。客人在等位期间产生了不必要的恼怒，在就餐时可能会变成挑剔、难缠的消费者。

3. 排队管理的原则

客人是一种加入服务过程的潜在资源，即使每天只失去几个客人，但日积月累，餐厅的营业额会下滑。因此，制定相应的排队管理战略、缩短客人等待的心理时间、消除客人因等待而形成的负面影响，是餐厅经营者的基本职责。

（1）让客人知道服务人员知道他们在等待。派一名员工与等待的客人接触，使客人明白餐厅知道他们正在等待。

（2）让等候时间变得令人愉快。设置专门的等候区，并将其布置得宁静、素雅，播放舒缓的轻音乐，并将等候区与就餐区隔开，避免直接的刺激。

（3）有效利用客人的等待时间。客人在等待时无其他事可做，但会仔细、反复地熟悉周围的环境，餐厅应注意细节的安排和布置。

（4）建立清晰的排队规则。排队规则是在队伍中挑选下一位接受服务的客人。进入餐厅的客人会领到一个连续的号码，然后等待被叫号。调查发现，餐厅不仅是按到达的顺序排号，同时还要考虑到每台可接纳的就餐人数。也就是说，排队规则要复杂。

4. 排队管理的法宝

服务需求的波动是一件不可避免的事情。排队是绝对的，不排队是相对的，但服务系统可以通过使用主动和被动的方法来调节需求，降低服务需求的周期性变化。

（1）等候区的设置。每天都有排队的餐厅应专设等候区，放置一些舒适、小巧的沙发、椅子等。也可附设一个小酒吧，既便于客人聊天，又可提供开胃酒、饮料，增加餐厅的收入。

（2）等候区的装饰。将等候区与就餐区隔开，并将其布置得宁静、雅致，鲜亮的色彩、抒情的音乐可令人心情舒畅。同时，餐厅还可展示新菜品，提供当天的报纸或企业自办的报纸供客人阅读，设置定期更换的企业宣传栏，公布客人来信，张贴优秀员工的照片和事迹，发布促销活动通知等。

（3）差别价格转移需求。通过统计分析，确定本餐厅营业的高峰时段。餐厅可给在固定时间范围内结束用餐的客人一个折扣，也就是说，在排队形成之前或初期，向用餐完毕离去的客人提供优惠，鼓励10:50之前用餐的客人加快用餐速度，在11:30—11:40结账，为后来者提供餐位，避免等候时间过长。

（4）采用关怀服务。冬天送热饮、夏天送冷饮、为老人搬椅子、为小孩提供手偶玩具等方式，可使客人知道餐厅尽所能安排其就餐。调查发现，饮用了餐厅提供的免费饮料的客人，基本没有中途离去，犹豫中的客人不会享用餐厅提供的服务。

（5）提前开始服务。为等候的客人送上餐单点菜，待其座位确定，该餐单即可传出，缩短了客人在餐桌上等待的时间。

缩短客人等待的时间、提供快速的服务是各类餐厅经营的趋势，是一家餐厅的竞争优势。上述介绍的方法仅仅是排队管理的小技巧，是多数餐厅很容易做到的或已经做到的。仔细分析客人的就餐过程，我们会发现：客人等候的时间是从排队等待餐位开始的，到结账才结束。餐厅应有效利用客人的等待时间，找到持续盈利点。

Project 3

Preparation

项目三

餐前准备

项目概述 PROJECT SUMMARY

在餐厅中，不同岗位的工作人员都有其分内的工作，这些工作都是烦琐又具体的。这就要求工作人员在遵循“一切就绪、万事俱备”的原则下，按部就班、有条不紊地完成餐前准备工作。

在餐厅营业之前，餐厅经理或者主管会召开餐前例会，服务人员接受任务分配，了解自己所要服务的区域、餐厅当日的预订情况，掌握当日常客及 VIP 客人的需求及服务注意事项，熟悉菜单及当日特选菜、推荐菜等。餐前例会结束后，各岗位工作人员检查当值区域卫生及服务工作台物品准备情况。

充分的餐前准备工作是良好服务的开端。即使每家餐厅规模不同、性质各异，但为了有效经营，工作人员必须严格执行各种规程，做到布置规范化、操作程序化。

餐厅营业前的各项餐前准备工作关系着餐厅当日的运作。若是餐前准备工作没有做好，致使客人抵达后需要等待，将会让客人感觉餐厅的服务不专业、不用心。

项目目标 PROJECT OBJECTS

知识目标：了解餐前准备的工作项目；了解餐前例会的内容；掌握托盘、餐巾折花的基本知识。

技能目标：掌握托盘的使用方法；掌握常见中、西餐餐巾折花技能。

素养目标：具备精益求精的工匠精神；具备较强的服务意识、安全意识；具有较强的责任心与严谨的工作作风。

任务一：掌握餐前准备工作
Task 1: Master Pre-meal Preparation

案例导入

某酒店的 VIP 客人王先生致电酒店中餐厅，次日中午 12:00 他将在中餐厅宴请一位十分重要的法国客人。中餐厅十分重视王先生的来电，在餐前例会时，餐厅经理再次强调了中午接待 VIP 客人的注意事项，并且特意分配了工作经验丰富、服务细致周到的乔负责此次 VIP 接待。例会结束后，乔开始检查工作区域的物品准备及卫生情况。他不经意看到了餐桌上的摆台，立刻给经理打了一个电话，经理马上同意了他的整改方案。

原来，乔看到餐桌上还是摆着中餐厅的传统餐具，想到客人是一位法国人，有可能不会用筷子，等开餐后再去帮客人更换餐具，会降低餐厅的服务品质。于是，他在主宾的餐位补充上了刀叉。

中午，王先生带着他的法国朋友走进了餐厅，当看到餐位上不同往常的餐具时，王先生连连赞扬酒店的用心。而他的法国朋友也幽默地说："我没有提前告知餐厅我不会用筷子啊，你们真是神机妙算！"

思考讨论：如果乔没有想到为客人准备刀叉，在客人入座后根据其需求再准备，客人还会由衷感谢她吗？

知识准备

一、餐前例会 Pre-meal meetings

为了使员工可以及时获取信息、更好地为客人提供服务，在每个班次开始工作前，餐厅应要求员工准时参加例会。例会一般由餐厅经理或主管主持。餐前例会的主要内容如下：

In order to provide timely information and better service to guests, the restaurant should require employees to attend regular pre-meal meetings on time before each shift begins. The regular meeting is usually presided over by the restaurant manager or supervisor. The main contents of the regular pre-meal meeting are as follows:

表 3.1　　餐前例会的流程和标准

The Process and Standard of Pre-meal Meetings

	流程 Process	标准 Standard
1	开例会并告知员工相关的信息 Hold regular meetings to inform related information	餐厅的活动和相关安排： - 有关同事的正面信息（如奖励等）； - VIP 客人的名单，分享客人特殊爱好； - 当日预订； - 每日特选、应季食品； - 餐饮推广活动（新的计划和取得的进展）； - 沽清项目（食品、酒水）； - 上座率（人数、收入、平均消费）； - 行动要点（重要的、需要马上解决的事情）； - 仪容仪表检查； - 员工工作任务分派。 Activities and related arrangement： -Good information about colleagues (e.g. rewards); -List of VIP guests and their special preference; -Reservation; -Daily specials and seasonal food; -Catering promotion activities (new plans and progress); -Sold-out item (food and beverage); -Attendance rate (number of people, income and average consumption); -Action points (important and urgent things); -Appearance check; -Job assignment.
2	反馈信息和跟进 Feedback and follow up	收集员工的反馈意见并记录，如有可能及时跟进。 Collect feedback from employees, write down the suggestions and follow up if possible.

餐前例会时间不应太长，一般以 10 分钟左右为宜。每天要有固定的开会时间，通常午餐餐前例会在上午 10:00 或 10:30 进行，晚餐餐前例会在下午 4:00 或 4:30 进行。经理或主管开例会前要做好充分的准备，事先写下开会时要讲的工作要点。开会时要求员工列队，要以期望员工做好服务工作的态度去激励员工，讲话要清晰，气氛要轻松，让员工易于接受。另外，要定期请上级领导到会指导，及时传达上级的指示，做到上情下达、下情上报。

It should not cost too much time for the pre-meal regular meeting, generally around 10 minutes. There must be a fixed time for regular meeting every day, usually at 10:00 a.m. or 10:30 a.m. for lunch and 4:00 p.m. or 4:30 p.m. for dinner.The manager or supervisor should be well prepared for the regular meeting and write down the main points of the meeting in advance. During the meeting, all staffs should line up and be encouraged to do their job well. The manager or supervisor should speak clearly and create a relaxed environment to make it easy for employees to accept. Besides, the manager or supervisor should regularly invite the leaders do the meeting guidance, timely communicate instructions, pass the requires to the staff and transfer the feedback to the upper management.

二、准备工作 Preparations

餐前准备工作是餐厅服务人员在客人到达之前，按服务程序完成的一系列服务准备工作，是做好服务工作的开始。具体应做好如下准备：

Pre-meal preparation is a series of preparation completed by restaurant servers before guests' arrival. It is the beginning of good service. In particular, the following preparations should be done:

表 3.2　准备工作的内容和标准
The Content and Standard of Preparations

准备内容 Content	工作标准 Standard
环境及清洁卫生 Environment and cleaning	- 餐厅大门及周围环境干净整齐，地面、餐桌椅等干净无尘； - 餐具柜、服务车等符合卫生要求； - 餐具干净卫生，无破损； - 餐厅室温适宜，根据季节及营业时间将温度控制在 18℃～22℃。 - The restaurant door and the surrounding environment are clean and tidy. The floor, dining tables and chairs are clean and dust-free; - Sideboards and service carts should meet the hygiene requirements; - Tableware is clean and without damage; - Dining room temperature is appropriate. According to the season and operating time, control the temperature between 18℃ -22℃ .
设备检查 Equipment inspection	- 开餐前 1 小时检查所有照明设备、空调、背景音乐开关及音响设备是否正常； - 调节好室内灯光及音响。 - Check whether all lighting equipment, air conditioner, background music switch and sound equipment are normal running one hour before the meal; - Adjust indoor lighting and sound.
餐具、服务用品准备 Tableware and service supplies preparation	- 将所需要的餐用具消毒后放在备餐间或备餐桌上； -准备好服务用品（如各种托盘、开瓶工具、餐巾、牙签等）。 - Put the necessary tableware on the preparation room or table after disinfection; - Prepare service items, such as trays, bottle openers, napkins, toothpicks, etc.
摆台 Table setting	- 符合餐厅摆放要求； - 餐具干净卫生、无破损。 - Comply with the restaurant display requirements; - The tableware is clean and unbroken.

续前表

准备内容 Content	工作标准 Standard
酒水饮料准备 Beverage preparation	- 备好供应的酒水饮料、茶叶、开水、冰块等； - 检查酒水饮料的质量，发现问题，及时退回。 - Prepare beverage, tea, boiled water, ice, etc. - Check the quality of beverage. If there is any problem, return in time.
菜单准备 Menu preparation	- 备好零点及套餐菜单； - 熟悉菜单的内容； - 熟悉当天菜单的变化。 - Prepare a la carte and set menu; - Be familiar with the menu; - Be familiar with daily menu changes.
员工形象准备 Employees' image preparation	- 餐厅员工仪容仪表符合餐厅工作服务要求。 - The appearance of the restaurant staff should match the restaurant service requirement.
检查预订摆台 Check the reservation table	- 所摆餐位符合预订人数，摆放符合要求； - 指示牌、可用菜单干净，内容正确无误； - 餐台鲜花新鲜、美观。 - The table is arranged according to the number of reservation and the table setting requirements; - The signpost and menu are clean and correct; - The flowers on the table are fresh and beautiful.
准备迎接宾客 Get ready for the guests	- 一般由领位或迎宾员在开餐前 5 分钟站在餐厅门后，准备迎接宾客。 - Generally, the hostess stands behind the door of the restaurant 5 minutes before the meal and prepares to greet the guests.

此外，来餐厅用餐的客人，由于年龄、职业、身份、国籍、地区、性别等不同，用餐目的、标准及要求也各不相同。餐厅服务员要眼观六路、耳听八方，做到处处留心、时时细心、事事精心，要善于观察和判断客人的眼神、表情、举止、动作，要对各类宾客的各种用餐要求有心理准备，要因人而异，掌握好尺度，使服务接待工作恰到好处。

In addition, due to the age, occupation, identity, nationality, region, gender and other factors, the purposes, standards and requirements of the restaurant guests are different. Restaurant servers should be all eyes and all ears, and pay attention to everywhere, be careful at all times, be careful in everything, be good at observing and estimating the eyes, expressions, manners and actions of the guests, and be psychologically prepared for all kinds of guests' requests during meals. The service should vary from person to person. The servers should grasp a good scale to make sure the service is to the point.

任务实施

第一步：根据教师的知识讲解，各小组自行设定餐前例会情景。

Step 1: According to the teacher's explanation, the groups set up their own pre-meal meeting situation.

第二步：教师提示模拟训练要点，包括内容的设定、例会的流程、例会的要点等。

Step 2: The teacher prompts the key points simulation training, including the content setting, the regular meeting process, the regular meeting main points and so on.

第三步：以小组（8 人 1 组）为单位，其中，1 位学生扮演餐厅经理，另外 7 位学生扮演餐厅服务人员，分别模拟召开餐前例会（8 位学生轮流进行情景模拟）。

Step 3: Take the group (8 people per group) as a unit, in which one student acts as the restaurant manager, the other seven students play the role of restaurant server, respectively simulates the regular pre-meal meeting (eight students take turns to carry on the scene simulation).

任务评价

表 3.3 餐前例会评价表

Evaluation Form of Regular Pre-meal Meeting

评价事项 Evaluation Items	评价结果 Evaluation Result			备注 Notes
	达成 Achieve	部分达成 Partly Achieve	未达成 Fail	
情景内容的设定符合酒店实际经营情形。 The setting of the meeting situation is in line with the actual business operation of hotel.				
例会流程规范，内容正确。 The meeting process is normative, and the content is correct.				
例会的要点：对于酒店或餐厅重大政策或事件的公告；前一段时间服务表现及营业状况的点评；客人的用餐反馈；服务人员仪容仪表的要求；工作区域的分配；今日餐品说明；VIP 客人的注意事项；给员工加油打气的话语。 Key points of regular meeting: Announcement of major policies or events of the hotel or restaurant; Comments on service performance and business status of the previous period; Guests' feedback on dining; Requirements for the appearance of service personnel; Allocation of work areas; Daily food description; Notes for VIP guests; Encouragement for employees.				
语言组织与表达能力：表述正确、清晰；发音标准、声音洪亮。 Language organization and expression skills: Correct and clear expression; Standard pronunciation and loud voice.				
分工明确，团队协作。 Clear division of labor and good teamwork.				

拓展阅读

客人基本需求心理分析

对于大多数住店客人来说，在酒店就餐既是需要又是享受。客人对于餐饮的基本需求心理分析如下：

1. 营养

营养能改善人的正常生理功能和抗病能力。营养高低、搭配合理与否直接影响人的精力旺衰和工作效率的高低，甚至影响人的外貌及个性。由于营养离不开每天每餐的饮食质量，因此，客人希望餐厅提供的菜点能够符合其科学营养需求，并且要求标明餐食的营养成分及含量。现在客人还希望多食绿色食品。

2. 风味

风味是指客人用餐时，对菜肴或其他食品产生的总的感觉印象，它是影响食物挑选的最重要因素。风味是用餐者所品尝到的口味、嗅觉和质地等的综合感觉。

3. 卫生

客人都非常注意餐具及饮食环境的卫生。卫生是客人的基本生理需求，餐厅要重视卫生，确保客人不受病害的威胁。需要强调的是，每位餐饮行业从业人员都要严格遵守餐饮部制定的卫生工作条例。在客人眼里，服务人员的整洁卫生也是餐厅卫生的重要环节。

因此，为了满足就餐客人的需求，服务人员除了要做到让客人感到“宾至如归”，还要做到熟练掌握业务知识，迎合客人对营养和风味的需求。同时，对就餐客人求快和卫生的需求，应做到尽量缩短客人等候时间，做好清洁卫生工作。

任务二：托盘服务

Task 2: Tray Service

案例导入

小王是某旅游院校的一名大三学生。初次进入酒店做餐厅服务员，从来没有独立工作过的小王手忙脚乱，把客人需要的酒水、饮料一股脑儿地全放在了托盘上，结果在给客人斟倒酒水时，不小心将放在外侧的饮料瓶碰倒，致使饮料和酒水洒了一地，并且把一位客人的衣服给弄湿了。

思考讨论：如果你是小王，你应该怎么做？如果你是小王的领班，今后应该如何培训小王的端托服务技能？

知识准备

托盘是餐厅服务工作中用于运送各种物品的常用工具之一。因此，托盘操作的熟练程度十分重要。熟练掌握托盘操作技能可以提高工作效率、保证服务质量和规范餐厅的服务工作。

The tray is one of the common tools used to transport all kinds of items in restaurant service. Therefore, the proficiency of tray usage is very important. It can improve work efficiency, ensure service quality and standardize the service of restaurant.

一、托盘的种类与用途 Types and usage of trays

（一）托盘的种类 Types of trays

（1）按照托盘的制作材料，可分为木托盘、金属托盘和胶木防滑托盘。

According to the manufacture material of the tray, it can be divided into wood tray, metal tray and bakelite anti-slip tray.

（2）按照托盘的规格和形状，可分为大、中、小三种规格的长方形托盘和圆托盘。圆托盘中，直径大于 36cm 的为大圆托盘；直径为 32cm～36cm 的为中圆托盘；直径为 20cm～32cm 的为小圆托盘。长方托盘也按此规格分大、中、小三种。

According to the size and shape, it can be divided into large, medium and small three sizes of rectangular and round tray. The three sizes of round tray are as follows: the large tray has a diameter of more than 36cm; the diameter of the middle pallet is 32cm-36cm; the tray with a diameter of 20cm-32cm is the small tray. Rectangular trays are also divided into three sizes according to the specification: large, medium and small.

（二）托盘的用途 Usage of trays

（1）大方盘和中方盘用于装运菜点、酒水，收运餐具等重的器皿。

The large and medium rectangular trays are used to deliver heavy utensils such as course, wine and tableware.

（2）小方盘和大、中圆盘，一般用于摆台、斟酒、上菜、上饮料等。

Small rectangular tray, large and medium round tray, are usually used for table setting, pouring wine, serving dishes and drinks, etc.

（3）小圆盘和 6 英寸（15.24cm）小银盘主要用于递送账单、收款、递送信件等。

Small round tray and 6 inch (15.24cm) silver dish are mainly used to send bills, money, receipts, letters and other items.

二、托盘的使用 The use of trays

按所托物品轻重，有轻托和重托两种方式。物品重量在 5kg 以内的，适宜采用轻托方式；物品重量在 5kg 以上的，则采用重托方式。

According to the weight of the items, there are two ways: light and heavy holder. If the weight of items is within 5kg, it is suitable to use light holder , and if the weight of the goods is above 5kg, it is suitable to use heavy holder.

（一）轻托 Light holder

轻托又称"胸前托"。此法多用于中、小型托盘，有便于工作的优点。轻托的动作要领如下：

Light holder is also called "chest holder". This method is more used with medium and small trays, which is easy to work. The main points of the light holder are as follows:

（1）两肩平行，用左手。

Keep your shoulders parallel, and use your left hand.

（2）大臂与小臂垂直，呈 90°。

The angle between the upper arm and the lower arm is 90°.

（3）手掌掌心朝上，五指张开，指实而掌心虚。

The palm is upward, the fingers are open, the fingers are touching the tray and the palms is danging.

（4）手肘离腰部 15cm。

The elbow is 15cm from the waist.

（5）右手自然下垂或放于背后。

The right hand naturally droops or puts behind the back.

（二）重托 Heavy holder

重托又称“肩上托”。此法多用于大型托盘。重托的动作要领如下：

Heavy holder is also called “shoulder holder”. This method is usually used with large trays. The key points of the heavy holder are as follows:

（1）用左手。

Use the left hand.

（2）左手向上弯曲臂肘的同时，手掌向左转动手腕 180° 至肩上方。手掌略高出肩 2cm，五指自然分开，用五指和掌根部控制托盘的平衡。

Left hand bending elbow upward, at the same time, the palm wrists 180° to the left to the shoulder.The palm of your hand stand 2cm above the shoulders; the fingers naturally separated; balance the pallet with your fingers and palm base.

（3）托盘的位置以盘底不压肩、盘缘不近嘴、盘后不靠发为准。

The position of the tray should not be pressed to the shoulder, the edge of the tray should not be close to the mouth, and the hair should not be touched after the tray.

（4）右手应自然下垂摆动或扶住托盘的前内角。

The hand should swing naturally or hold the front inner corner of the tray.

目前，为了安全省力，餐饮企业一般不采用大型托盘，多用小型手推车递送重物。

At present, in order to serve with safety and convenience, catering enterprises generally use multifunctional small carts to deliver heavy items instead of large trays.

表 3.4 托盘的使用步骤、技能要求和操作规范
The Process, Skill Requirement and Operation Specification of the Use of Trays

步骤 Process	技能要求 Skill Requirement	操作规范 Operation Specification
理盘 Preparing	1. 根据装运物品选择托盘； Pick the tray based on the items; 2. 垫上垫布； Pad the placemat; 3. 防滑。 Non-slip.	1. 托盘应洗净、擦干； The trays should be clean and dry; 2. 垫布平铺整齐。 The placemat should be tiled and neat.
装盘 Setting	根据物品形状、体积、使用先后顺序等进行合理装盘。 According to the shape,volume, usage order of the object to set the tray.	1. 较重、较高的物品放在里面，较轻、较低的物品放在外面； Put heavier and taller items inside and the lighter and lower objects outside; 2. 先用的物品放在前面、上面，后用的物品放在里面、下面； Put the prior used items in the front and above; put others inside and below; 3. 物品重量应分布得当。 The weight should be well distributed.

续前表

步骤 Process	技能要求 Skill Requirement	操作规范 Operation Specification
起盘 Taking	保持托盘的平稳，汤汁不洒、菜肴不变形。 Keep the tray stable, the soup not spill out, dishes nondeformable.	1. 先将托盘的 1/3 托至操作台外； Place one third of the tray outside the counter; 2. 左手托住托盘底部，掌心位于底部中间，右手握住托盘； The left hand holds the bottom of the tray, puts the palm in the middle of the bottom, and the right hand holds the tray; 3. 如托盘较重，则先屈膝，用力托住托盘后起身，然后用手掌托住盘底。 If the tray is heavy, bend the knee first, then lift the tray up, and use the palm to hold the bottom.
托盘行走 Walking	步伐轻盈、稳健，汤汁不洒，身体挺直、略向前倾。 The pace is light and steady, the soup can not be spilled out. The body should be straight and slightly forward.	行走时要注意周围情况，能较好控制行走速度。 Pay attention to the surroundings, control the walking speed.

任务实施

第一步：教师讲解托盘基本知识并进行示范。

Step 1: The teacher explains the basic knowledge of the tray and demonstrates it.

第二步：按照下表以小组为单位（5 人 1 组）进行训练。

Step 2: Train in groups (5 people per group) according to the form below.

表 3.5　托盘操作训练表
The Training Form for Tray Service

训练内容 Training Content	托木块练习 Blocks-holding Exercise	托瓶练习 Bottle-holding Exercise	托盘行走练习 Walk-with-tray Exercise
训练方法 Training Method	所需物品：干净托盘、秒表（计时器）、砖形木块 2 块。 具体步骤：让每位学生练习托木块 2 个。 Required items: clean tray, stopwatch (timer), 2 brick type wood block. Procedure: Let the student practice holding 2 pieces of wood block.	所需物品：干净托盘、秒表（计时器）。 具体步骤：让学生托酒瓶 3～6 瓶。 Required items: clean tray, stopwatch (timer). Procedure: Ask students to hold 3-6 bottles.	所需物品：干净托盘、秒表（计时器）、不同酒瓶（啤酒、葡萄酒）4～6 个、水杯 1 只、障碍物若干（椅子）摆成 S 形。 具体步骤：让学生托盘行走。 Required items: clean tray, stopwatch (timer), 4-6 different bottles (beer, wine), water glass, several obstacles (chairs) placed in the shape of S. Procedure: Let the students walk with the tray.

续前表

训练内容 Training Content	托木块练习 Blocks-holding Exercise	托瓶练习 Bottle-holding Exercise	托盘行走练习 Walk-with-tray Exercise
训练要求 Training Requirements 根据班级人数分为几个小组；每10人一行，面对面站立进行训练；每组参加人员的练习时间为10分钟，时间到即停止操作。 Divide the class into several groups according to the number of the students; Every 10 students in a row, stand face to face; The practice time for each group of participants is 10 minutes, and the operation must stop when the time is up.	女生端托时间不少于2分钟，男生不少于5分钟；依照操作标准进行；逐渐增加重量。 The time for female students is not less than 2 minutes, and the male students not less than 5 minutes. Exercise in accordance with the operation standards; Gradually increase the weight.	高物练习，学会调整托盘重心；依照操作标准进行操作，可逐渐增加重量。 Practice with high object, learn to adjust the gravity of the tray; Exercise in accordance with the operation standards; The weight can be gradually increased.	每位学生进行多物托盘行走练习；行走时必须绕过每个障碍物，而且做到规范正确、迅速。 Each student does the walking exercise with the tray which is put on several items;Walk and bypass every obstacle; The action should be standard and quick.
注意事项 Notes	操作规范，重量不要增加太快。 Operate on the basis of specification, and do not increase the weight too fast.	操作规范，重量不要增加太快。 Operate on the basis of specification, and do not increase the weight too fast.	托盘行走平稳、姿势优美；行走时保持盘内物品的平衡；托盘时注意做到平、稳、松。 Walk smoothly with the graceful posture;Keep the balance of the items in the tray while walking;The action should be stable and relaxed.

任务评价

表 3.6 托盘操作评价表
The Evaluation Form of Tray Service

项目 Items	操作程序及标准 Operation Process and Standard	分值 Value	得分 Score
理盘 Preparation	保持托盘干净整洁，无油渍、无水迹。 Keep the tray clean and tidy, without oil or water stains.	3	
装盘 Setting	物品摆放整齐、美观、合理。 The objects are arranged neatly, nicely and properly.	10	
起托 Action	起托方法正确。 The lifting method is correct.	2	
	端托时姿势正确，手臂成直角。 Hold the tray correctly with arms at right angles.	3	
	六个支点受力。 Holding with six fulcrum.	5	

续前表

项目 Items	操作程序及标准 Operation Process and Standard	分值 Value	得分 Score
起托 Action	托盘不靠腹，手臂不撑腰。 The tray is not supported by abdomen, and the arms are not supported by the waist.	2	
	表情自然、动作大方、保持微笑。 Look naturally, act naturally and keep smile.	3	
	上身挺直、头正、肩平、眼睛目视前方。 Keep the body straight, head straight, shoulders flat, and eyes look straight ahead.	2	
	左手托盘。 Hold the tray with left hand.	3	
	理盘平稳，物品不歪、不倒，不发出声响。 The tray setting is stable, and the object is not tilted, fallen, or makes any noise.	5	
	不允许翻盘。 Tipping over the tray is forbidden.	40	
端托行走 Walk with the tray	行走步伐轻盈。 Walk lightly.	5	
	遇障碍物避让自如。 Avoid obstacles freely.	5	
卸盘 Unloading	姿势正确。 Correct posture.	5	
	盘内物品不歪、不倒。 The contents of the tray are not tilted or fallen.	5	
	卸盘后物品摆放整齐。 After unloading the tray, the articles should be put neatly and tidily.	2	
最终得分 Final Score			

拓展阅读

托盘的重要性

餐饮经营者会对餐厅环境的塑造费尽心思，却往往忽略一个细节，即餐厅服务中必须使用的重要工具——托盘。精美的餐品搭配合适的托盘，更能彰显餐厅的品位。

《随园食单》中记载有“美食不如美器”，并且提出菜肴出锅后“煎炒宜盘，汤羹宜碗，参错其间，方觉生色”，这就是对美食、美器、美饰的精炼总结。许多餐厅经营者觉得为客人提供高档餐具就足够了，其实不然。若将托盘的搭配纳入美器的考量范围，整体效果会更佳。

任务三：餐巾折花
Task 3: Napkin Folding

案例导入

某饭店宴会部的小王接待了一位日本客人小泉先生。小泉先生详细了解了酒店的服务情况后，预订了3天后40人的高档宴会，并提出了宴会要求，交付了订金。3天后宴会部按照小泉先生的要求做好了一切准备工作，并根据时令季节选用了优雅的荷花造型的餐巾折花。当迎宾员将其中的几位日本客人引领到餐桌时，客人十分不悦。

思考讨论：客人为什么不悦？如果你是该宴会部的服务员，接下来该怎么做？

知识准备

一、餐巾及餐巾折花 Napkins and napkin folding flowers

餐巾又称“口布”，是一种正方形布巾。客人在用餐过程中将餐巾压置于骨碟下面或者置于大腿上。餐巾是餐桌上常备的一种保洁用品，客人可以用其擦去手上或嘴上的油渍，防止酒水、汤汁滴洒到衣服上。

Napkin, which is also called “mouth cloth”, is a square cloth towel, and is placed under a plate or on the lap during the meal. Napkins are a kind of cleaning equipment that guests can use to wipe off oil stains on their hands or mouth to prevent alcohol or soup dripping on their clothes.

最早的餐巾折花是直接折成正方形，平放在餐盘上。直至1639年，意大利人将餐巾折叠发展成为一种观赏艺术。餐巾最重要的作用是清洁，因此，从卫生角度出发，餐巾折花花样越简单越好。同时，简单的餐巾折花也可以节省服务人员的时间，方便客人打开使用。

The earliest napkin folding flowers were directly folded into a square, put flat on the plate. Until 1639, the Italians developed napkin folding into an ornamental art. The most important role of napkins is cleaning, so from the view of hygiene, napkins should be as simple as possible. At the same time, simple napkin folding can also save the service time, and it’s convenient for guests to open and use.

餐厅为了营造气氛、美化餐桌，有时候需要选择不同颜色、不同造型的餐巾折花，因此，餐桌上会出现各种不同动植物造型的餐巾折花。

In order to create the atmosphere and beautify the dining table, sometimes the restaurant needs to choose different colors and shapes of napkins to fold flowers. As a result, there will be various forms of animals and plants made by napkins on the table.

餐巾折花可分为杯花、盘花与环花三种。杯花是将餐巾折好造型之后放置于水杯中，水杯去除之后即散开，常用于中餐厅摆台及各类中式宴席。盘花折叠成形后，可独立放置于餐盘中或者餐桌上，常用于西餐厅。由于盘花折叠简单、可独立成型，因此也常见于中餐厅。环花是将餐巾平整卷好或者折叠成造型后套在餐巾环内。餐巾环也称为餐巾扣，材料有塑料、瓷质、银制、骨制、象牙等。除此之外，餐巾环还可以用彩色丝带或丝穗带代替。餐巾环花通常放置在装饰盘或餐盘上，给人以传统、简洁和雅致的感觉，中西餐厅皆可使用。

Napkin folding flower can be divided into cup flower, plate flower and wreath. The cup flower is to fold the napkin and put it in the water cup. The flower will disappear when taken out of the cup. It is often used in the Chinese restaurant and all kinds of Chinese banquet. Plate flower can be placed independently on the plate or on the dining table. It is often used in western restaurants because it is easy to fold and can be shaped independently. Therefore, it is also common in Chinese restaurants. The wreath is to roll the napkin or fold it into shape and put it in the napkin ring. Napkin ring, which is also known as napkin buckles, can be made by different materials like plastic, porcelain, silver, bone, ivory, etc. In addition, napkin rings can also be replaced by colored ribbons or spikes. The wreath is usually placed on a decorative plate or dinner plate to give the guests a traditional, concise and elegant feel, which are available in both Chinese and western restaurants.

西餐厅比较偏爱白色且样式简单的餐巾，中餐厅的餐巾变化较多，色彩也较为丰富。

Western restaurants prefer white and simple style napkins. The napkins used in Chinese restaurants are more changeable and colourful.

餐巾的材质以纯棉最受欢迎，这种材质不仅吸水性好，而且折花易于成型。混纺材质的餐巾吸水性差，且折花时不易成型。

Pure cotton is still the most popular napkin material. It's not only because it has good water absorption, but also the flower folding easy to shape.The napkin of blended material has poor water absorption and is not easy to form when folding flowers.

二、餐巾花的摆放要求 The display requirements of table napkin flowers

餐巾花的应用比较广泛，大至国宴小到家宴都可以用餐巾花来摆台装饰。总的摆设要求是整齐美观、搭配得当、使用方便、便于观赏，尽可能与台布、餐具的色调相结合。餐巾花在摆放时要注意以下几点：

Napkin flowers are widely used from state banquet to family dinners. The overall furnishing requirements are neat and beautiful, decorate with proper collocation, easy to use, easy to watch, as much as possible to combine with tablecloth and tableware. The following points should be noted when placing napkins:

（一）区别插摆 Distinguished arrangement

餐巾花一般插入水杯或摆放在盘中，因此要区别插摆。底部较大的花型宜插入水杯中，需要平摊摆放的花形则适宜搁置在盘里。餐巾花插入水杯中的深度要适当，一般插在水杯深度的 2/3 为宜，露在外面的部分为观赏部分，因此插放的时候应该要注意调整花型。由于杯子是透明的，因此杯子内的部分也不能忽视，应该线条清楚，忌乱插乱塞。摆放在盘里的餐巾花要正、要稳。

Napkin flowers are generally inserted into the cup or placed in the plate, so it's important to distinguish the methods. Napkin flowers with larger bottom should be inserted into the water cup, those which need to be laid flat is suitable for placing on the plate. The napkin flower should be inserted into the cup at a suitable depth, generally 2/3 of the depth of the cup, and the exposed part is the ornamental part. Therefore, it should be paid attention to the perfection of the pattern when inserting. Because the cup is transparent, so the part in the cup can not be ignored, which should be clear, and away from random plugging. The napkin flowers placed on the plate should be straight and steady.

（二）搭配得当 Properly matched

餐巾花的品种要搭配得当，凸显主位，其他宾客位置的花形应高低均匀，错落有致。同桌摆放时，要将品种、形状相似的花形，或高低、大小相似的花形，错开并对称摆放，一般不宜将相同花型摆放在一起。

The varieties of napkin flower should be matched properly to highlight the host and other guests. When placing the napkin flower on the same table, the varieties, shape, height, size of the flower should be considered. It must be staggered and symmetrical placed, and never put the same pattern together.

（三）注意朝向 Paying attention to the orientation

餐巾花要注意摆放的朝向，应将观赏性的一面对着宾客席位。餐巾花摆放要注意距离匀称，整齐一致，不能挡住餐具和餐台上的其他用品，也不能影响服务操作。

Pay attention to the orientation of napkin flowers. The view side should face to the guests. Napkin flowers should be placed evenly and neatly, neither block tableware and other items on the table, nor affect service operation.

三、常见餐巾折花及折叠步骤 Normal napkin flower holding style and process

表 3.7 餐巾花折叠步骤（盘花）

Napkin Flower Folding Process（Plate Flowers）

名称 Name	步骤 Process	完成图 Graphic Model
金字塔 Pyramid	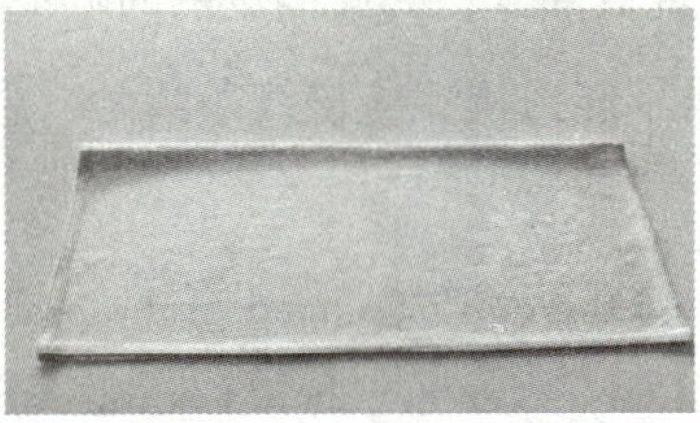	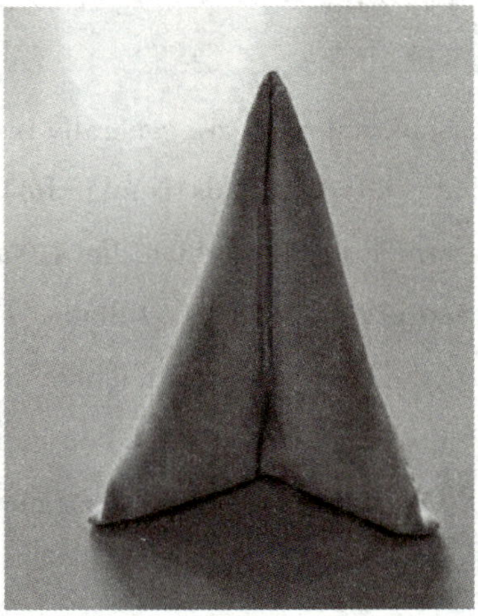

济公帽（僧帽） Mitral	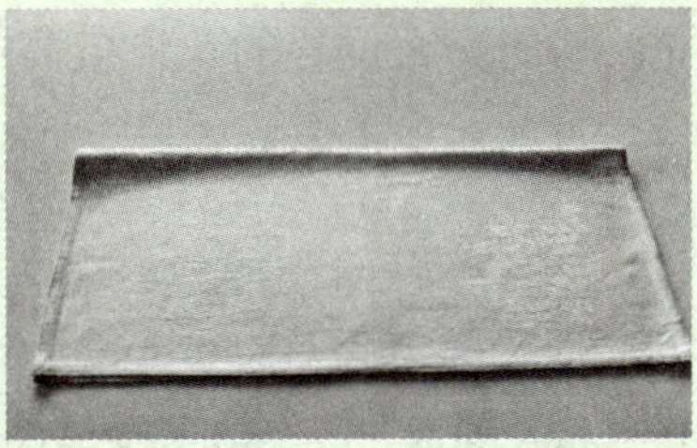	

续前表

名称 Name	步骤 Process	完成图 Graphic Model
济公帽（僧帽） Mitral	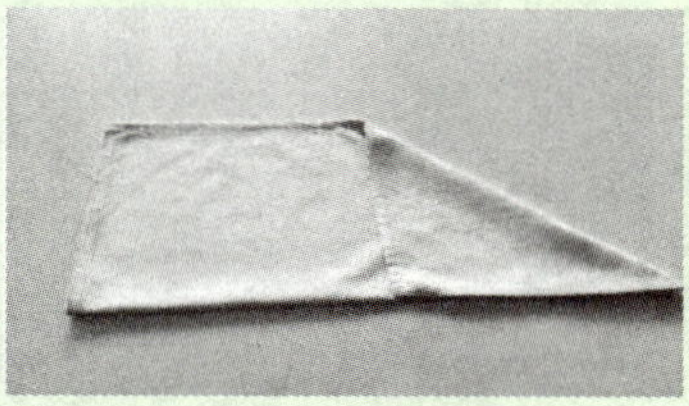 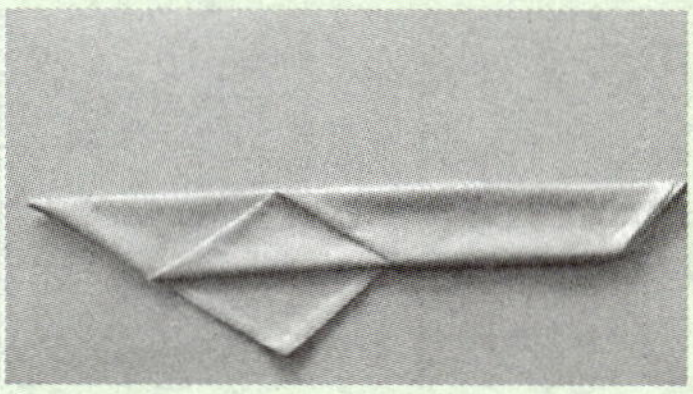 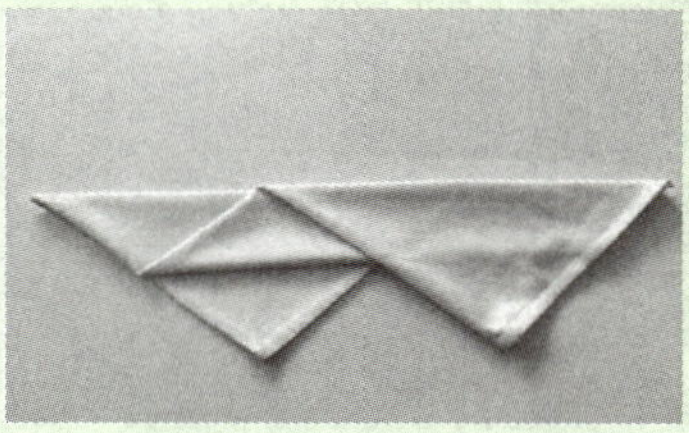  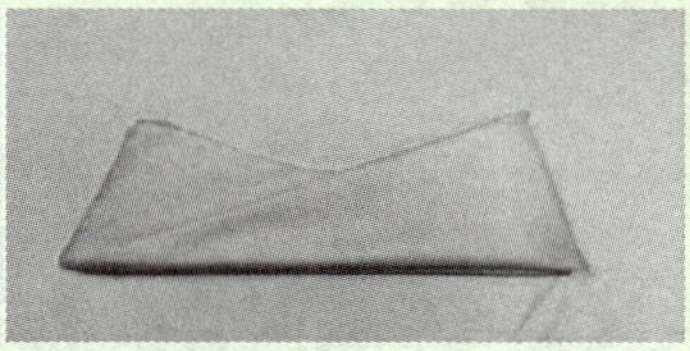	
法国褶 French Plait	 	

续前表

<table>
<tr><th>名称
Name</th><th>步骤
Process</th><th>完成图
Graphic Model</th></tr>
<tr><td rowspan="3">法国褶
French Plait</td><td>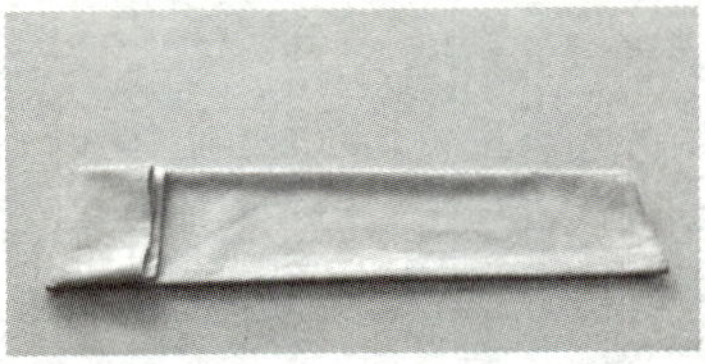</td><td rowspan="3">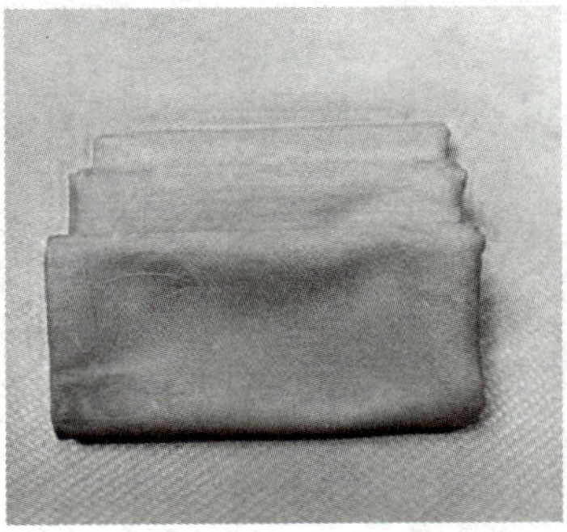</td></tr>
<tr><td></td></tr>
<tr><td></td></tr>
<tr><td rowspan="4">帐篷
Tent</td><td>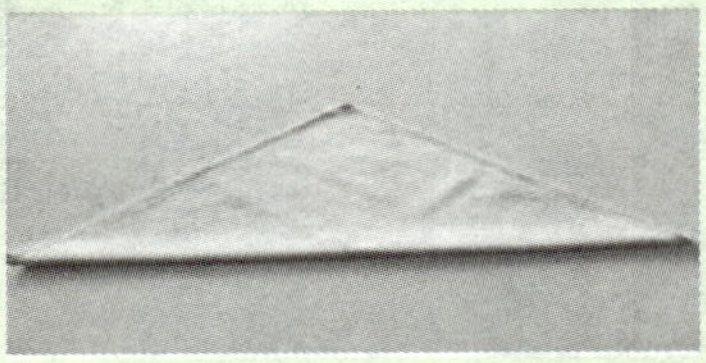</td><td rowspan="4">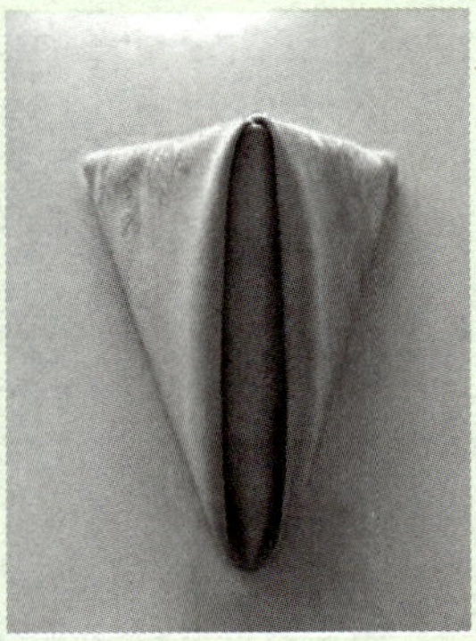</td></tr>
<tr><td></td></tr>
<tr><td></td></tr>
<tr><td>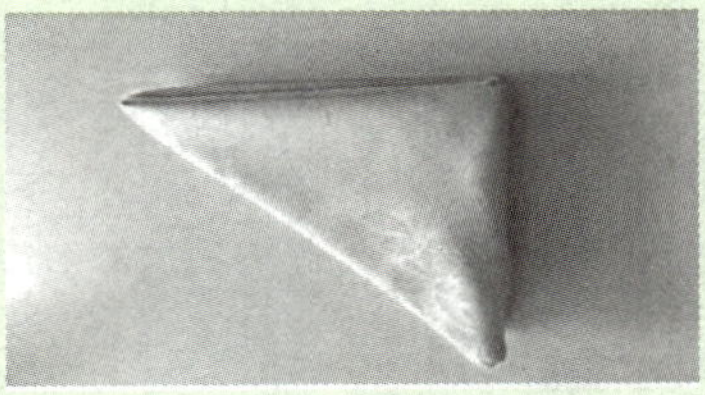</td></tr>
</table>

续前表

名称 Name	步骤 Process	完成图 Graphic Model
蜗牛 Snail	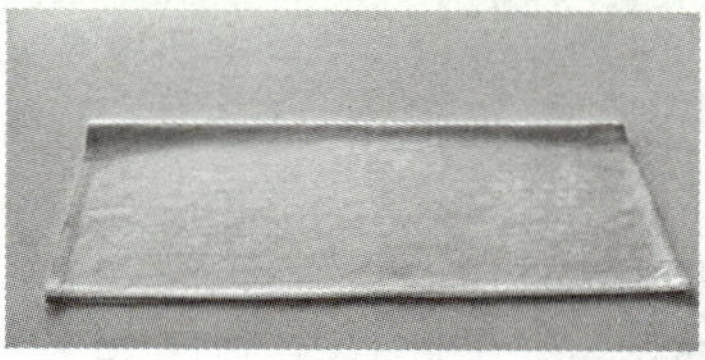  	
圆锥帽 Conical Hat	  	
星光灿烂 Starry Night	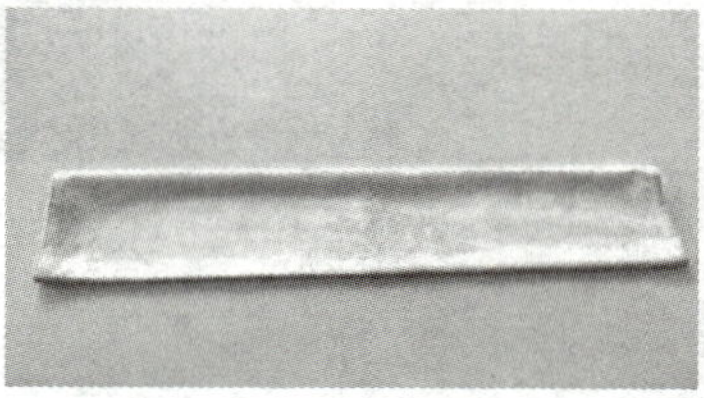	

续前表

名称 Name	步骤 Process	完成图 Graphic Model
星光灿烂 Starry Night		
	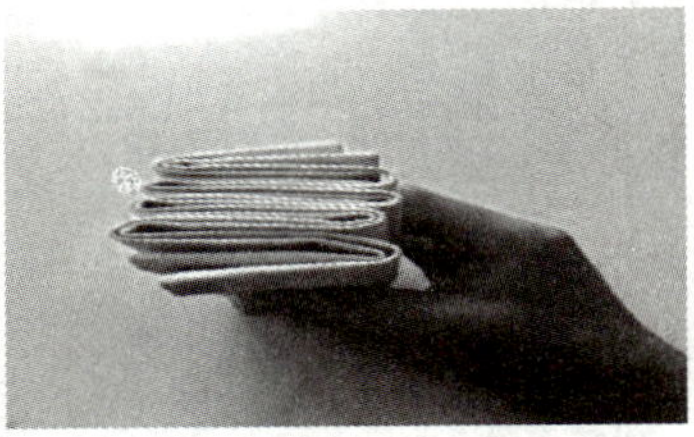	

帆船 Sailing Boat	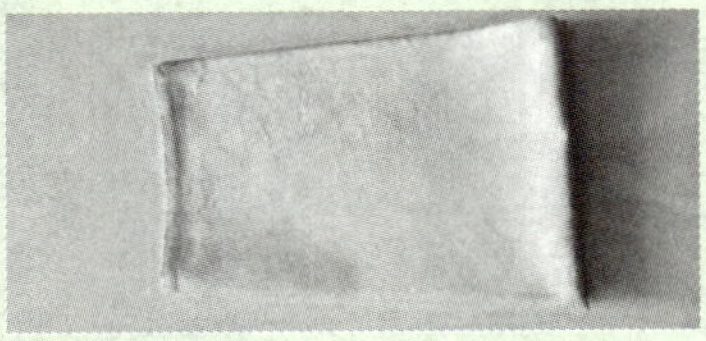	

续前表

名称 Name	步骤 Process	完成图 Graphic Model
帆船 Sailing Boat	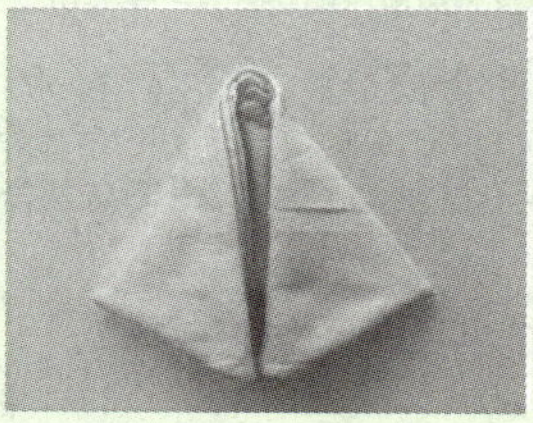	
	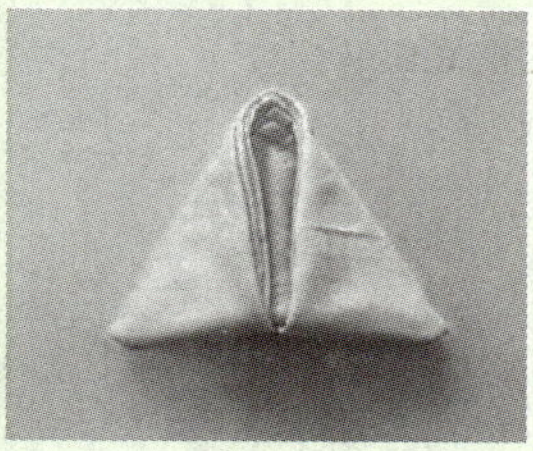	
	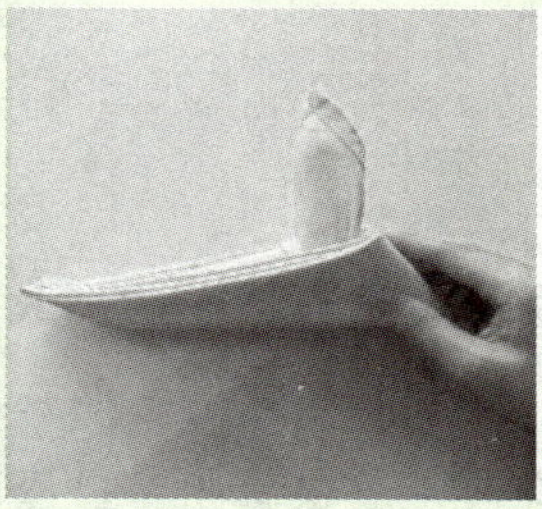	

任务实施

第一步：教师示范讲解餐巾及餐巾折花的基本知识。

Step 1: The teacher demonstrates the basic knowledge of napkins and napkin folding.

第二步：教师示范杯花的折叠。

Step 2: The teacher demonstrates the folding of cup flowers.

第三步：教师示范盘花的折叠。

Step 3: The teacher demonstrates the folding of plate flowers.

第四步：以小组为单位（5 人 1 组）进行餐巾折花训练，每人至少练习折出 5 种杯花、5 种盘花。折花要求手法正确、花型美观大方。

Step 4: Take the group as a unit (5 people per 1 group) for napkin folding training. Each person should practice folding at least 5 cup flowers and 5 plate flowers. Folding requires correct technique and elegant pattern.

任务评价

表 3.8 餐巾折花操作评价表
The Evaluation Form of Napkin Folding

考核内容 Content	考核要点 Key Points	分值 Value	得分 Score
餐巾折花 Napkin Folding	折出 5 种杯花、5 种盘花。 Finish five kinds of cup of flowers, and five kinds of plate flowers.	50	
	折叠均匀整齐，造型美观。 The flowers are uniform, tidy and beautiful.	30	
	手法规范。 The skills are standard.	10	
	操作卫生。 The process is free of contamination.	10	

拓展阅读

餐巾的起源与发展

中国古代典籍中就有宴会使用“餐巾”覆盖食物和擦手的记载。明清时期，宫廷和贵族宴会出现了高档的锦缎绣花餐巾。可以说，餐巾并非完全是舶来品。

西方餐巾的历史久远。古希腊和古罗马贵族一直保持用手进食的习惯，所以在用餐完毕后，他们会用一条毛巾大小的餐巾来擦手。更讲究一点的贵族会在擦完手之后在洗指钵内洗手。洗指钵里除了盛着水，还盛有玫瑰花瓣。古埃及人还在钵体中放入杏仁、肉桂和橘花。到了 17 世纪，餐巾除了实用之外，其观赏性也越来越受到重视。公元 1680 年，意大利已有 20 多种餐巾的折法，如教士用的挪亚方舟形，贵妇人用的母鸡形，以及普通人喜欢用的小鸡、乌龟、公牛、熊、兔子等形状，形态各异。

我们使用的现代餐巾是一种中西合璧的产物，被广泛应用于各式餐厅服务中，成为餐厅和服务的一个重要组成部分。

Project 4

Table Setting

项目四

摆　台

项目概述 PROJECT SUMMARY

摆台，是指餐桌上供客人使用的餐具摆设放置的状况。整体的餐桌摆设，除了包括最初的台布铺设和最终桌面的装饰摆放之外，还包括餐具的排列，花瓶、调味品的放置等。各餐厅有不同形态的摆台，不论如何摆设均应该以安全、卫生、合理、整齐、统一以及服务的便利性为出发点。

餐厅的摆台是否合理、美观将会极大地影响客人的用餐体验。无论是台布材质的选取、颜色的搭配，还是餐、酒具的材质与品质，都需要餐厅经营者用心关注。

因为饮食文化的差异，中、西餐摆台在布料选择、器具使用上有着很大的不同。在理解饮食文化差异的基础上，再探讨中、西餐摆台的原则与方法，更能体现出餐厅服务的品质。

项目目标 PROJECT OBJECTS

知识目标：了解中、西餐摆台的原则；掌握中、西餐摆台所需要的器具；掌握中、西餐摆台的步骤。

技能目标：熟练进行中、西餐台布的铺设；熟练进行中、西餐台面的摆设。

素养目标：具有强烈的民族自信与文化自信；具备精益求精的工匠精神；具有强烈的职业责任感；具备创新意识。

任务一：中餐摆台
Task 1: Chinese Restaurant Table Setting

案例导入

王先生来到某酒店中餐厅，领位员将他引领至其所预订的牡丹亭包间。牡丹亭包间在走廊的尽头，到达该包间需途经其他几个包间。王先生在行走的过程中随意地看了看左右两边的包间，其中一个荷花亭包间的门半掩着，可以看到里面的摆台情况。王先生看到圆桌上已经摆好了餐具，但是每个餐位上都用餐巾盖住整套餐具，很是奇怪，就随口问这位领位员："为什么要把餐巾盖在餐具上面？"领位员的回答是："这样就不会落灰了！"王先生一脸惊讶，等走进牡丹亭包间后，王先生立即吩咐服务员将餐桌上的所有餐巾都换了新的。

思考讨论：餐厅客用物品如何规范使用？

知识准备

一、铺台布 Spread the tablecloth

台布是餐厅摆台必备的物品之一。台布的规格及颜色的选择，应与餐台的大小、餐厅的风格协调一致。

As a part of table setting, the size, color and style of tablecloth should be in line with that of the restaurant.

（一）台布的种类 Category of the tablecloth

台布的种类有很多，因纯棉材质吸水性能好，大多数餐厅广泛使用纯棉提花台布。台布的图案有团花、散花、工艺绣花及装饰布等。台布的颜色多种多样，但多数餐厅选用白色。台布的颜色要与餐厅的风格、装饰、环境相协调。通常来说，台布的形状有正方形、长方形和圆形三种。中餐摆台中，正方形常用于方台或圆台，圆形台布主要用于圆台。

Among numerous kinds of tablecloth, cotton cloth is outstanding in water absorption which is widely used in current restaurants. The patterns of tablecloth vary from single cluster, bunches, craft embroidery to decorative fabric usually against white background which, on most occasions, is determined by the style, decoration and ambience of the restaurant. The shape of the cloth ranges from the square—which is frequently applied to square and round tables in Chinese setting—to rectangle and round ones—which goes for round tables.

（二）台布的规格 Size of the tablecloth

正方形台布的规格有多种，应根据餐桌的大小选择适当规格的台布。如 140cm × 140cm 的台布适用于 90cm × 90cm 的方台；160cm × 160cm 的台布适用于 100cm × 100cm 或 110cm × 110cm 的方台；200cm × 200cm 的台布适用于直径 170cm 的圆台；220cm × 220cm 的台布适用于直径 180cm 或 200cm 的圆台。圆形台布的规格各有不同，一般的圆形台布多需定制，即根据餐台的大小将台布制成直径大于餐台直径 60cm 的圆形台布，使台布铺于餐台上时圆周下垂 30cm 为宜。

The size of tablecloth is determined by the size of the table. For example, a 140cm × 140cm cloth applies to a 90cm × 90cm square table; a 160cm × 160cm one corresponds to a 100cm × 100cm or 110cm × 110cm square table，a 200cm × 200cm tablecloth is suitable for a round table of 170cm diameter; a 220cm × 220cm one caters for a round table of 180cm or 200cm diameter. Normally, round shape tablecloth is customized under the principle, whose furthest range is 60cm longer than that of the table. By doing so, the rest 30cm can circle around and be hung off the table.

（三）台布铺设 Laying the tablecloth

台布铺设是将台布舒适平整地铺在餐桌上的过程。铺台布之前，服务人员应将所需餐椅按就餐人数摆放于餐台的四周，使之呈三三两两的并列状。然后，服务人员应将双手洗净，并对准备铺用的每块台布进行仔细检查，发现有残破、油渍或褶皱，则不能使用。最后，根据餐厅的装饰、布局确定席位。操作时，服务人员应将副主人位处餐椅拉开至右侧餐椅边，然后站立在副主人餐椅处，距餐台约 40cm，将选好的台布放于副主人的餐台上。

Laying the tablecloth is a process to gently and evenly pave the cloth on the table. Before that, the server should put chairs around the table according to the amount of diners, align them by twos and threes. Then, the server should clean his hands before committing to the process; examine every cloth to make sure that it’s clean without any loophole, stain or wrinkle. At last, place chairs according to the direction and design of the table. When performing the layout, the server should move out the chair of the deputy host first, then stand in its place, keep a distance about 40cm to the side of the table, and put on the tablecloth.

（四）铺台布的三种方法 Three ways to spread the tablecloth

1. 推拉式铺台 Push-and-pull

推拉式铺台，即用双手将台布打开后，放至餐台上，将台布贴着餐台平行推出去再拉回来。这种铺法多用于零点餐厅或较小的餐厅。

Push-and-pull is to lay the cloth on the table, open and push it along the facet of the table, then pull back to adjust to an optimal position. This method commonly applies to a la carte and small restaurants.

2. 撒网式铺台 Cast-net

撒网式铺台，即用双手将台布打开，平行打折，呈右脚在前、左脚在后的站立姿势，双手将打开的台布提拿起来至胸前，双臂与肩平行，上身向左转体，下肢不动。在右臂与身体回转时，台布斜着向前撒出去。将台布抛至前方时，上身转体回位并回复至正位站立，这时台布应平铺于餐台上，台布的中心应与台面中心重合。抛撒时，动作应自然、潇洒。这种铺法多用于宽大场地或技术比赛场合。

Cast-net is to open the tablecloth parallelly on both sides, and stand firmly on the ground with the right foot set in front of the left one. The server should lift the cloth to chest at the same level of the arm, then move the upper body to the left with rest stay unmoved. When the upper body turns back, the server should cast the cloth diagonally forward. When the tablecloth lands on the table, make sure the center of the cloth overlap with that of the table. This method applies to restaurant with enough space or to skills competitions.

3. 抖铺式铺台 Shake the tablecloth

抖铺式铺台，即用双手将台布打开，平行打折后将台布提拿在双手中，身体呈正位站立式，利用双腕的力量，将台布向前一次性抖开并平铺于餐台上。这种铺台方法适合于较宽敞的餐厅。

Shake is to open the tablecloth parallelly on the two sides. The server should stand in a forward position and shake the cloth by the power of wrists until it's widely open. This method applies to restaurant with spacious ground.

表 4.1 中餐台布铺设操作流程
The Operation Procedure of Laying Tablecloth in Chinese Restaurant

操作程序 Operation Procedure	动作要领 Essentials of Exercise	图示 Examples
开（抖）台布 Shake	1. 站于主人位； Stand in the host's position; 2. 双手将台布向餐位两侧尽可能地拉开。 Hold two sides of the cloth and pull them apart as far as possible.	

续前表

操作程序 Operation Procedure	动作要领 Essentials of Exercise	图示 Examples
拢台布 Hold	1. 双手拇指和食指捏住台布； Hold the tablecolth between thumb and forefinger; 2. 双手收拢于前身，身体略前倾。 Fold the tablecloth in front of you with both hands and lean forward slightly.	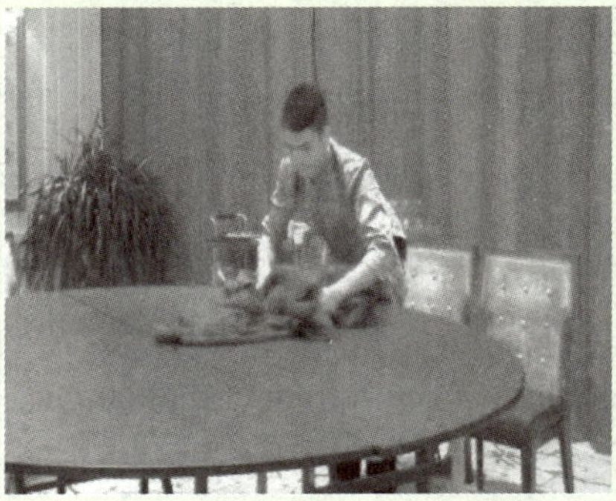
推（撒/抖铺）台布 Push/Cast/ Shake and Push	推： Push： 1. 双手把台布沿桌面迅速用力推出； Rapidly push the cloth along the table facet; 2. 双手捏住台布边角不要松开。 Hold the sides of the cloth firmly. 撒： Cast： 1. 腰向左转或向右转，手臂随腰部的转动并向侧方挥动； Turn your waist either to the left or to the right, when turning back, the movement of arms go with that of the waist; 2. 除捏台布边角的拇指和食指，其他手指松开。 Hold the cloth with your thumb and index finger with the rest fingers in relax. 抖铺： Shake and Push： 1. 双手拇指和食指捏住台布，平行打折后将台布提拿在双手中； Hold the tablecloth between thumb and forefinger on its two sides; Lift the tablecloth by two hands after parallel folding; 2. 身体呈正位站立式，利用双腕的力量，将台布向前一次性抖开并平铺于餐台上。 Stand forward, shake the cloth and lay it on the table with the help of the wrists.	  

续前表

操作程序 Operation Procedure	动作要领 Essentials of Exercise	图示 Examples
台布定位 Locate	1. 台布下落时缓慢把台布拉至桌子边沿靠近身体处； As it lands, gently pull the cloth to the side of the table besides your body; 2. 调整台布的中心位置，使台布中心和台面中心重合； Adjust the center of the cloth to make sure its center overlaps with that of the table; 3. 台布凸缝朝上，中心线对准正副主人位。 The convex side of the cloth should face upward with the center line pointing directly towards the seat of the host and deputy host.	 
放转盘 Set the Turntable	把转盘放在转轴上，转轴处在桌子正中。 Set the turntable and make sure the spindle is in the middle.	

（五）注意事项 Notices

铺台布时，台布不能接触地面，台布中间折痕的交叉点应正好在餐台的中心处；台布的正面凸缝朝上，中心线直对正、副主人席位；四角呈直线下垂状，下垂部分距地面距离相等；铺好的台布应平整无皱褶。铺好台布后，应将拉出的餐椅送回原位。还应注意铺台布时的手部力量：避免拉台布力量过大；避免推台布力量不够；避免两手用力不均匀。

When spreading the tablecloth, it should be kept away from the ground. The intersection should overlap with the center of the table, and the convex side of the cloth face upward with center line pointing directly towards the seat of host in the front and deputy host at the back. The server should make sure the cloth doesn't have wrinkle on the facet with its four edges hanging evenly to the ground, and put the chairs back when finishing. The server should pay attention to the strength when spreading the tablecloth: Do not pull the cloth with too much strength; Do not pull the cloth too gentle; Do get even strength on both sides.

二、摆台 Table setting

摆台，就是在餐台上摆放各种餐具的过程。

Table setting is the process of putting the tableware on the table.

（一）中餐宴会摆台的程序及规范 The procedure and standard of Chinese banquet table setting

表 4.2　　中餐宴会摆台的程序及规范

The Procedure and Standard of Chinese Banquet Table Setting

操作程序 Operation Procedure	操作标准与要求 Operation Standard and Requirements	图　示 Examples
1. 铺台布 Lay the tablecloth	1. 位置：站在主人位右侧的副主人位； Position: Stand on the seat of deputy host;which is on the right side of the host's seat; 2. 方法：推拉式、抖铺式或撒网式； Methods: Push-and-pull, shake, cast-net; 3. 标准：正面朝上，一次到位，台布十字折线居中，不偏斜；台布凸缝朝上，对准正副主人餐位；台布四角下垂均匀；台布下垂四角与桌腿平行，与地面垂直。 Standard: Put tablecloth upward on the table and finish during the first try as possible; Make sure the center of the cloth is in the middle of the table and the convex side pointing towards the host's and deputy host's seat; Make sure the four edges of the cloth hang evenly to the ground with the surface parallel with the legs of the table and perpendicular to the ground.	  

续前表

操作程序 Operation Procedure	操作标准与要求 Operation Standard and Requirements	图 示 Examples
2. 拉椅 Pull the chair	将餐椅摆放在餐台周围。圆桌摆放呈“三三两两式”；方桌摆放呈“两两一一式”或“对称式”；从主位开始，将餐椅正对餐位，椅子之间距离相等，与桌边相距 1.5cm。 Arrange seats around the table. For round tables, place the seats into a form of “three-three-two-two”; For square ones, place the seats into a form of a symmetrical array or “two-two-one-one”, aiming to the center of the table and place the seat starting from the host’s seat; Keep the equal distance between seats with a 1.5cm distance to the side of the table.	 
3. 摆放转盘和中心装饰物 Place turntable and centerpiece	1. 8 人以上餐台应摆转台；转盘居中摆放，与餐台同心，注意检查转盘旋转是否灵活。 Set a turntable for a group of more than eight people; Make sure the center of the turntable is concentric with that of the table; Check to see if the turntable can rotate smoothly to perform the task. 2. 摆放中心装饰物，装饰物规格与餐桌比例恰当，外形美观，具有较强观赏价值；中心装饰物要与宴会主题相符，同时起到烘托和点缀主题的作用。 Put the centerpiece whose specifications are appropriate to the table. It should have a beautiful appearance with a strong ornamental value. It should be accord with the banquet theme, and play the role of foiling and embellishing the theme.	 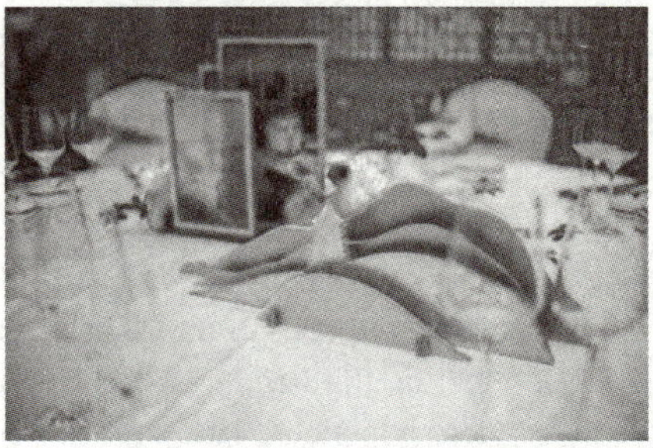 

续前表

操作程序 Operation Procedure	操作标准与要求 Operation Standard and Requirements	图　示 Examples
4. 摆餐饮具 Set the tableware	要求：使用托盘操作，从主人位开始，按顺时针方向依次摆放；摆放餐具时要求轻放，注意卫生标准要求。 Requirements: Hold the tray and distribute the wares in clockwise order from the host’s seat; Handle them gently and be aware of the sanitation. （1）骨碟定位：拿骨碟边缘，摆在席位正中，间距相等，距桌边 1.5cm，店徽或图案对齐。 Locate the plate: Hold the edge of the plate and place it on the table aligning to the center of each seat, and keep a 1.5cm gap between each other. If a pattern or logo is present, make sure to place them in a unanimous position. （2）汤碗、汤勺和味碟：味碟放在骨碟正上方，距骨碟 1cm；汤碗放在骨碟左上方，距味碟 1cm，勺置于碗中，勺把向左。汤碗和味碟的横向直径在一直线上。 Soup bowl, spoon and sauce dish: Set a sauce dish in the front, and leave 1cm to the nearest side of the plate. Set the soup bowl on the top left of the plate, and leave a 1cm gap to the sauce dish. Put the spoon in the bowl with its handle pointing to the left. Maintain the three items horizontally in the same level. （3）筷架、筷子和牙签：筷架摆在骨碟的右侧，位于筷子上部 1/3 处；筷子、长柄勺摆在筷架上，长柄勺距骨碟右侧边缘 3cm，尾端离桌边 1.5cm；筷子图案向上，后端距桌边 1.5cm；牙签摆放在筷子和长柄勺中间，牙签套正面朝上，底部与长柄勺齐平。 Chopsticks rack, chopsticks and toothpick: Place the rack to the right of the plate at the top third end of the chopsticks. Then, set chopsticks, ladle on the rack. Leave 3cm between the ladle and the plate with a 1.5cm gap between its end and the edge of the table. Keep the same distance between the end of chopsticks and the edge of the table. If a pattern or logo is present, make sure the painted side is in the front. Lay the toothpick in between the chopsticks and ladle with its front side facing upward and	（1）  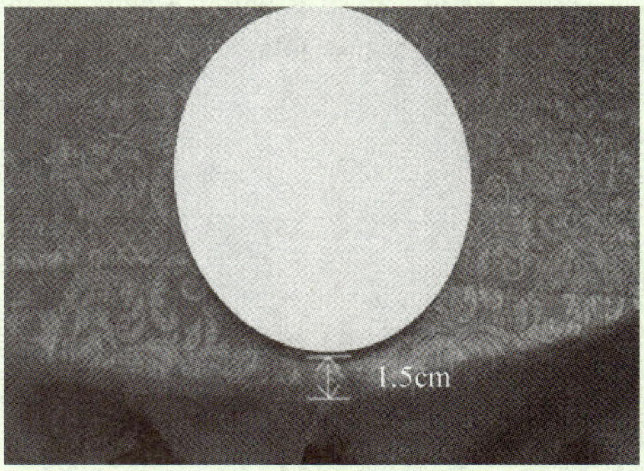 （2）  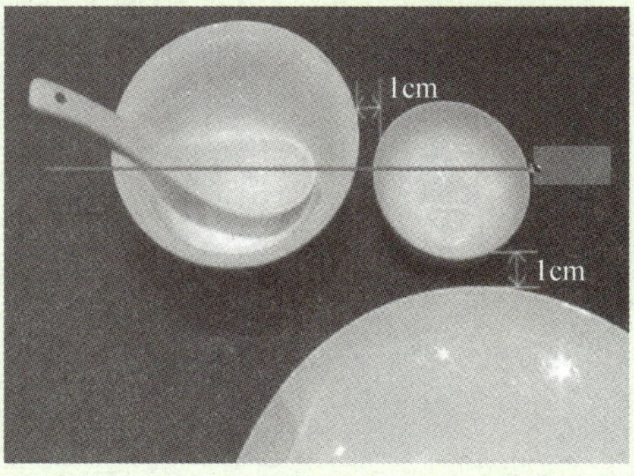

续前表

<table>
<tr><th>操作程序
Operation Procedure</th><th>操作标准与要求
Operation Standard and Requirements</th><th>图 示
Examples</th></tr>
<tr><td>4. 摆餐具
Set the tableware</td><td>its end should be aligned to the ladle's.
（4）公用餐具：公筷架、公用勺、公筷放置于正、副主人位的正前方，公筷架距离转台 5cm～8cm，公勺在外，公筷在里，勺柄向右。
Public tableware: Serving chopsticks rack, spoons and chopsticks should be put in front of the host's and deputy host's seat. Make sure there is a 5cm-8cm distance between the serving chopsticks rack and the turntable. And place the serving chopsticks inside, serving spoon outside and the handle to the right.
（5）水杯、葡萄酒杯和白酒杯：葡萄酒杯放在味碟正上方，葡萄酒杯右侧摆放白酒杯，左侧摆放水杯，三杯成斜直线，与水平线呈 30 度角，各杯肚间距 1cm。如果折的是杯花，水杯待餐巾花折好后一起摆上桌。
Water glass, wine glass and short glass (for Chinese liquor): Place the wine glass in front of the sauce dish, lay a short glass to its right and a water glass to its left. Make sure there is a 1cm gap between each glass and are on the same level at 30 angles to their horizontal layout. If the table will be decorated with cup flower, the water glass should be put on the table after the cup flower is done.</td><td>（3）

（4）

（5）
</td></tr>
</table>

续前表

操作程序 Operation Procedure	操作标准与要求 Operation Standard and Requirements	图示 Examples
5. 摆放餐巾花 Arrange table napkin flowers	中餐宴会可以摆设杯花，也可摆放盘花。应位置摆放得当，美观大方。Napkin flower can be cup flower or plate flower during a Chinese banquet. Napkin flowers should be placed properly,beautiful and dignified.	
6. 复查 Double check	摆台后要检查台面摆设有无遗漏，摆放是否规范、符合标准。After the process is finished, check and make sure the quantity and quality of the setting which should be accord with the standard.	

（二）中餐零点摆台的程序及规范 The procedure and standard of a-la-carte service table setting

表 4.3 中餐零点摆台的程序及规范 The Procedure and Standard of A-la-carte Service Table Setting

操作程序 Operation Procedure	操作标准与要求 Operation Standard and Requirements	图示 Examples
餐前准备 Preparation	1. 将摆台前的餐具准备齐全，干净卫生，无破损；Prepare all the tableware which are clean and undamaged; 2. 摆台时服务人员保持双手干净；The service staff should keep their hands clean when setting the table; 3. 检查餐桌椅是否干净、齐全。Check whether the dining table and chairs are clean and complete.	

续前表

操作程序 Operation Procedure	操作标准与要求 Operation Standard and Requirements	图　示 Examples
铺台布 Lay the tablecloth	1. 位置：站在主人位右侧，副主人位。 Position: Stand on deputy host's seat, to the right of the host's. 2. 标准：不管是方桌还是圆桌，台布四周下垂部分都要均等。餐桌上的台布要求正缝朝上，餐厅内所有台布的正缝方向一致。 Standard: Put tablecloth upward on the table. Make sure the center of the cloth is in the middle of the table with the surface of the cloth hanging parallel to the legs of the table and perpendicular to the ground no matter it's a square or round table. 3. 铺设的台布要求平整、挺括，无皱褶、无破损；台布铺好后开始摆台。 The tablecloth should be flat and neat without crimp damage; Set the table after the tablecloth is laid.	 
摆放餐具 Set the tableware	要求：摆台时需按用餐的要求配备和摆放餐具；使用托盘操作，从主人位开始，顺时针方向依次摆放；摆放餐具时要求轻放，注意卫生标准。 Requirements: The tableware should be equipped and placed according to the requirements of dining. Hold the tray and distribute wares in clockwise order from the host's seat. Place the tableware gently and look out for sanitation. 1. 骨碟定位：拿骨碟边缘，摆在席位正中，间距相等，店徽或图案对齐。 Locate the plate: Hold the edge of the plate and place it on the table aligning to the center of the seat with equal distance between. If a pattern or logo is present, place them in a unanimous position. 2. 汤碗、汤勺：在骨碟左上方放口汤碗，勺置于碗中，勺把向左。 Soup bowl and spoon: Place the soup bowl to the top left of the plate. Put the spoon in the bowl with its handle pointing to the left. 3. 筷架、筷子、长柄勺：筷架摆在骨碟的右侧，长柄勺和筷子摆在筷架上，长柄勺距骨碟右侧边缘 3cm，图案向上，筷子后端距桌边 1.5cm。	

续前表

操作程序 Operation Procedure	操作标准与要求 Operation Standard and Requirements	图示 Examples
摆放餐具 Set the tableware	Chopsticks rack，chopsticks and ladle: Place the rack to the right of the plate. The ladle and chopsticks are placed on the rack, and the ladle has 3cm distance from the right edge of the plate. Make sure the end of the chopsticks is 1.5cm away from the edge of the table. If there is a pattern on chopsticks or its wrapper, make sure the painted side is in the front. 4. 酒杯：在骨碟右上方摆水杯和葡萄酒杯（水杯在左，葡萄酒杯在右）；两者间距 1cm，横向直径在一条线上；葡萄酒杯底部与筷子对齐。 Wine glass: Lay the glasses on the top right side of the plate with the water glass on the left and the wine glass on the right. Make sure the horizontal diameter of the three items is on a line. The bottom of the wine glass is aligned to the chopsticks'. 5. 调味瓶、花瓶等应摆放整齐。 The seasoning bottle, vase and other tableware should be put in order.	
摆放餐巾花 Arrange table napkin flowers	餐巾花可根据情况选择花型，位置摆放得当，美观大方。 The shape can vary according to specified occasions and is required to stand elegantly on the plate.	

任务实施

第一步：教师介绍中餐摆台的相关知识。将中餐实训室布置成 2 个区域：零点区域和宴会（包间）区域。

Step 1: The teacher introduces the knowledge of Chinese table setting, and arranges the Chinese training room into two areas: the a la carte area and the banquet (private room) area.

第二步：教师演示台布的铺设、中餐零点摆台及宴会的摆台，并提醒学生相关注意事项。

Step 2: The teacher demonstrates the laying of tablecloth, the Chinese table setting and reminds students of the matters needing attention.

第三步：以小组（5 人 1 组）为单位，根据教师演示的步骤，分别完成中餐零点及宴会摆台练习。2 组同学在 2 个区域同时进行（5 位学生轮流进行摆台练习）。

Step 3: Work in groups (5 persons per 1 group) to complete the Chinese a la carte and banquet table setting exercises according to the steps demonstrated by the teacher. Two groups of students do exercises in two areas at the same time (Five students take turns to set the table).

第四步：以小组为单位，各抽取一名同学进行中餐宴会摆台考核，并进行评价和总结。

Step 4: Select one student from each group exercise the Chinese banquet table setting, and then the teacher evaluates and summarizes by the settings.

任务评价

表 4.4 中餐宴会摆台评价表

The Evaluation Form of Chinese Banquet Table Setting

评价内容 Evaluation Items	评价标准 Evaluation Standard	分值 Score	小组自评 Self-evaluation (20%)	小组互评 Peer-evaluation (30%)	教师评价 Teacher-evaluation (50%)	综合得分 Subtotal
铺台布 Lay the tablecloth	操作标准、规范 Operate according to specifications	15				
拉餐椅 Pull the chair	操作标准、规范 Operate according to specifications	15				
摆放餐具 Set the tableware	操作标准、规范 Operate according to specifications	20				
摆放公用餐具 Set the serving tableware	操作标准、规范 Operate according to specifications	10				
摆放杯具 Set the glasses	操作标准、规范 Operate according to specifications	20				
摆放调料瓶、花瓶等 Set the seasoning bottles, vases, etc.	摆放位置正确 Correct placement	10				
团队精神 Teamwork	分工明确，团队合作 Clear division of labor, and good teamwork	10				
合计得分 Total						

评分标准（按 100 分制）：81～100 分为“优秀”；71～80 分为“良好”；60～70 分为“合格”；60 分以下为“不合格”。

Scoring standard（On a scale of 100）: 81-100 points as “Perfect”; 71-80 points as “Good”; 60-70 points as “Pass”; 60-below points as “Fail”.

拓展阅读

G20 峰会国宴餐具及菜单介绍

2016 年，二十国集团领导人峰会（The G20 Summit）在浙江杭州召开。中方为欢迎二十国集团领导人精心准备的国宴（state banquet）和国宴餐具也引起了人们的关注。这套玛戈隆特“西湖盛宴”（the West Lake feast）G20 国宴餐具系列的设计团队来自上海，其设计创作灵感（inspiration）来源于水和自然景观。整套餐具体现出“西湖元素、杭州特色、江南韵味、中国气派、世界大国”的 G20 国宴布置基调。

图 4.1　玛戈隆特“西湖盛宴”G20 国宴餐具

国宴餐具的图案（graphic pattern）采用富有传统文化审美（traditional culture aesthetic）的“青绿山水”元素，以工笔带写意的笔触创造，布局含蓄严谨（careful and precise）、意境清新，所有图案设计均取自西湖实景。例如，茶和咖啡瓷器用具系列，设计灵感来源于西湖的荷花（lotus）、莲蓬（seedpod of the lotus）造型，壶盖提揿（the lid of the kettle）酷似水滴。

图 4.2　G20 杭州峰会冷菜拼盘餐具

此届 G20 峰会的会标图案是用 20 根线条描绘了一个桥型轮廓（bridge shaped outline

of the configuration)。桥，在这套国宴餐具中，不仅体现在图案上，器具（appliance）的造型中也融入了桥的元素。冷菜拼盘（hors d'oeuvres）半球形的尊顶盖提揪设计，源自西湖十景之一的"三潭印月"（three pools mirroring the moon）；尊顶盖上半部图案创意则来源于"满陇桂雨"（Sweet Osmanthus Rain at Manjuelong Village），以杭州市花桂花与江南翠竹自然相互依偎展开。

图 4.3 G20 杭州峰会餐具

G20 杭州峰会欢迎晚宴菜单
The Welcome Dinner Menu of G20 Hangzhou Summit

冷盘 Hors d'Oeuvres
清汤松茸 Pine Mushroom Soup
松子鳜鱼 Sweet and Sour Mandarin Fish with Pine Nuts
龙井虾仁 Stir-Fried Shrimps with Longjing Tea Leaves
膏蟹酿香橙 Orange-Flavored Crab Meat
东坡牛扒 Hangzhou-Style Fillet Steak
四季蔬果 Braised Vegetables
点心 Pastries
水果、冰激凌 Fruits and Icecream
咖啡和茶 Coffee and Tea
张裕干红 Red Wine Changyu 2012, Beijing China
张裕干白 White Wine Changyu 2011, Beijing China

任务二：西餐摆台

Task 2: Western Restaurant Table Setting

案例导入

某咖啡集团X总裁将于三日后在某酒店西餐厅邀请朋友一起用餐，该酒店管理层高度重视此次VIP接待，并特意安排酒店相关人员对餐台进行了设计。

本次接待所设计的西餐台面强调简约与优雅，突出“低调中的奢华”，符合各位贵宾良好的文化背景与审美水准。整个台面借助餐具、台布与主题装饰物的完美搭配和色彩组合，用低调而和谐的方式诠释奢华，以理性而睿智的态度演绎客人讲究的品质和典雅悠适的生活态度。精心挑选的质地优良的台布，彰显出高雅的商务格调；与台布相同颜色、质地的口布，让整个用餐环境温馨、惬意，使客人可以在轻松愉悦的氛围中把酒畅谈。

同时，此次餐台设计选取世界顶级品牌的金属餐具，色泽明快，与台布交相辉映，高贵典雅，体现出此次宴请的规格和品质。装饰盘、面包盘、黄油碟等瓷制品也独具特色，全部由“瓷都”景德镇知名窑炉定制，品质上乘，充分体现出西餐宴会应有的优雅格调。

桌面正中为独具匠心的创意插花，淡绿色的康乃馨紧紧地簇拥在一起，寓意着对生活的热情与生命的活力。晶莹的花瓶中堆满可爱的咖啡豆，不时散发出淡淡的咖啡香，浓情之意，尽于此处展现。

宴请结束后，X总裁对酒店此次用心设计的台面与接待服务十分满意，特意给酒店留下了感谢信。你认为该酒店西餐厅的餐台设计有何独特之处？

知识准备

一、台布铺设 Tablecloth laying

台布铺设之前，服务人员要先做如下检查工作：

Before laying the tablecloth, the servers should do the following inspections:

（1）选取的台布是否正确；

Whether the tablecloth is correct;

（2）桌面是否干净；

Whether the desktop is clean;

（3）餐桌是否平稳。

Whether the table is stable.

西餐台布铺设操作流程如下：

The operation procedures of laying tablecloth in western restaurant is as follows:

表 4.5　　西餐台布铺设操作流程

The Operation procedures of Laying Tablecloth in Western Restaurant

<table>
<tr><th colspan="2">操作流程
Operation Procedures</th><th>图示
Examples</th><th>注意事项
Notices</th></tr>
<tr><td>1</td><td>站于餐桌一旁，将台布的开口折边朝向自己和右边，打开台布。
Stand besides the table, make the folded edge of the tablecloth toward the right side of the body and open the tablecloth.</td><td>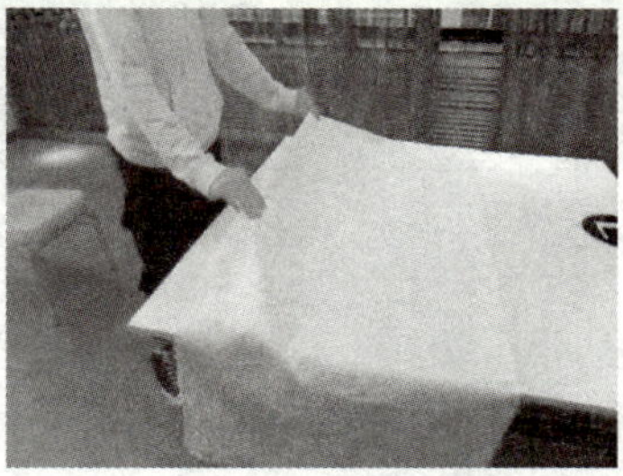</td><td rowspan="3">1. 台布下垂约 30cm；
2. 放置餐椅后，台布中心折痕应与餐椅中心对齐；
3. 台布折痕的中心点在餐桌正中央。
1. Make the tablecloth hang about 30 cm;
2. After the dining chairs are placed, the center crease of the tablecloth is aligned to the center of the dining chairs;
3. The center of the tablecloth crease is in the middle of the dining table.</td></tr>
<tr><td>2</td><td>用拇指和食指夹住台布的最上层，食指与中指夹住中间单层台布。
Hold the top tier of the cloth between the thumb and forefinger and hold the middle tier with the forefinger and middle finger.</td><td>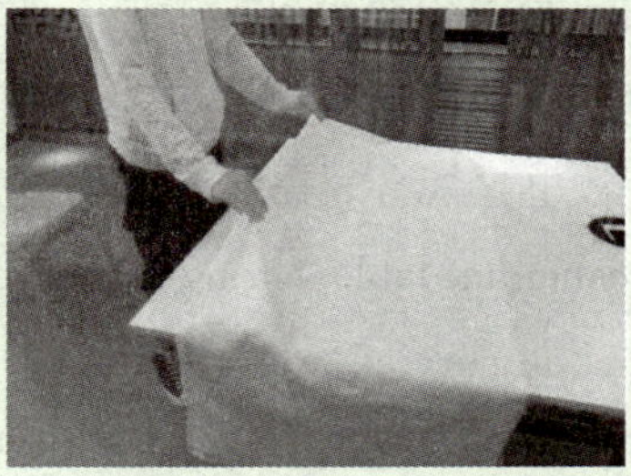</td></tr>
<tr><td>3</td><td>食指与中指夹住台布，向外张开至桌边，身体微弯，两脚一前一后，台布往前抛出；松开食指与中指后，将台布往后轻拉，直到台布覆盖整个桌面。
Make sure that the tablecloth is clamped between the index finger and middle finger, and is pulled to the table edge; Make the body slightly bent, one leg forward and one leg back; Throw the tablecloth and gently pull it back until it covers the entire table.</td><td>
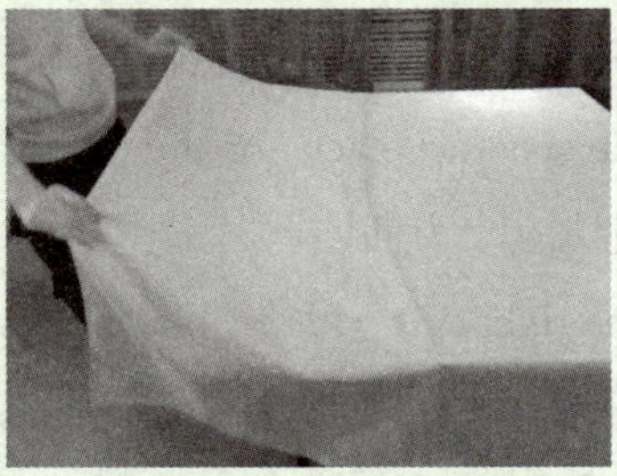
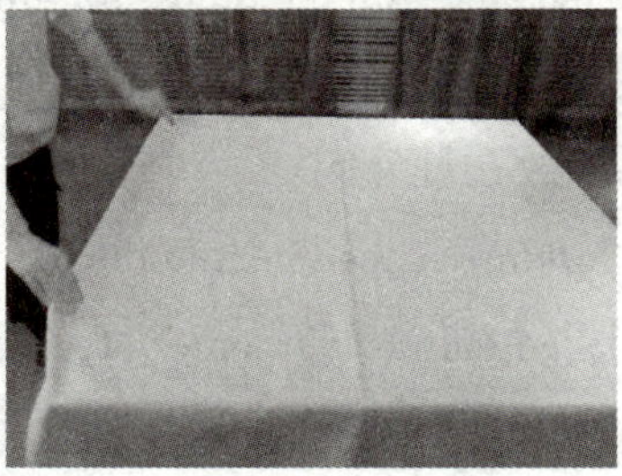</td></tr>
</table>

续前表

	操作流程 Operation Procedures	图示 Examples	注意事项 Notices
4	调整台布，使四周下垂均匀。 Adjust the tablecloth so that it hangs evenly around.		

二、摆台 Table setting

一般来说，西餐摆台较中餐摆台更加多样。西餐厅种类繁多，服务方式及其台面摆设也不尽相同。西餐摆台的主要依据是餐厅的定位及客人所点菜品。除了服务及使用便利之外，安全卫生及整齐一致也是摆台时需要考虑的因素。

Normally, western restaurant table setting is more diversiform than Chinese. Western dining-room is assorted, so that the service operation is also different as the table setting. Western restaurant table setting is mainly arranged according to the orientation of the restaurant and the dishes ordered by the guests. In addition to the convenience of service and use, safety, hygiene and tidiness are also factors to be considered when setting the table.

西餐摆台的原则如下：

The principles of western restaurant table setting are as follows:

（1）餐具应以展示盘或口布为定位，由内往外依顺序整齐摆放。汤匙摆放在右侧，通常放于主餐刀的外侧。

Tableware should be positioned on the display plate or table napkin, and be placed in order from inside to outside. The spoon is placed on the right side, usually outside the main knife.

（2）刀类摆放在右侧，刀刃向内。

Place the knife on the right side with the blade inward.

（3）叉类摆放在左侧，叉齿向上。

Place the fork on the left side with the prong upward.

（4）主餐刀与主餐叉紧邻展示盘放置，也就是放于最内侧。其余餐具依供餐顺序依次往外摆放，最先使用的摆放在最外侧。

The main knife and fork are placed next to the display plate, which is the innermost side. The rest of the tableware is placed outwards in order of serving, and the one which will be first used is placed at the outermost side.

（5）面包盘、黄油碟摆放在左侧，面包盘中心与装饰盘中心对齐，黄油碟左侧边沿与面包盘中心在一条直线上。

The bread and butter dishes are placed on the left side. The center of the bread dish is aligned to the center of the decorative dish. The left edge of the butter dish is in line with the center of the bread dish.

（6）黄油刀摆放在面包盘上，横跨于盘子上方，握把朝右、刀刃向下；或放于盘子右侧，刀刃朝左。

The butter knife is placed on the bread plate, across the plate. The grip is facing right with the blade downward, or on the right side of the plate with the blade facing left.

（7）甜品叉、匙横放于上侧，甜品叉握把朝左，紧邻展示盘；甜品匙握把朝右，置于甜品叉上侧。

The dessert fork and spoon are placed horizontally on the upper side. The handle of the dessert fork faces left, next to the display plate, and the handle of the dessert spoon faces right on the dessert fork.

（8）水杯摆放于主餐刀正上方，酒杯依顺序摆放在水杯右下方，呈直线排列。

The water cups are placed directly above the main knife, and the wine cups are arranged in a straight line on the lower right side of the water cups.

（9）咖啡匙不预先摆放在餐桌上。

Coffee spoons are not pre-setted on the table.

一般的西餐厅，无论是客人单点还是吃套餐，事先都是只摆放基本餐具，待客人开始点餐之后，才会依照客人所点餐食增减所需餐具。

General western restaurant will put basic tableware only beforehand. After the guest orders the menu, the server can add or remove the tableware according to the guest's order.

依照欧洲的传统，基本的餐具包括：口布、主餐刀叉、面包盘、黄油刀、水杯、红葡萄酒杯和椒盐瓶。通常，我们在高级西餐厅还会看到展示盘，口布也是置于展示盘上。在许多非正式的西餐厅，仅能看到口布和主菜刀叉。

According to the European tradition, basic tableware includes: cloth, knife and fork, bread plate, butter knife, water glass, red wine cup, pepper and salt shaker.Usually, we will see the display plate in the high-end western restaurant, in which the cloth is also placed on the display plate.In many informal western restaurants, we can only find cloth laid out with a knife and fork for the main course.

下面我们将以西式早餐、午餐、晚餐做西餐摆台的详细举例。

Next, we will take western breakfast, lunch and dinner as examples.

（一）西式早餐摆台 The table settings of western breakfast

西式早餐主要分为欧陆式早餐和美式早餐，其摆台如下：

Western breakfast is mainly divided into continental breakfast and American breakfast. The table is set as follows:

表 4.6　　西式早餐摆台

The Table Settings of Western Breakfast

早餐类别 Breakfast Category	图示 Examples
欧陆式早餐：供应餐点较为简单，包括面包、果酱、奶油、咖啡或红茶。所需要的餐具为餐盘、餐刀、叉、咖啡杯组、口布、椒盐瓶等。 Continental breakfast is a simple meal consisting of bread, jam, cream, coffee or black tea.The tableware needed is plate, knife, fork, coffee cup set, table napkin, salt and pepper shaker, etc.	
美式早餐：供应餐点较为丰富，包括肉类、蛋类、芝士、面包、水果、咖啡或红茶。需要的餐具有餐盘、餐刀、叉、面包盘、黄油刀、咖啡杯组、口布、椒盐瓶等。 American breakfast is a rich meal consisting of meat, eggs, cheese, bread, fruit, coffee or black tea.The tableware needed is plate, knife, fork, bread plate, butter knife, coffee cup set, table napkin, salt and pepper shaker, etc.	

（二）西式午、晚餐摆台 The table settings of western lunch and dinner

一般而言，西餐厅只预先摆放基本餐具，再根据客人点餐及需要更换及增减所要的餐具。下面我们将列举基本午、晚餐摆台，基本单点摆台及套餐摆台。

General speaking, restaurant only puts basic tableware in advance. According to the guest’s order, the server will add or remove tableware. Next, we will list the basic settings of western lunch and dinner, and the basic a la carte order and set menu tableware setting.

表 4.7 西式午、晚餐摆台

The Table Settings of Western Lunch and Dinner

餐具摆设 Tableware Setting	图示 Examples
基本摆设：餐具包括展示盘、主餐刀叉、口布、水杯、椒盐瓶。 Basic setting: the tableware includes display plate, main knife and fork, table napkin, water glass, salt and pepper shaker.	
单点摆设：餐具包括展示盘、主餐刀叉、水杯、面包盘、黄油刀、口布、椒盐瓶等。 A la carte order table setting: the tableware includes display plate, main knife and fork, water glass, bread plate, butter knife, table napkin, salt and pepper shaker, etc.	
套餐摆设（不含前菜）：餐具包括展示盘、主餐刀叉、沙拉刀叉、汤匙、甜品叉、甜品匙、水杯、酒杯、口布、面包盘、黄油刀、椒盐瓶等。 Set-meal table setting (excluding appetizer): the tableware includes display plate, main knife and fork, salad knife and fork, spoon, dessert fork, dessert spoon, water glass, wine glass, table napkin, bread plate, butter knife, salt and pepper shaker, etc.	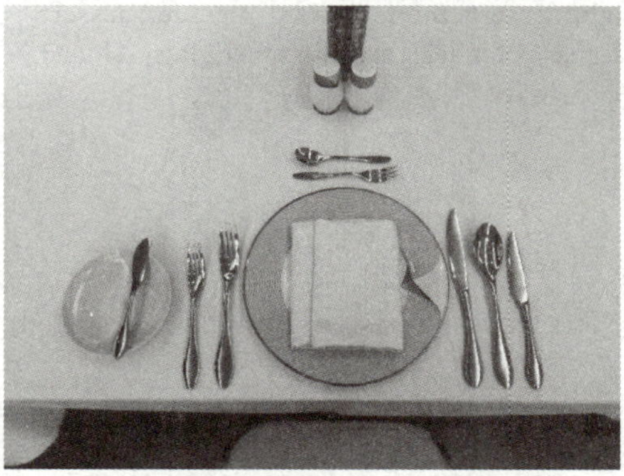
套餐摆设（含前菜）：餐具包括前菜刀叉、沙拉刀叉、汤匙、主餐刀叉、甜品叉匙、酒杯、展示盘、口布、面包盘、黄油刀、水杯、椒盐瓶等。 Set-meal table setting (including appetizer): the tableware includes appetizer knife and fork, salad knife and fork, spoon, main course knife and fork, dessert fork and spoon, wine glass, display plate, table napkin, bread plate, butter knife, water glass, salt and pepper shaker, etc.	

续前表

餐具摆设 Tableware Setting	图示 Examples
单点沙拉：餐具包括沙拉刀叉、口布、水杯、椒盐瓶。 Single salad: the tableware includes salad knife and fork, table napkin, water glass, salt and pepper shaker.	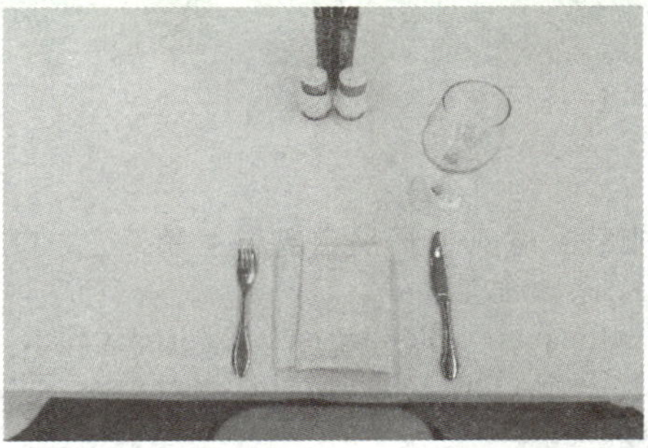
单点意面：餐具包括餐叉、餐匙、面包盘、黄油刀、口布、水杯、椒盐瓶。 Single pasta: the tableware includes fork, spoon, bread plate, butter knife, table napkin, water glass, salt and pepper shaker.	
单点甜品：餐具包括甜品叉匙、口布、水杯、椒盐瓶。 Single dessert: the tableware includes dessert fork and spoon, table napkin, water glass, salt and pepper shaker.	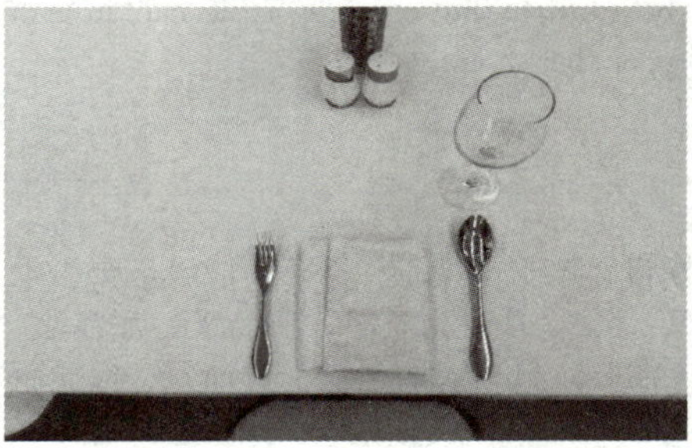

西式宴会的摆台步骤及原则如下：

The table setting of western banquets needs to follow these procedures and principles:

表 4.8 西式宴会摆台

The Table Settings of Western Banquets

摆台步骤及原则 Procedures and Principles	图示 Examples
摆放展示盘及口布于每个餐位的中央位置，展示盘距离桌沿约 2cm； Place the display plate and table napkin at the center of each seat with a 2cm distance from the edge of the table;	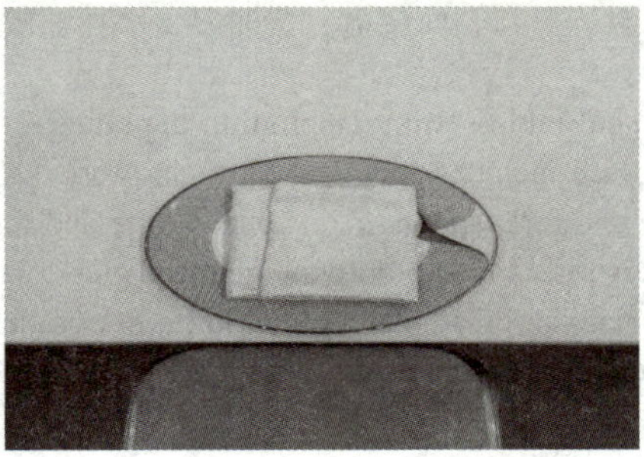

续前表

摆台步骤及原则 Procedures and Principles	图示 Examples
摆放主餐刀于餐盘右侧，餐刀下缘与餐盘平齐，刀刃向左； Place the main knife on the right side of the plate with the handle of the knife aligned to the plate, and the blade faced to the left;	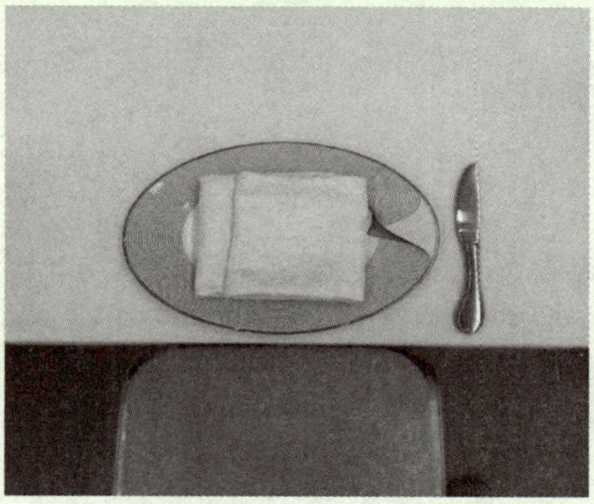
摆放汤匙于餐刀右侧，汤匙下缘与餐盘平齐； Place the spoon on the right side of the knife with the bottom of the spoon aligned to the plate;	
摆放沙拉刀于汤匙右侧，沙拉刀下缘与餐盘平齐； Place salad knife on the right side of spoon, keep the bottom of salad knife aligned to the plate;	
摆放主餐叉于餐盘左侧，餐叉下缘与餐盘平齐，刀刃向左； Place the main fork on the left side of the plate, the bottom of the fork aligned to the plate, and the blade faced to the left;	

续前表

摆台步骤及原则 Procedures and Principles	图示 Examples
摆放沙拉叉于主餐叉左侧，沙拉叉下缘与餐盘平齐； Place the salad fork on the left side of the main fork and keep the bottom in line with the plate;	
摆放面包盘于沙拉叉的左侧，面包盘下缘与展示盘下缘平齐； Place the bread plate on the left side of the salad fork, and the bottom of the bread tray is aligned to the bottom of the display plate;	
摆放黄油刀于面包盘右侧，距离面包盘右侧边缘 2～3cm； Place butter knife on the right side of the bread plate with a distance of 2-3 centimeters from the right edge of the bread plate;	
摆放甜品叉、匙于展示盘正上方，甜品叉握柄朝左，甜品匙握柄朝右； Place the dessert fork and spoon above the main plate with the handle of dessert fork faced left, and the handle of dessert spoon faced right;	

续前表

摆台步骤及原则 Procedures and Principles	图示 Examples
摆放水杯于餐刀正上方 2～3cm 处； Place the water glass at 2-3 centimeters above the knife;	
摆放酒杯于水杯右下方，呈 45 度角直线摆放； Place the wine glass in a straight line at a 45 degrees angle below the right of the water glass;	
摆放花瓶、椒盐瓶于餐桌中央处。 Place vases, salt and pepper shaker at the center of the table.	

任务实施

第一步：教师首先介绍西餐摆台的相关知识。

Step 1: The teacher introduces the relevant knowledge of western restaurant table setting.

第二步：教师演示西餐摆台的台布铺设，西餐早、午、晚餐及西式宴会的摆台，并提醒学生相关注意事项。

Step 2: The teacher demonstrates the laying of table cover, table setting of western breakfast, lunch, dinner and banquet, and reminds students of the relevant matters needed attention.

第三步：以小组（5 人 1 组）为单位，根据教师演示步骤，完成西餐的早、午、晚餐及西式宴会摆台练习（5 位学生轮流进行摆台练习）。

Step 3: Take the group (5 people per group) as the unit, complete the table setting practice of western breakfast, lunch and dinner and banquet according to the steps of the teacher's demonstration (5 students take turns in setting up exercises).

第四步：以小组为单位，各抽取一名同学进行西餐宴会摆台考核。

Step 4: Take one student from every group to examine the table setting of western dinner banquet.

任务评价

表 4.9 西餐宴会摆台评价表

The Evaluation Form of Western Banquet Table Setting

评价内容 Evaluation Items	评价标准 Evaluation Standard	分值 Score	小组自评 Self-evaluation（20%）	小组互评 Peer-evaluation（30%）	教师评价 Teacher-evaluation（50%）	综合得分 Subtotal
台布 Tablecloth	台布中凸线向上； The tablecloth's convex line should be put upward; 台布四边下垂距离合适并均等； Four sides of the tablecloth droop evenly; 铺设操作最多四次整理成形。 Operate max up to four times to achieve the final effect.	5				
餐椅摆放 Chair setting	餐椅边沿与下垂台布间距离合适并均等； Keep a suitable and equal distance between edge of chair and hanging tablecloth; 从主人位开始按顺时针方向摆设； Arrange clockwise from the host; 操作从餐椅正后方进行。 The operation should be completed behind the chair.	5				

续前表

评价内容 Evaluation Items	评价标准 Evaluation Standard	分值 Score	小组自评 Self-evaluation （20%）	小组互评 Peer-evaluation （30%）	教师评价 Teacher-evaluation （50%）	综合得分 Subtotal
装饰盘 Decorative plate	从主人位开始按顺时针方向摆设； Set the plate clockwise from the host position; 各盘盘边与桌边距离合适并均等； Keep the distance between the edge of each plate and the edge of the table appropriate and equal; 装饰盘中心与餐位中心一致； The center of the decoration plate should be consistent with the center of the table; 手持盘沿右侧操作。 Operate with the hand holding the right side of the plate.	30				
刀、叉、勺 Knife, fork and spoon	刀、叉、勺摆放整齐、距离合适并均等，距桌边距离相同； Knives, forks and spoons should be placed tidily with a proper and equal distance from the table; 各个餐位餐具布局对称，餐具间距离合适并均等。 Each tableware's layout is symmetrical, and the distance between tableware is appropriate and equal.	30				
面包盘、黄油刀 Bread plate and butter knife	面包盘中心与展示盘中心平齐。 The center of the bread plate and display plate should be kept on the same level.	10				
杯具 Glass	水杯于餐刀正上方 2～3cm 处； The water glass is placed above the knife with a distance of 2-3 centimeters; 酒杯于水杯右下方 45 度角直线摆放。 Place the wine glass in a straight line with the water glass at a 45 degree angle.	15				

续前表

评价内容 Evaluation Items	评价标准 Evaluation Standard	分值 Score	小组自评 Self-evaluation（20%）	小组互评 Peer-evaluation（30%）	教师评价 Teacher-evaluation（50%）	综合得分 Subtotal
椒盐瓶、花瓶等 Salt and pepper shakers, vases, etc	摆放位置正确。Put them on the right position.	5				
合计得分 Total						

评分标准（按 100 分制）：81～100 分为“优秀”；71～80 分为“良好”；60～70 分为“合格”；60 分以下为“不合格”。

Scoring standard（On a scale of 100）：81–100 points as “Perfect”；71–80 points as “Good”；60–70 points as “Pass”；60–below points as “Fail”.

拓展阅读

西餐餐具的起源

吃西餐时，我们会用到西餐餐具。西餐餐具十分繁杂，大大小小的餐具对于没怎么吃过西餐的人来说，是一件令人非常头痛的事情。但是，正是因为有了这些餐具，才让我们觉得，吃西餐是一件十分精致而享受的事情。西餐餐桌上每一种餐具都有着不同的起源。

1. 餐叉

西餐餐叉最早出现在 11 世纪意大利托斯卡纳地区，最早只有两个叉齿。当时的神职人员对叉子非常抵制，他们认为，人类只能用手去碰触上帝所赐予的食物，而托斯卡纳人创造餐具是受到了撒旦的诱惑，是一种亵渎神灵的行为。意大利史料中记载：一个威尼斯人在用叉子进餐后，于数日内死去。其实，他很可能是感染瘟疫而死去，但神职人员认为，他是遭到了惩罚，劝诫大家不要再用叉子吃东西。

12 世纪，餐叉进入盎格鲁－撒克逊王国。据说，当时的贵族们并不喜欢用叉子进餐，却常常把叉子拿在手里，当作决斗的武器。

对于 14 世纪的英格兰人来说，叉子仍然只是舶来品。当时的大部分欧洲人都喜欢用刀把食物切成块，然后用手放进嘴里。如果一位男士用叉子进食，那就表示，他不是一个“挑剔鬼”，就是一个“娘娘腔”。

18 世纪，法国大革命爆发。由于法国贵族偏爱用四个叉齿的叉子进餐，于是叉子变成地位、奢侈、讲究的象征，之后便变成必备餐具。

2. 餐刀

餐刀很早便在人类的生活中占有重要的地位。早在数亿年前，人类的祖先就开始使用石刀作为工具。刀子挂在腰上除了用来割肉，还可用来御敌防身。只有有地位、身份的头目们才能有多把不同用途的刀子。

路易十三在位期间，深谙政治谋略的黎塞留公爵不仅为法国跻身欧洲的主要强国做出了贡献，即便是对于一般生活细节，这位主教也留下了深远影响。当时的餐刀顶部并不是我们今天所熟悉的椭圆形状，而是有锋利的刀尖。很多官僚政要在用餐之余，会把餐刀当牙签使用。黎塞留公爵不满这一现象，因而命令家中仆人把餐刀的刀尖磨成椭圆形，不准客人当着他的面用餐刀剔牙。影响所及，法国上下吹起了一阵“将餐刀刀尖磨钝”的旋风。

3. 汤匙

汤匙的历史也非常久远。早在旧石器时代，亚洲地区就出现过汤匙。古埃及的墓穴中曾发现过木、石、象牙、金等材料制成的汤匙。金匠生产的金银汤匙多为礼品。

Project 5

Order Service

项目五

点餐服务

项目概述

PROJECT SUMMARY

随着信息时代的到来，信息化成为餐厅发展的必然趋势之一。如今，越来越多的餐厅和酒店开始关注餐饮点菜系统，并逐渐使用餐饮点菜软件代替人工管理。在移动互联网的推动下，点菜系统电子化将成为餐厅和酒店在信息时代制胜的砝码之一。

然而，点餐系统只是提高餐厅工作效率、减少点餐失误、提升餐厅规范管理的工具，餐厅要想为客人提供独一无二的优质服务，还需要人工点餐的存在。

点餐服务是餐厅服务员必须具备的基本技能。由于客人的饮食喜好、饮食习惯、饮食方法不同，以及对于餐厅所供应产品的熟悉程度、风味、价格等要求不同，因此点餐员只掌握基本的服务技能是不够的，还要学会因人而异地灵活推销菜品、应对突发状况，为餐厅带来最大化收益。

点餐员对菜单的熟悉程度以及对菜品的了解程度，会影响客人的整体用餐评价。点菜服务水准的高低，直接关系到顾客满意度，以及酒店效益和声誉，因此做好酒店点菜服务是一项非常重要的工作。

点餐服务考查的是员工的专业知识技能、自我管理技能和可迁移技能，检测的是员工对菜单的熟悉程度、对菜品烹饪工艺的了解、对客沟通能力、引导能力以及自我管理水平。

项目目标

PROJECT OBJECTS

知识目标：掌握点菜所需要的基础知识及点菜的基本流程。

技能目标：掌握点菜服务的方法；灵活运用点菜推销技巧。

素养目标：具备民族自信；具备节约意识；具备服务意识与安全意识；爱岗敬业、具备不断突破自我、勇于创新的意识。

任务一：中餐点菜服务
Task 1: Chinese Dish-ordering Service

案例导入

某年5月的一个周末，某饭店203房间接待了一场家宴，加孩子共有10位客人。一开始，客人点的是380元的烤鸭套餐，并在看菜单时问服务员："姑娘，菜不够吃的时候再加吧！"服务员说："可以的，不够吃的时候再给您点。"餐中的时候，客人加了两个家常菜。但因为服务员没有告诉客人加菜需要另付费用，所以当客人在看账单的时候就问道："服务员，怎么这两个菜加钱了呢？"服务员立刻向客人解释，这两道菜不在客人点的套餐内。客人皱了皱眉头。当给客人结账时，服务员将这件事情告诉了主管，主管立刻拿了份果盘，去房间里给客人道歉，客人的态度也很好，说："小姑娘，以后一定要说明白了，不然就不给你们结账了。"

思考讨论：客人为什么对账单产生疑惑？

知识准备

一、点菜前的准备工作 Preparation before taking order

（1）了解菜单上菜肴的制作方法、烹调时间、口味特点和装盘要求。

Be familiar with the recipe, cooking time, flavor characteristics and the requirements of dishing up of the cuisine on the menu.

（2）了解菜单上菜肴的单位，即一份菜的规格和分量等，通常以大盘、小盘、斤、只等来表示。

Be familiar with the units on the menu, such as the quantity of the cuisine. The size of the plate, weight or the number are usually used as the unit.

（3）掌握客源国和地区的饮食习惯和菜肴知识，了解客人口味及饮食需求，便于给出好的建议。

Master the dietary habits and dishes of the guests from different countries and regions, and be familiar with guests' taste and dietary requirements which could help give better recommendations to the guests.

（4）掌握不同人数的客人所需要菜肴的组成和分量。

Master the components and amounts of dishes required by different groups of guests.

（5）掌握上菜顺序、时机和作料搭配。

Master the order sequence, timing and seasonings.

二、中餐点菜的基本服务流程 Service procedures of taking order in Chinese restaurant

中餐点菜的基本服务流程从形式上看比较简单，包括递送菜单、问候客人、点菜、介绍推荐、记录菜名和复述确认。

with regard to the form, it seems more simple of the service procedures of taking order in Chinese restaurant, which includes delivering the menu,greeting the guest, taking order, introducing and recommending dishes,recording dishes. repeating and confirming.

表 5.1 中餐点菜的服务流程和标准

The Procedures and Standard of Ordering Service in Chinese Restaurant

服务流程 Service Procedures	服务标准 Service Standard	注意事项 Notes
1. 递送菜单 Deliver the menu	通常在迎宾服务中，由迎宾员（服务员）递上菜单。 In general, the host/ hostess(waiter/waitress) will deliver the menu to the guest.	若餐厅使用平板电脑或手机扫码点餐的方式，则不需要递送菜单，但服务员需指导客人如何使用。 If the restaurant takes order through mobile phone or iPad, the waiter or waitress should instruct the guest how to take order if they need.
2. 问候客人 Greet the guest	1. 礼貌问候客人，如："晚上好，先生。很高兴为您服务！" Greet the guest with courtesy and say,"Good evening, sir. I'm glad to do the service for you!" 2. 介绍自己； Introduce yourself; 3. 询问客人是否可以点菜，如："请问现在可以为您点菜吗？" And then, ask if the guest is ready to order, such as "May I have your order, please?"	
3. 点菜 Take order	1. 为客人点菜时，要站在客人的左侧，身体略向前倾，认真倾听客人的叙述。 Stand on the left side of the guest, lean forward slightly and listen carefully to the guest. 2. 中餐一般都是按照上菜的顺序为客人点菜。一般遵循"先凉菜，后热菜；先荤菜，后素菜；先风味，后一般菜；先菜肴，后汤品、点心、酒水"的顺序。 Generally, the sequence of order taking is according to the sequence of serving dishes. Normally, the rules are "Cold dish before hot dish; Meat or fish before vegetable; Special/typical local dish before ordinary dish; Dishes before soup, dessert and drink".	1. 点菜前给客人留出一定的选择时间； Give the guest some time to choose before ordering, and you can say: "Please take your time." 2. 礼貌地询问客人是否可以点菜； Ask gently,"May I have your order now?" 3. 在等待客人阅读菜单（手机端点菜或平板电脑点菜）的时候应该保持耐心，尽量详细地回答客人的提问，耐心向客人解释菜单上的菜品的原料、口味、制作工艺等。 Be patient while waiting for the guest who is reading the menu (mobile ordering or tablet orders). And answer questions in as much detail as possible. Explain the materials, taste or the method of the dishes patiently to the guest.

续前表

服务流程 Service Procedures	服务标准 Service Standard	注意事项 Notes
4. 介绍、推荐菜肴 Introduce and recommend dishes	1. 熟悉菜单，对于客人所点菜肴做到了如指掌。 Be familiar with the menu and the dishes. 2. 服务员应该体贴客人的需要。推荐菜肴时首先询问客人的喜好和禁忌，然后根据客人的需要，推荐餐厅特色菜、特价菜等，注意荤素搭配、价格合理，不可一味推荐高价菜品。 A waiter should be considerate of the needs of the guests. Ask about guests' preferences and taboos when recommending dishes. The expression of "How would you like (that, them) prepared/done?"will be appropriate. Then recommend some restaurant specials according to the needs of the guests. Pay attention to the balance portion of vegetables and meat, and reasonable price.	1. 遇到客人所点菜肴已经售完，则应表示歉意，并向客人推荐其他菜品； Please apologize if the food that guests ordered is sold out, and say,"Sorry, we haven't any...."Then, recommend other dishes to guests such as"Why don't you try..., it's delicious, too." 2. 如果某样菜肴烹制时间比较长，要向客人说明。 If a dish takes a long time to prepare, explain it to the guest with "I'm afraid it will take some time to prepare, would you mind it?"
5. 记录菜名 Record dishes	清楚准确地记录不同客人所点的菜肴，避免混淆。 Clearly and accurately record the dishes ordered by different guests to avoid confusion.	注意身体姿势，不可将点菜单放在餐桌上填写。 Be careful to body posture, and do not place the order sheet on the table.
6. 复述确认 Repeat and confirm	1. 复述客人所点的菜肴，请客人确认； Repeat the food ordered by the guest, and let the guest confirm it; 2. 询问客人是否需要酒水饮料，记清客人所点的酒水饮料； Ask about if the guests want any drinks and record the drinks that guests ordered; 3. 服务人员收回菜单，并向客人表示"请稍等"或告知客人大约等待的时间； Take the menu back after taking order, and the server should tell the guests about the waiting time; 4. 迅速下单。 Place the order quickly.	注意填写内容齐全，菜肴与酒水分开、冷菜与热菜分开；部分餐厅使用电子点菜系统或移动端点菜应用，系统会自动将点菜单联网传至厨房和传菜部，更加方便快捷。 The order written down by the server should be complete. Make sure the dishes are separated from the wine, and the cold dishes are separated from the hot dishes.The electric order system used by some restaurants will automatically send the order to different relative department in time which is more convenient.

然而，要将这些步骤有机地结合起来，达到客人满意的效果，并不是一件简单的事情。由于不同的客人在对菜食的喜好程度、饮食习惯、方法、要求等方面也不相同，因此需要在点菜的过程中区别对待。

However, it is not easy to combine these procedures organically to achieve a satisfactory result. Due to the preference, eating habits, eating methods, requirements and other aspects of food by different guests, the server needs to treat differently during the ordering process.

三、点菜服务的方法 The method of dish-ordering service

在接受客人点菜时，服务员要掌握方法并具备灵活处理问题的能力。

When taking orders for the guests, the waiter should master the method and could handle problems flexibly.

一般的点菜服务的方法有如下几种：

The methods of ordering service are as follows:

（一）程序点菜法 Regular ordering method

该方法是指按冷菜、热菜、酒水、主食的程序进行。

This method refers to the order process of cold dishes, hot dishes, drinks and staple food.

（二）推荐点菜法 Recommendation method

该方法是指向客人推荐店内的招牌菜、特色菜、时令菜、创新菜等。

The method is to recommend the restaurant's signature dishes, specialties, seasonal dishes, innovative dishes, etc.

（三）推销点菜法 Sales promotion method

该方法要按客人的消费动机来推销。

This method refers to promoting dishes according to guests' consumption motivation.

1. 便餐 Luncheonette

来餐厅吃便餐的客人有各种情况：有外地来出差、旅游和学习的客人，为就近解决吃饭问题；有居住在附近的居民，因某种情况而来用餐等。这些客人要求菜点经济实惠、品种不要太多、上菜速度快，所以应主动介绍价廉物美、制作时间短的菜肴。

Diners come to the restaurant for luncheonette in a variety of reasons: for people on a business trip, travel or study nearby, they want to solve the problem of eating; for people living nearby, they have some other reasons. These guests demand affordable options with not too much variety, but they ask for the serving speed. So the waiter should recommend the high quality and inexpensive dish with short cooking time.

2. 调剂口味 Spice up the taste

客人慕名而来想品尝餐厅的风味特色、名菜、名点，或者是专门为某一道菜肴而来。在这种情况下，要注意多介绍一些有特色的菜肴，数量上要少而精。

Guests are attracted to a restaurant by its famous dish. In this case, the waiter should pay attention to introducing some special dishes which is simplified but with great quality.

3. 宴请 Fete

如商务、结婚、祝寿等各类宴请。这类宾客有些会讲究排场，需注意菜肴精美。

In the case of business, marriage or birthday fete, some of the guests will pay attention to the ostentation; therefore, the waiter should emphasize the delicacy of the dishes when recommending dishes.

4. 聚餐 Party

如朋友、同事聚会。要求热闹，能够边吃边谈，对菜肴要求一般，品种丰富而不多，精细而不贵。

In the case of a party with friends or collegues, the guests usually ask for warm atmosphere in which they can talk while eating, so they do not have too much demand on dishes. Generally, the dishes which are numerous in variety but not too much, delicate but not too expensive will be preferred.

（四）心理点菜法 Psychological method

该方法应按照客人的特性来进行推销。

This method is to promote dishes according to the guest's characteristics.

1. 炫耀型 Show-off type

这类客人情感丰富，重友情、好面子、爱炫富，对菜肴不求快只求好。

This type of guests are emotional, concerned about friendship and face-saving, love to show off the wealth, so they ask for good quality but not fast service.

2. 茫然型 Blank type

这类客人可能是很少在外用餐，不知道哪个餐厅好，不知道吃什么好，就餐知识和经验比较缺乏。

This type of guests may seldom dine out. They do not know which restaurant is good or what they want to eat. They are lack of the knowledge and experience.

3. 习惯型 Habitual type

这类客人表现为喜好某一餐厅的风味、某一厨师的名气、偏好一种或几种菜肴。在为这类客人服务时，应注意与客人打招呼，并可询问："××先生，是和上次一样，还是另外点菜？我们饭店推出了您以前没有尝过的新菜，是否品尝一下？"

This type of guests prefer for the flavor of a restaurant, a chef's reputation, one or several dishes. When serving such guests, pay attention to greeting the guests, and ask "Mr. ××, would you like the same dish as last time, or would you like to order something else? We have a new dish which you have never tasted before. Would you like to try it?"

四、点菜推销的语言技巧 The language skills of selling the dish

（一）使用选择式问句 Use Selective questions

用选择性的推销语言询问客人，更容易使客人做出决定。例如："请问您是喝红茶还是绿茶？"而不说"请问您喝茶吗？"

It is easier for the guests to make decisions by asking them in a selective promoting language. For example, the waiter could ask,"Would you like black tea or green tea?" rather than ask,"What kind of tea would you like?"

（二）语言的加法 Addition of language

罗列菜肴的优点向客人介绍，让客人对菜肴感兴趣。例如："这道菜不仅味道好，而且原料十分新鲜，含有多种维生素，还对虚火等症状有辅助疗效。"

Introducing the advantages of the dishes to the guests could make guests interested in dishes. For example, the waiter could introduce to the guest,"This dish is not only delicious, but the ingredients are very fresh and contain a variety of vitamins. In addition, it has auxiliary curative effect on deficiency fire and other diseases."

（三）语言的减法 Subtraction of language

向客人说明本店特色，表示如果没有吃到会很遗憾，或者说明假如现在不吃这道菜会怎样。例如："这种银鱼只有太湖一带的水域中才有，您如果现在不品尝，回家后将很难有机会品尝到了。"

Explain the characteristics of the specials of the restaurant to the guests. Tell them it would be a pity if they didn't taste it. For example, the waiter could say,"This kind of whitebait is only found in the waters around Lake Taihu. If you don't taste it now, it will be difficult for you to taste it when you return home."

（四）语言的除法 Division of language

将一份菜的价格分为若干份，使其看来不贵。例如："一品鱼翅锅虽然要 200 元一份，但 10 个人平均下来不过 20 元，您只花 20 元就能品尝到这道美味菜肴了。"

Divide the price of a dish into several parts to make it seem less expensive. For example, the waiter could say,"A shark fin soup pot is 200 yuan, but the average cost of 10 people is only 20 yuan. You can spend only 20 yuan to taste this delicious dish."

（五）语言转折法 Transition of language

首先顺着客人的意思，然后委婉地转折，既维护客人的面子，又能顺利推销产品。例如："这道菜的价格确实有些贵，但其原料比较名贵，成菜工艺较为复杂，口味别具特色，您不妨一试。"

The waiter should follow the guest first, then gently turn to other meaning which could not only maintain the guest's face, but also promote the product smoothly. For example, the waiter could say,"This dish is really expensive, but its materials are precious, the cooking process is complex, and the taste is unique, so you might try it as well."

（六）借名人之口法 By celebrity

顾名思义，就是借名人的赞美推销自己的产品，让客人感到值得购买。例如："毛泽东曾赞誉过湖北的武昌鱼，您如果品尝一下一定会有同感"或者"当年乾隆皇帝下江南吃过'叫花鸡'这道菜，对此赞誉有加，您是否品尝一下？"

It is the method through the praise of famous people to promote the products and make the guests feel worthy to purchase. For example, "This is the blunt-snout bream praised by Mao Zedong, you must like it as well." "Years ago, the Emperor Qianlong came to Jiangnan and had tasted this dish called 'Jiaohua chicken'. This dish received highly praise for its taste, would you like to try it?"

（七）赞语法 Praise method

即在介绍菜肴时使用赞语。例如："这道'杏鲍菇三色明虾球'是我们这里的招牌菜之一，您不妨尝尝。"

It refers to the use of compliments in the introduction of dishes. For example, the waiter could say,"This 'pleurotus eryngii with three color prawns' is our specialty dish, would you like to try?"

（八）亲近法 Be close to guest

这个方法多用于对熟悉客户的推销。例如："今天我介绍一道好菜，是我们餐厅最新推出的特色菜肴，您尝尝如何？"

This method is mostly used for promoting to the familiar customers. For example, the waiter could say,"I'd like to recommend this new dish for you which is our special, would you like to try?"

任务实施

第一步：教师导入本节情景设定：晚餐时，一位外国客人史密斯和几个朋友来到××中餐厅用餐，史密斯先生第一次来到中国，想让服务员为他们推荐一些特色菜。

Step 1: The teacher introduces the settings of this section: During the dinner time, a foreign guest Smith and his friends came to ×× Chinese restaurant for dinner. Mr. Smith came to China for the first time and asked the waiter to recommend some special dishes for them.

第二步：教师讲解点菜的方法和注意事项，并列出常用的中英文点菜用语，以供学生练习和参考。

Step 2: The teacher explains the methods and precautions of ordering food, and lists some phrases and vocabularies of the dish-ordering service for students to practice and refer to.

常用语

Useful Expression

- 请问现在可以点菜了吗？

Can I take your order now?/May I take your order now?/Would you like to order?

- 这是菜单，先生。

Here's the menu, sir.

- 我要看看这道菜是否还有，先生。

I'll see if the dish is available, sir.

- 请问要来点什么喝的？

Would you like something to drink?

- 先生，这道菜恐怕要花 15 分钟来准备。您介意等一会儿吗？

I'm afraid the dish will take about 15 minutes to prepare, sir. Would you mind waiting?

第三步：给出示范案例，并予以示范。

Step 3: The teacher gives cases and demonstrates it.

示范案例

Demonstration Case

（A：服务员，S：史密斯先生）

（A: Waiter, S: Mr. Smith）

A：先生，您想点些什么菜？

What would you like to order, sir?

S：我想尝尝中国菜。

I'd like to try some Chinese food.

A：您以前在我们餐厅吃过中国菜吗？

Have you had any Chinese food here before?

S：没有。

No, I haven't.

A：我们有不同风格的中国菜，但我不确定您喜欢哪种。

We serve different styles of Chinese food here, but I'm not sure which one you prefer.

S：我也不知道。你能为我推荐一些吗？

I have no idea. Could you recommend some to me?

A：当然，粤菜较清淡，北京菜味道较重，四川菜通常比较辣。

Well, Cantonese food is rather light, Beijing food is heavy, and Sichuan food is usually spicy.

S：哦，我了解了。我喜欢辣的食物。

Oh, I see. I'd like to have spicy food.

A：如果是这样，那我推荐您尝尝四川菜。大多数四川菜是麻辣口味，但它们也有其他口味的。

If so, I suggest you have a taste for Sichuan food. Most Sichuan dishes are spicy and hot, but they have different tastes.

S：真的吗？那你可以推荐一些给我吗？

Really? So, do you have something special?

A：麻婆豆腐和青红椒炒牛肉片比较有特色。

I think the Mapo Tofu and Sliced Beef with Green & Red Pepper are quite special.

S：好吧，我就点这些。

All right, I'll have them.

A：您还要点其他的吗？

What else would you like to order?

S：让我想想，我点一份宫保鸡丁。

Let me see. I'd like Kung Pao Chicken.

A：您想喝点汤吗？四川酸辣汤非常美味。

Would you like some soup? The Sichuan Hot and Sour Soup are very delicious.

S：好的。

Fine.

A：您想要米饭跟菜一起上吗？

Would you like to have some rice to go with them?

S：是的，谢谢。

Yes, thank you.

第四步：以小组（5人1组）为单位，其中，1位学生扮演服务员，另外4位学生扮演史密斯先生和他的同行朋友，服务员运用不同的点菜推销方法进行中英文中餐点菜（各小组学生轮流进行情景模拟，使用的推销方法不能重复）。

Step 4: Work in groups (5 persons per group), in which one of the students acts as a waiter, and the other four students act as Mr. Smith and his friends. Use different selling methods of dish-ordering in Chinese and English (Each group of students take turns to carry out scenario simulation, and the selling method cannot be used repeatedly).

任务评价

表 5.2　　点菜的推销方法评价表

The Evaluation Form of Dish-ordering Promotion Method

评价内容 Evaluation Items	评价标准 Evaluation Standard	分值 Score	小组自评 Self-evaluation（20%）	小组互评 Peer-evaluation（30%）	教师评价 Teacher-evaluation（50%）	综合得分 Subtotal
递送菜单 Passing the Menu	操作正确规范，用语标准。Standard operation and correct expression.	20				
点菜推销方式 Promotion Method	使用正确的推销方式。Use the right sales promotion method.	20				
推销语言 Selling Language	根据模拟情景选用适当的推销语言。Choose the appropriate selling language.	30				
应变能力 Strain Capacity	灵活应变不同的情况。Be flexible to different situations.	20				
团队精神 Team work	分工明确，团队协作。Clear division of labor and good teamwork.	10				
合计得分 Total						

评分标准（按 100 分制）：81～100 分为“优秀”；71～80 分为“良好”；60～70 分为“合格”；60 分以下为“不合格”。

Scoring Standard (On a scale of 100): 81–100 points as “Perfect”; 71–80 points as “Good”; 60–70 points as “Pass”; 60–below points as “Fail”.

拓展阅读

中国八大菜系

菜系，是指在一定区域内由于地理环境、气候、物产、文化传统以及习俗等因素的影响，在饮食上形成的各具特色的、被人们认可的、具有代表性和系统性的菜肴。中国地域辽阔，民族众多，因此各地区饮食口味不尽相同。总体来讲，中国饮食可以大致分为八大菜系。

1. 山东菜系

山东菜系由济南菜系和胶东菜系组成，清淡、不油腻，以其香、鲜、酥、软而闻名。因为使用青葱和大蒜作为调料，山东菜系通常较辛辣。同时，山东菜系注重汤品，清汤清澈新鲜，油汤则外观厚重、味道浓重。济南菜系擅长炸、烤、煎、炒，胶东菜系则以海鲜烹饪而闻名。代表菜有：葱烧海参、糖醋鲤鱼、德州扒鸡等。

2. 四川菜系

四川菜系是世界上最著名的中国菜系之一。四川菜系以其香辣而闻名，味道多变，着重使用红辣椒，搭配使用青椒和花椒，调配出经典、刺激的味道。此外，大蒜、姜和豆豉也被应用于烹饪过程中。野菜和野禽常被选用为原料，油炸、无油炸、腌制和文火炖煮是四川菜系基本的烹饪技术。代表菜有：宫保鸡丁、麻婆豆腐、水煮鱼等。

3. 广东菜系

由于大多数华侨来自广东，因此广东菜也是国外知名度最高的中国地方菜系之一。广东菜系的味道清、淡、脆、鲜，常用猛禽走兽来烹饪出有创意的菜肴。它的基础烹饪方法包括烤、炒、煸、深炸、炖和蒸。其中蒸和炒最常使用，可保存食材的天然风味。除此之外，广东厨师还非常注重菜肴的艺术感。代表菜有：烤乳猪、脆皮烧鹅、上汤焗龙虾等。

4. 福建菜系

福建菜系由福州菜、泉州菜、厦门菜组成，以其精选的海鲜，漂亮的色泽，甜、酸、咸和香的味道而出名。最特别的是其卤味。代表菜有：佛跳墙、太极芋泥、荔枝肉等。

5. 江苏菜系

江苏菜系，又叫淮扬菜，发源于扬州、淮安。淮扬菜以水产作为主要原料，注重原料的鲜味。其雕刻技术十分珍贵，尤以瓜雕著名。淮扬菜的烹饪技术包括炖、烤、焙、煨等，特色是淡、鲜、甜、雅，味道强而不重、淡而不温。代表菜有：松鼠鳜鱼、四喜丸子、清炖蟹粉狮子头等。

6. 浙江菜系

浙江菜系由杭州菜、宁波菜、绍兴菜组成，以其菜肴的鲜、柔、滑、香而闻名。杭州菜是三者中最出名的一个。代表菜有：西湖醋鱼、龙井虾仁、东坡肉等。

7. 湖南菜系

湖南菜系由湘江地区、洞庭湖区域和湘西的地方菜肴组成，以其极辣的味道为特色。红辣椒、青辣椒和青葱在这一菜系中是必备品。代表菜有：腊味合蒸、东安仔鸡、剁椒鱼头等。

8. 安徽菜系

安徽菜系，简称“徽菜”，因徽州而得名，随徽州商人的崛起而发展。徽菜厨师注重烹饪的温度，擅长煨炖，通常会加入火腿和方糖来改善菜肴的味道。代表菜有：李鸿章杂烩、腌鲜鳜鱼、黄山炖鸽等。

任务二：西餐点菜服务
Task 2: Western Dish-ordering Service

案例导入

王先生带着客户到某西餐厅用餐，这家西餐厅的牛排很有名。王先生一行落座后，每人点了一份主厨推荐牛排。由于餐厅比较忙碌，服务员在客人点餐后没有确认点单信息就急忙帮客人下单了。

牛排端上来后，客人发现牛排还在“滴血”，就叫来服务员确认。服务员承认，由于一时忙碌忘记询问客人需要几分熟，但又解释说，大部分来店的客人都喜欢餐厅五分熟的牛排，王先生等人可以试试，或重新加工一下。客人拒绝食用，也不接受端回厨房重新加工。

服务员只好叫来经理来处理这件事情。经理了解了整个事件之后，立刻道歉，询问了每位客人需要几分熟后，安排厨房重新做了牛排，并给客人免费提供了冰激凌甜点。客人对经理的处理方式很满意，留下来享用了牛排和甜点。

此案例中，服务员在为客人点餐时漏掉了哪些细节？在事件发生后，服务员应该如何与客人沟通并灵活处理呢？

知识准备

点菜服务完美与否对客人整个用餐过程是否融洽起着至关重要的作用。如果在这一服务环节让客人产生了不愉快，即使食物再美味，心情也可能挽救不回来。因此，了解客人的基本情况，高水平地推荐菜品是一个优秀的点餐员应该具备的最基本技能。点餐员除了需要准确研究客人心理，还需要对菜品了如指掌，包括菜品的成分、营养价值、菜品典故、适合人群以及成品的口感和分量的大小等。具备这些基本的理论知识后，点餐员还需要懂得点餐礼仪和点餐流程，如菜单的递送顺序、递送角度等。

The perfect presentation of ordering service plays an important role in the harmony of the whole dining process. If the guest is unhappy in this stage, even if the food is delicious, his mood may not be saved. Therefore, understanding the basic situation of guests and recommending dishes tactfully is the most basic knowledge that a good attendant should have. In addition to accurately studying guests' psychology, the attendant also needs to know the menu adequately, including the ingredients of the dishes, nutritional value, allusions related, target crowd, the size and weight of the finished products and other details. With these basic theoretical knowledge, the attendant also needs to understand ordering etiquette and process, such as the order of delivering menus to customers, the delivery angle, etc.

一、递送菜单 Passing the menu

（1）站在客人右侧呈递菜单时，轻轻将菜单放在客人餐位中间，注意菜单正面标识朝上。

When the menu is presented on the right side of the guest, gently place the menu in the middle of the guest's table and pay attention to the front sign of the menu facing up.

（2）原则上每位客人一份菜单，当无法满足时应告知客人。

In principle, each guest has a menu and should be informed when it is unsatisfactory.

（3）呈递菜单时注意女士优先的原则，然后沿着餐桌以顺时针方向依次递送给客人。

Pay attention to the principle of "ladies first" when presenting menus, and then deliver them clockwise to the guests along the dining table.

（4）菜单递送完毕后，可暂时离开客人餐桌，给予客人充分的时间翻看菜单。

After the menu is delivered, the attendant can leave the guest's table temporarily and give the guests enough time to take a look.

（5）主动向客人介绍餐厅推荐菜品。

Take the initiative to introduce the restaurant's recommended dishes to the guests.

二、接受点叫 Acceptance of a la carte

（一）接受点叫餐前饮品或酒水 Accept pre-meal drinks or drinks

（1）先介绍餐厅的相关饮品及酒水，由女主人或女士开始依顺时针方向点叫餐前饮品，然后是男士。

Introduce the related beverage in the restaurant. Order the pre-meal drinks clockwise from the hostess or lady, followed by the man.

（2）若西式宴会客人较多，可将客人所点饮品写在餐位平面图上。

If there are more guests at a western-style banquet, the drinks ordered by the guests can be written on the seat distribution map.

（3）开具点餐单。

Make an order.

（4）依客人所点，到吧台取出所点酒水及饮料。

Depending on what the guests ordered, go to the bar and take out the drinks.

（二）接受点菜 Accept orders

（1）关注客人查看菜单的进程，当发现客人有需要点菜的趋势时，立刻上前接受点菜。

Pay attention to the process of menu checking. When you find that the guests have a tendency to order, go ahead and accept the order immediately.

（2）点菜顺序：西式宴会点餐先从主人开始，依顺时针方向点菜；夫妻或情侣，以男士为先；若无法分辨主人，可视谁先准备点菜，然后从该客人开始按顺时针方向依次点菜，或由年长者开始。

The sequence of ordering: For western-style banquet order, it starts from the host, and continues in a clockwise order; For couples, take the man as the first; If the attendant can not distinguish the host, just see who is preparing to order first, and then start with this person and continue clockwise, or from the elderly.

（3）点菜时站在客人左侧，手持点菜单，不可将菜单放到客人餐桌上，稍微弯腰倾听客人点餐并记录。

Stand on the left side of the guest when ordering. Hold the menu with hands and never put the menu on the guest's table. Bend slightly to listen to the guest's order and record it.

（4）为客人点菜时，可以适当向客人推荐或介绍餐厅特色菜品。

When ordering for guests, recommend or introduce the restaurant's special dishes appropriately.

（5）当客人不知如何点菜时，向客人解释菜品相关内容及烹调方法等。

When the guest does not know how to order, explain the relevant contents and cooking methods to the guest.

（6）当菜品有多种烹饪方法时，需要特别注意的事项应向客人详细解释，并问明客人需求。如牛排要几分熟、需要哪种沙拉酱等。

When there are several kinds of cooking methods, and some special matters needed attention, the attendant should explain to the guests in detail and ask about their needs. For example, the attendant can say,"How would you like your steak?"or "What kind of salad dressing do you need?"

（7）按照西餐出菜顺序详细记录客人点单，并向客人重复确认无误后下单。

Make a detailed record of the order according to the sequence of the western food, and repeat to make the confirmation from the guests before placing the order.

（8）收回菜单，向客人致谢。

Take the menu back and thank the guests.

（三）接受点叫餐后甜品及饮料 Accept desserts and beverage

（1）介绍餐厅推荐甜品及饮料，注意女士优先的原则，按顺时针方向一一接受点叫，并做好记录。

Introduce desserts and beverage recommended by restaurants. Pay attention to the principle of "ladies first". Accept orders clockwise and keep records.

（2）若客人点咖啡或茶，要问明冷、热，是否需要糖、奶等具体细节。

If a guest orders coffee or tea, ask for specific details such as the temperature, and whether he/she needs sugar or milk.

三、西餐点餐基本流程 Basic process of western dining order

西餐在菜单的安排上与中餐有很多不同点。在这里我们以讲解高档西餐厅、普通西餐厅和咖啡厅的点餐服务流程为主。

Western food is different from Chinese food in menu arrangement. Here we mainly explain the ordering service process of high-end western restaurants, ordinary western restaurants and cafés.

（一）高档西餐厅的点餐服务 High-end western restaurant's ordering service

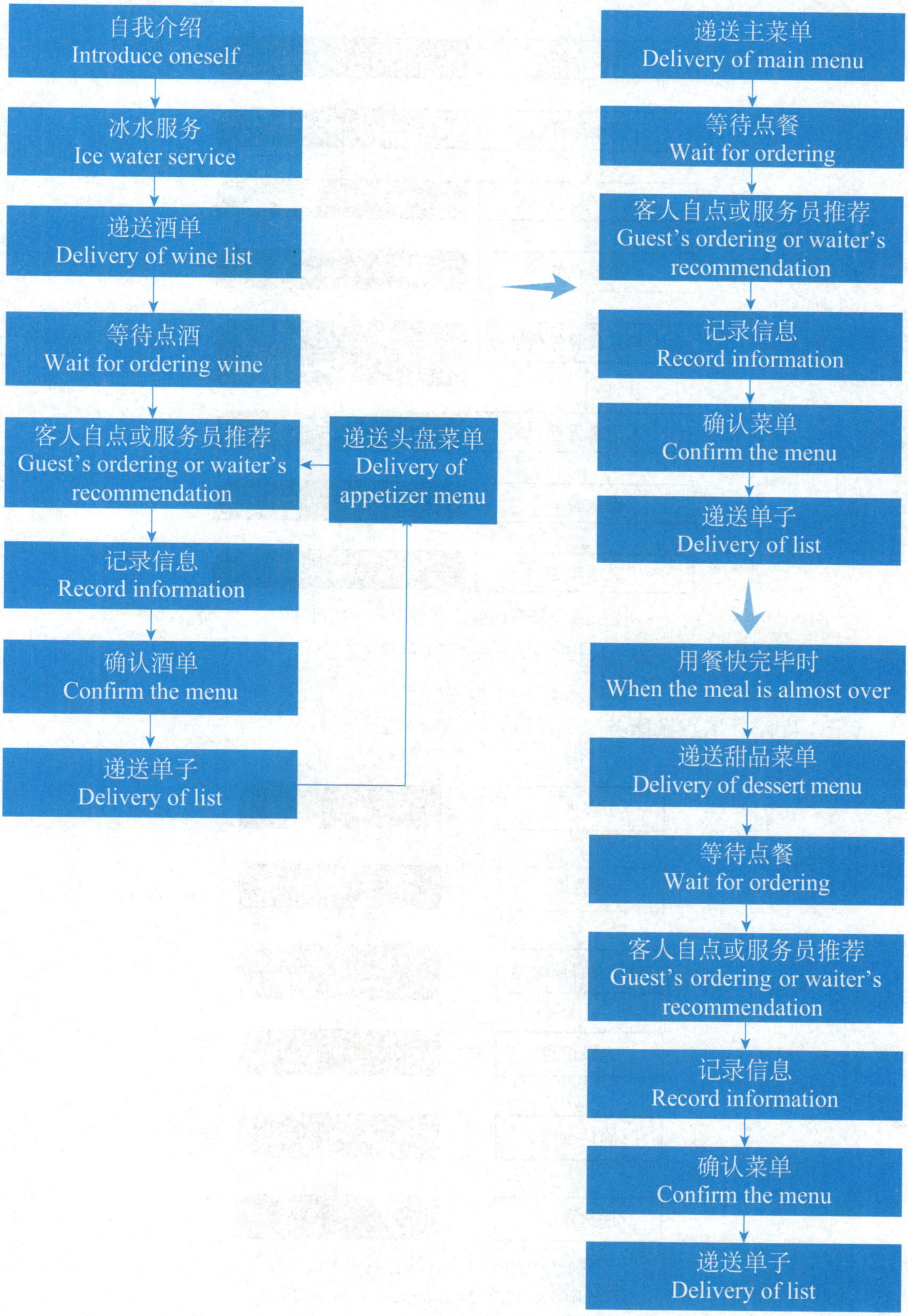

图 5.1　高档西餐厅点餐服务基本流程
Basic Process of High-end Western Restaurant's Ordering Service

（二）普通西餐厅的点餐服务 Ordinary western restaurant's ordering service

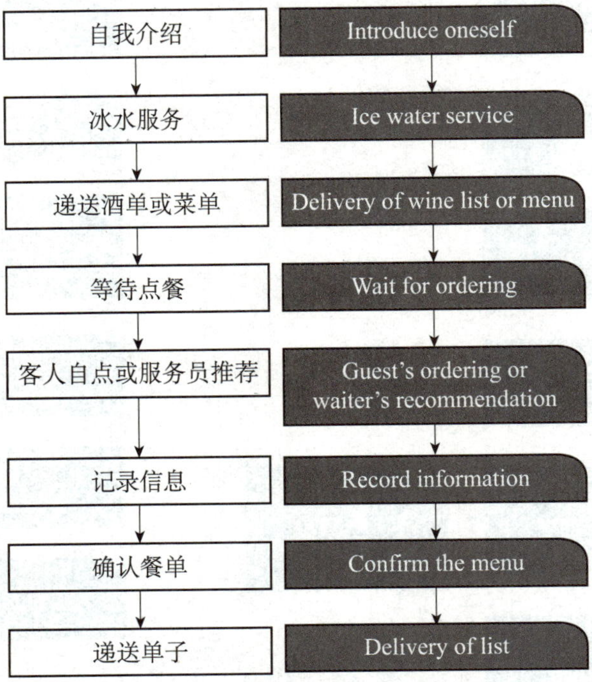

图 5.2　普通西餐厅点餐服务基本流程

Basic Process of Ordinary Western Restaurant's Ordering Service

（三）咖啡厅的点餐服务 Ordering service in café

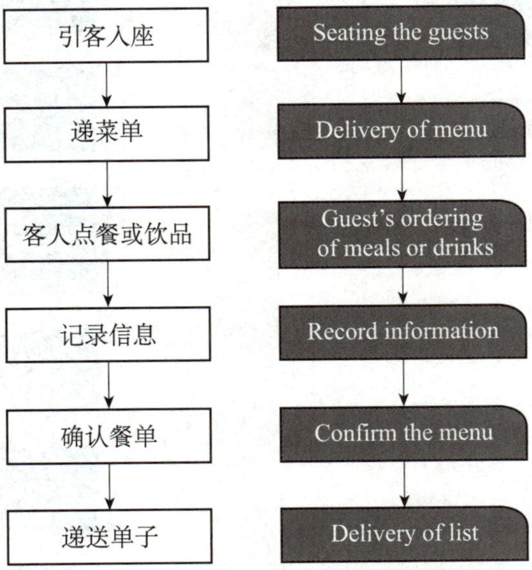

图 5.3　咖啡厅点餐服务基本流程

Basic Process of Ordering Service in Café

任务实施

第一步：教师讲解西餐点餐的相关知识，并做出演示。

Step 1: The teacher explains the relevant knowledge of western meals and make demonstrations.

第二步：教师导入本节情景设定：李先生打电话预订了一家高档西餐厅 4 人位置（3 男 1 女）。随后李先生一行四人来到该餐厅用餐，在服务员的介绍下，4 位客人点了相同的餐前开胃饮料，女士点了鸭胸肉，李先生点了五分熟的牛排，另外两位男士点了全熟的羊排。

Step 2: The teacher introduces the settings of this section: Mr. Li called to reserve for four people (3 men and 1 woman) in an upscale western restaurant. Then Mr. Li and his friends came to the restaurant for dinner. Under the introduction of the waiter, they ordered the same pre-meal drinks. The lady ordered duck breast, Mr. Li ordered medium steak, and the other two ordered well-done lamb chop.

第三步：以小组（5 人 1 组）为单位，其中，1 位学生扮演餐厅服务员，另外 4 位学生扮演点餐客人，分别模拟进行点餐服务（5 位学生轮流进行情景模拟）。

Step 3: Work in groups (5 people per group), in which one student acts as the restaurant waiter, and the other four students act as guests. Simulate the ordering service respectively (5 students take turns to do the scenario simulation).

任务评价

表 5.3 餐饮点餐评价表

The Evaluation Form of F&B Ordering Service

评价内容 Evaluation Items	评价标准 Evaluation Standard	分值 Score	小组自评 Self-evaluation（20%）	小组互评 Peer-evaluation（30%）	教师评价 Teacher-evaluation（50%）	综合得分 Subtotal
递送菜单 Deliver the menu	操作正确规范，用语标准。Standard operation and correct expression.	30				
介绍餐厅特色酒水 Introduce the specific beverage	用语规范，表述正确。Standard and correct expression.	30				
介绍餐厅特色菜品 Introduce the specific dishes	用语规范，表述正确。Standard and correct expression.	20				

续前表

评价内容 Evaluation Items	评价标准 Evaluation Standard	分值 Score	小组自评 Self-evaluation（20%）	小组互评 Peer-evaluation（30%）	教师评价 Teacher-evaluation（50%）	综合得分 Subtotal
记录客人点餐内容 Record information	准确记录每位客人的点餐需求，并复述确认。Record clearly, and repeat to confirm.	10				
团队精神 Team work	分工明确，团队协作。Clear division of labor and good teamwork.	10				
合计得分 Total						

评分标准（按 100 分制）：81～100 分为“优秀”；71～80 分为“良好”；60～70 分为“合格”；60 分以下为“不合格”。

Scoring Standard (On a scale of 100): 81–100 points as “Perfect”; 71–80 points as “Good”; 60–70 points as “Pass”; 60–below points as “Fail”.

拓展阅读

餐饮点菜系统

随着互联网时代的到来及信息化技术的发展，点菜系统被普遍使用。无论是在豪华的五星级酒店，还是在街头时尚餐饮店，都可以看到其身影。下面，我们就来看看餐饮点菜系统与传统手写点菜的区别。

点菜系统主要由软件部分和硬件部分两大块组成。与传统手写点菜相比，点菜系统具有以下优势：

（1）提高效率，点菜、提交、下单同步进行，规范管理；

（2）及时更新酒店介绍、新菜谱信息，提升餐厅管理水平；

（3）餐厅营业状况数据分析一目了然，并兼容大部分餐饮管理软件；

（4）比手工点菜管理方式更方便、简洁、高效；

（5）有效降低了出错率。

点菜系统实现的是“菜谱 + 无线点菜系统 + 餐饮管理系统”的综合功能。

（1）同一道菜可根据餐桌的类型，如包房、VIP 包房等，增加菜品价格；

（2）安装简单，软件可自动检测并完成菜品更新和软件更新；

（3）支持一次下单、多处打印，且每处可以设置打印模板以实现个性化需求，支持后备打印机；

（4）可根据客户要求创建操作语言包；

（5）可远程管理订单，查看就餐、付费、消费情况；

（6）可导出统计资料，如每张桌、每道菜、每天、每周、每月的消费情况，服务员递送的菜量情况等；

（7）支持拼音或者语音搜索菜品，可呼叫前台服务，如加菜、结账、倒茶等；

（8）可开台、并台、移动订单，并于后台自动生成费用清单；

（9）可对每个菜品增加做法、配料说明、不同的大小规格等，菜品价格根据做法、配料、大小规格自动变化；

（10）支持自助设计皮肤和语音包；

（11）支持在平板电脑上查看、更新每张桌的就餐情况，如人数、已点菜单、已上菜单、未上菜单；

（12）可通过平板电脑，看到厨房的实时监控画面；

（13）有独立介绍页面，可放餐厅介绍视频、餐厅介绍图片等；

（14）支持仓库管理、成本自动核算、会员打折管理等；

（15）支持桌面应用程序锁定功能，开启此功能，平板电脑将只显示点菜界面，不可进行浏览网页、游戏等操作，也可输入密码解除锁定；

（16）界面灵活，待机图片可自行翻动，可以播放合适的广告图片。

Project 6

Beverage Service

项目六

酒水服务

项目概述

PROJECT SUMMARY

酒水服务是餐饮服务的重要组成部分，酒水服务水平的高低直接影响客人的感受及其酒水消费水平。在酒水服务中，工作人员既要做到服务标准化、规范化，又要做到个性化、程序化，为酒店创造良好的声誉和经济效益。

项目目标

PROJECT OBJECTS

知识目标：掌握各种酒水饮料的基础知识及服务要求。

技能目标：掌握酒水服务的服务流程，灵活运用酒水的斟倒技巧。

素养目标：具备文化自信；具备节约意识；具备服务意识与安全意识；爱岗敬业、具备团结合作、勇于创新的意识。

任务一：认识酒水
Task 1: The Basic Knowledge of Beverage

案例导入

不可忽视的酒水服务

近年来，餐饮业持续保持快速的发展，更是受到了影视媒体的关注。明星真人秀节目《中餐厅》第二季的播出，让普通老百姓更加深入地了解了葡萄酒的知识。在第 7 期节目中，以明星赵某为店长的、位于法国的中餐厅迎来了“神秘客人”——法国科尔马市的市长及几位市领导。科尔马“最高”规格的服务考验，使得“店员们”都压力山大。

因为知晓法国人对葡萄酒的喜爱程度，店长很快意识到这些客人可能需要葡萄酒。于是，她首先通知店员打开一瓶常温的 2002 年的红葡萄酒，先醒酒，做足准备；然后吩咐店员给客人上了红葡萄酒与杯子。但店员苏某（非专业）并不了解如何斟倒酒水，也不知道正确的斟酒顺序，所以一直跑到后厨向店长求助。店长非常了解葡萄酒，并及时帮忙做好了各项斟酒服务。在一切都很顺利地进行时，科尔马市长品尝完葡萄酒后微微一笑，提出了一个建议：“红葡萄酒其实应该再冰一点儿。”

对于葡萄酒来说，温度很重要。这在酒水服务中也是非常容易被忽视的细节。科尔马市长的建议很好，给酒水服务人员提出了更高的细节要求。

思考讨论：如果你来接待科尔马市长，你会提前做哪些准备工作？

知识准备

一、酒水的基本知识 Basic knowledge of alcoholic beverage

（一）酒的概念 The concept of alcoholic beverage

酒是一种用水果、谷物、花瓣或其他含糖或淀粉的植物，经过发酵、蒸馏等方法酿造而成的一种含酒精的饮料。基本上，任何含有 25%～75% 的乙醇、可以喝的液体，都可以称为“酒精饮料”。

Alcoholic beverage is produced by fruit, cereal or other plants with sugar or starch through the method of fermentation, distillation and so on. Basically, every kind of drinkable liquid with 25%–75% alcohol can be called “alcoholic beverage”.

（二）酒的分类 The classification of alcoholic beverage

（1）按生产工艺，酒可以分为酿造酒、蒸馏酒、混合酒，这也是国际流行的分法。

According to the produce technology, alcoholic beverage can be classified as fermented wine, distilled wine and mixed wine, and this is the international and popular classification method.

（2）按生产原料，酒可分为果类、谷物类、杂物类。

According to the product material, alcoholic beverage can be classified as fruit sort, cereal sort and sundries sort.

（3）按服务性质，酒可以分为餐前酒、餐后酒、佐餐酒。

According to the character of service, alcoholic beverage can be liquor classified as aperitif, dessert wine and table wine.

（4）按不同的制作方法，酒可分为白酒、黄酒、啤酒、葡萄酒。

On the basis of different production methods, alcoholic beverage can be classified as spirit, yellow rice wine, beer and wine.

二、常见酒水 Common alcoholic beverage

源远流长的中国文化中，酒文化有着重要的地位。作为饮料中的“排头兵”，酒水的具体品种成百上千。就目前而言，在国内所见较多的酒水主要有白酒、啤酒、葡萄酒、香槟酒、白兰地、威士忌及鸡尾酒等。它们也都是各类酒中的代表。为了更好地掌握这些主要酒水的特点，以便对其正确、有益地加以应用，我们将对它们分别进行介绍：

Within the historic culture of China, the culture of alcoholic beverage has an important status. There are different kinds of alcoholic beverage in the world. The common kinds of alcoholic beverage in China are spirit, beer, wine, champagne, brandy, whisky, cocktail and so on. They are all representatives in each kind of alcoholic beverage. In order to better understand the characterics of these main alcoholic beverage and use them correctly and properly, we will introduce them respectively:

（一）白酒 Spirit

在这里所提到的各种酒水，除白酒之外，都是从西方国家传进来的舶来品。只有白酒是地地道道的中国货。其他酒统称“洋酒”。

Besides the spirit, all the alcoholic beverage mentioned here are exotic. The only native alcoholic beverage in China is spirit. Other alcoholic beverage are called “imported wine”.

1. 白酒的特点 Characteristics of spirit

白酒，亦名烧酒、白干。它是高粱、玉米、番薯等粮食或某些果品，经发酵、蒸馏制成的一种酒类。酒质无色（或微黄）透明，气味芳香纯正，入口绵甜爽净，酒精含量较高，属于典型的烈酒。白酒在我国各地均能生产，但因工艺的差别而分成各种香型。当前最著名的白酒有茅台酒、五粮液、剑南春、西凤酒等。

The spirit is alcoholic beverage made from sorghum, corn, sweet potato or other fruits through fermentation and distilling which can be also called as "Shaojiu" or "Baigan". The spirit has no color or a yellowish color with good smell and a little bit sweet flavor. At the same time, the spirit has a high alcohol level. It can be fermented all over China, but divided into various types because of the different technology. The most famous brands of spirit in China are Moutai, Wuliangye, Jiannanchun and Xifeng.

2. 白酒的饮用 How to drink spirit

白酒可以净饮干喝，也可以用来助菜下饭，有时还可以泡药作引。不过，白酒不可与其他酒类的汽水、可乐等软饮料混合同饮，不然极易醉酒。

The spirit can be drunk directly, help to eat food, and sometimes it also can be used as a medicine guiding drug. But it cannot be drunk with other soda wine, coke and so on at the same time. Otherwise, it'll be easy to get drunk.

在正式场合喝白酒，讲究以专用的瓷杯或玻璃杯盛酒。它们“襟怀”不大，所以喝白酒讲究“酒满敬人”和“一饮而尽”。喝白酒时，一般不需要加温、加冰，或用水稀释。

In formal occasion, the spirit should be put in the porcelain cup or glass. When cheering with people, you need to drink off the spirit at one time. At the same time, you don't need to heat, put ice or use water to dilute the spirit.

（二）啤酒 Beer

啤酒是人类最古老的酒精饮料之一，是继水和茶之后世界上消耗量排名第三的饮料。啤酒于 20 世纪初传入中国，属外来酒种。在国外，人们主要把啤酒看作是一种日常饮料，而非真正的酒。不过，对许多中国人来讲，它却是一种最著名、最受欢迎的“洋酒”。

Beer is one of the most historic alcoholic beverage in the world and it ranks the third in the consumption of beverage after water and tea. Beer is exotic which was introduced to China at the beginning of the 20th century. In western countries, people always take the beer as a daily beverage, not wine. But, for many Chinese, it is the most famous and popular "foreign wine".

1. 啤酒的特点 Characteristics of beer

啤酒，又称“麦酒”，它是一种以大麦和啤酒花为主要原料，经发酵制成的低酒精度酒。啤酒含有大量的泡沫和浓郁的香味，味道微苦，酒精度一般在 4°（20℃时的 100ml 酒中含乙醇 4ml, 以下同）左右。

Beer is also called “ale wine”. It is a low alcoholic beverage made of barley and hops through fermentation. Beer has a low alcoholic level of about 4°. (The alcoholic level refers that there is 4ml ethyl alcohol in 100ml wine when the temperature is 20℃, similarly hereinafter.) It has a lot of bubbles with full aroma, tastes a little bitter.

目前，世界各国都生产啤酒，但它主要分为德国式、捷克式、丹麦式三大类型。根据酿制工艺的差别，啤酒又有生啤、熟啤之分。较为著名的啤酒品牌有德国的贝克、荷兰的喜力、丹麦的嘉士伯、美国的百威、日本的朝日和中国的青岛。

At present, beer is produced all over the world, but it is mainly divided into German, Czech and Danish styles. According to the difference of brewing technology, there are draft beer and flaschebier. The famous beer brands include Beck’s (Germany), Heineken (Holland), Carlsberg(Denmark), Budweiser(USA), Asahi(Japan), Tsingtao (China).

2. 啤酒的饮用 How to drink beer

饮用啤酒时，一般应使用倒三角形或带把的啤酒杯，饮用时啤酒的最佳温度在 7℃左右，所以不要加冰或久冻。喝啤酒时，讲究大口饮用。

Using the invert triangle glass or beer glass with handle is the popular way to drink beer. When the temperature of the beer is 7℃ , it tastes the best. When drinking beer, you need not to put ice or froze the beer for a long time.

在国外，啤酒是上不了筵席的。但是在国内，啤酒可以在社交聚餐中露面，也可作为消暑解渴的饮品。

In foreign countries, beer cannot appear on the formal dinner. But in China, beer can be drunk on different social occasions. It is also taken as a beverage to quench people’s thirst.

（三）葡萄酒 Wine

目前，在饮酒方面，国内与国外同步的恐怕只有葡萄酒了。作为正式宴会中的佐餐酒，葡萄酒一直是首选。

At present, wine is probably the only one that is popular in China and abroad. As an table wine in a formal banquet, wine has always been the first choice.

1. 葡萄酒的特点 Characteristics of wine

葡萄酒，即以葡萄为主要原料，经发酵酿制而成的一种酒类。它的酒精含量不高，味道清美，富含营养。根据颜色的差别，葡萄酒可分为白葡萄酒、红葡萄酒和桃红葡萄酒。根据糖分含量的差别，又可将葡萄酒分为干、半干、微干、微甜、半甜、甜等几种。这里的“干”意思是“基本不含糖分”。葡萄酒的酒精含量在 12° 左右。世界上最著名的葡萄酒产地在法国的波尔多地区。

Wine is an alcoholic beverage which is made from grape through the fermentation method. It has low alcoholic level with good taste and nutrition. By the different colour of wine, it can be classified into white wine, red wine and pink wine. By the different level of sugar in wine, it can be classified into dry, half-dry, micro-dry, micro-sweet, half-sweet, sweet, etc. The meaning of "dry" is that there is almost no sugar in wine. The common alcoholic level of wine is 12°. The best famous place to produce great wine is Bordeaux in France.

2. 葡萄酒的饮用 How to drink wine

葡萄酒不但可以佐餐，也可以单独饮用。不同的葡萄酒，喝的时候对酒的温度要求也有差别。白葡萄酒宜在 7℃左右饮用，故可适量加冰块。而红葡萄酒则在 18℃左右饮用最佳，故不宜加冰块。喝葡萄酒时，要用高脚玻璃杯。喝白葡萄酒时，要捏着杯脚；而喝红葡萄酒时，则讲究握住杯身。喝葡萄酒时兑可乐或雪碧的做法是不正确的。

Wine is not only taken as a table wine, but also can be drunk directly. Different wine has different drinking temperature to create good taste. Just like white wine, the best temperature is 7℃, so it can be added with ice in moderation. And the best drinking temperature for red wine is 18℃, so drinking without ice will be better. Goblet is a good choice for people to drink wine. When you drink white wine, you can hold the goblet's foot. When you drink red wine, you can hold the bowls. Mixing the wine with coke or sprite is a wrong way to drink wine.

桃红葡萄酒，又称"玫瑰红葡萄酒"。它的口味、喝法与白葡萄酒略同。因其颜色美丽，多为女性所喜欢。

Pink wine is also called "rose wine". Its flavor and drinking method is similar with white wine. Because of its beautiful color, most of female like it.

（四）香槟酒 Champagne

香槟酒在我国的知名度在逐渐提高，其饮用场合也越来越广泛。

Champagne is becoming more and more popular in China. It is used in different occasions.

1. 香槟酒的特点 Characteristics of champagne

香槟酒，又称"发泡葡萄酒"。实际上，它是一种以特种工艺制成的、富含二氧化碳的、起泡沫的白葡萄酒。因其以法国香槟地区所产最为著名，故称为香槟酒。酒精含量在 10° 左右，口感清凉、酸涩，且有水果香味。

Champagne is also called "sparkling wine". In fact, it is a white wine with carbon dioxide and bubbles which is produced by special method. Due to its famous wine region which named Champagne district in France, the wine is called Champagne. Champagne has 10°alcoholic level with acid taste and fruit smelling flavor.

2. 香槟酒的饮用 How to drink champagne

香槟酒以 8℃左右饮用为佳，故在饮用之前，需将其临时放于冰桶中。开瓶时，可稍作摇晃，然后再起走瓶塞。届时，它就会连泡带酒一同喷涌而出，增添欢快的气氛。饮用香槟酒，宜用郁金香形的高脚玻璃杯，并应以手捏住杯脚。香槟酒可用来佐餐、祝酒，也可以单独饮用，或者是在庆典、仪式上为人助兴。

The best drinking temperature of champagne is around 8℃ , so before drinking it, you should put the bottle in the ice bucket. You should shake the bottle when you want to open it. Then open the cork, and champagne will pull out to create a happy atmosphere. The tulip glass is suitbable for drinking champagne, and you need to hold the foot of the glass while drinking. Champagne can be used to be a table wine, drink a toast or drink alone in different occasions such as formal dinner, ceremony or party.

（五）白兰地 Brandy

在所有洋酒中，白兰地是最为名贵的。它一度与威士忌和茅台酒并称为“世界三大名酒”。

Brandy is the most precious wine comparing with all foreign wines. It is one of the “Top 3 World’s Famous Wine” with whisky and Moutai.

1. 白兰地的特点 Characteristics of brandy

白兰地也是葡萄酒家族里的一员，它是用葡萄干发酵之后蒸馏精制而成，故又称“蒸馏葡萄酒”。它的酒精度约为 40%，酒色金黄，苦涩醇美。世界上著名的白兰地酒品牌有马爹利、轩尼诗、人头马、拿破仑等，并以产于法国干邑地区，避光储存较久的为佳。

Brandy is one kind of wine which use fermented raisin through distillation method to produce, so it is also called as “distilling wine”. Its alcoholic level is 40% vol. It has an golden color and a little bitter taste. There are some famous brands of brandy in the world, such as Martell, Hennessey, Remy Martin, Napoleon and so on. And the Brandy produced in Cognac in France which is kept out of the sun and has a long time storage is the best all over the world.

2. 白兰地的饮用 How to drink brandy

与白酒有所差别，以白兰地为代表的洋酒多数是以盎司计量的，故此它不讲究“酒满敬人”。饮白兰地的最佳温度为 18℃，所以应将其盛装在专用的大肚、收口、矮脚杯内，饮用时先以右手托住杯身观其色彩，并以手掌为其加温。待其香味弥漫时闻其酒香，再慢慢地小口品尝。若将其一饮而尽，只会被看作没有品位的“草莽英豪”。

As the representative of the foreign wines, brandy is measuring in ounces which is different from the spirit. So you don’t need to drink off at one time. The best drinking temperature is 18℃ , so it should be put into the brandy glass with big bowl and small top. When drinking brandy, you should look the color first and use hand to warm it, then take a little bit wine after smelling its fragrance. Drinking off brandy at one time will be treated as rude people.

（六）威士忌 Whisky

如果说白兰地是洋酒之中的“贵族”，那么物美价廉的威士忌则是洋酒中的“草根王子”。

If brandy is the nobility of wines, then whisky is “the grassroots prince”.

1. 威士忌的特点 Characteristics of whisky

威士忌是一种用谷物发酵酿造而成的烈性蒸馏酒。它的口味浓郁、刺激，酒精含量约为 40°。在世界各国生产的威士忌中，首推英国苏格兰地区生产的威士忌，其知名品牌有尊尼获加、威雀等。

Whisky is a hard liquor which uses grain to produce through the fermentation method. It tastes of rich and stimulated flavor with a 40°alcoholic level. Compared with other countries' whisky, the whisky in Scotland of the UK is the best whose famous brands include Johnnie Walker and the Famous Grouse, etc.

2. 威士忌的饮用 How to drink whisky

威士忌可以直接饮用，不过加入冰块、苏打水或姜汁后，其味道更好。喝威士忌时，最好使用特别的平底小玻璃杯，耐心细致地慢慢品尝。威士忌不仅可以在家自酌自饮，也可以在酒吧里喝。

Whisky can be drunk directly and it also can be added ice, soda water or ginger liquid to make the flavor better. Drinking whisky should use small glass with flat base and taste it as slowly as possible. Whisky can be drunk in home or bars.

（七）鸡尾酒 Cocktail

鸡尾酒是目前中国人在不同社交场合中接触较多的一种酒。

Cocktail is the famous wine in different social occasions in China.

1. 鸡尾酒的特点 Characteristics of cocktail

准确地讲，鸡尾酒并非某一品种的酒，而是一种混合型的酒。它是用各种不同的酒，以及果汁、汽水、蛋清、糖浆等其他饮料或液体，按一定的比例，以特别的技法调配而成的。它的口味有浓有淡，酒精的含量有多有少，但其配合之后，则是奇光异彩，闪烁好似雄鸡之尾，故被称为“鸡尾酒”。鸡尾酒有好几千种，其中比较知名的有马提尼、曼哈顿、红粉佳人、血腥玛丽、亚历山大、天使之吻等。

Accurately speaking, cocktail is not a single kind of wine, but a mixed wine. There are different kinds of cocktail using fruit, soda, egg white and other soft drinks with special percent to produce. Its flavor can be fresh or rich, the alcoholic level can be high or low. After the mixing, the cocktail will be colourful and shiny like the tail of a cock, which is the origin of its name. There are thousands of cocktails in the world, such as Martini, Manhattan, Pink Lady, Bloody Marry, Alexander, Angel's Kiss and so on.

2. 鸡尾酒的饮用 How to drink cocktail

鸡尾酒适用于多个场合，如酒吧、聚会场所或家中。为了便于观赏其独具特色的丰富色彩，最好用高脚广口玻璃杯来盛鸡尾酒。一般不适宜把各种不同的鸡尾酒混杂在一起喝。

Cocktail can be used widely in bars, parties or at home. To enjoy the special beautiful color of cocktail, the best choice of the container is goblet with wide mouth. Don't mix different cocktail while drinking.

任务实施

第一步：课前布置任务：各小组（5～6 人为一组）通过查阅资料，了解啤酒、葡萄酒、鸡尾酒、白酒等不同种类的酒水的特点、作用及如何饮用。要求每组选择一种酒水制作 PPT, 并在课堂上进行现场介绍。

Step 1: Assign the tasks before class: Each group (5–6 people per group) should learn about the characteristics, functions and how to drink different types of drinks such as beer, wine, cocktail and Chinese spirit by looking up relevant materials. Each group is required to choose a kind of wine to make PPT, and gives a presentation in class.

第二步：教师根据学生所做的课堂介绍，点评各小组的任务完成情况，并展开讲解本节内容。

Step 2: According to the presentation given by students, the teacher reviews the task completion of each group and gives a lecture of this section.

第三步：结合教师的讲授内容，讨论一个好的侍酒师应具备哪些能力和服务品质。各组独立完成报告，不少于 800 字。

Step 3: Discuss the competence and service quality of a good sommelier according to what the teacher has taught. Each group should finish the report independently, no less than 800 words.

任务评价

表 6.1　“如何做一名优秀的侍酒师”报告评价表

Evaluation Form of The Report of “How to be A Good Sommelier”

评价内容 Evaluation Items	评价标准 Evaluation Standard	分值 Score	小组自评 Self-evaluation（20%）	小组互评 Peer-evaluation（30%）	教师评价 Teacher-evaluation（50%）	综合得分 Subtotal
精神面貌 Mental Attitude	态度认真，积极主动。Good attitude and be proactive.	20				
报告质量 Quality of Report	文字表达流畅，字数不少于800字；Smooth writing, and the word number is not less than 800 words;	40				
	排版格式规范，内容条理清晰；Normative format and clear content;	10				
	阐述观点明确；Clear viewpoints;	20				
	有创新性。Be creative.	10				
合计得分 Total						

评分标准（按100分制）：81～100分为“优秀”；71～80分为“良好”；60～70分为“合格”；60分以下为“不合格”。

Scoring Standards (On a scale of 100): 81–100 points as “Perfect”; 71–80 points as “Good”; 60–70 points as “Pass”; 60–below points as “Fail”.

拓展阅读

酒水的开启与保管

在酒水服务中，开瓶也是检验侍酒师基本技能的一个方面。这里，我们介绍一些瓶装酒水的开启注意事项。

一、酒水的开启

1. 白兰地、威士忌、伏特加的开瓶方法

（1）验酒。左手持瓶颈，右手托瓶底，酒牌面对客人，待客人确认无异议后方可开酒。

（2）去除瓶口包装膜。白兰地、威士忌、伏特加瓶口一般都包有胶膜纸或锡纸，正常都可以用指甲划开，划不开时可借助开瓶器的螺旋钉划开。

开瓶大致分为两种：一种是去除包装膜后，直接拔出塞子饮用，其代表有轩尼诗、蓝方；另一种是去除包装膜后，瓶口还含有小圆珠，无须担心，这时可直接倒酒。若倒不出，则瓶口朝下，对准酒杯，轻轻晃动瓶身（晃动时小圆珠会移位，酒自然就会流出来，但注意晃动瓶子时动作要优雅），其代表有黑方和绝对伏特加。

2. 葡萄酒的开瓶方法

（1）将瓶口的封套撕开，并用擦布将瓶口擦拭干净。

（2）将螺旋钉的尖端插入木塞的中间（如果插在边上，会容易导致木塞断裂或者有木碎片掉进酒里），再按顺时针方向钻入木塞。

（3）螺旋钉钻进木塞后，将金属支点放在瓶口，一只手握着瓶肩，另一只手握住开瓶器的把手，提起来，木塞就可被拔出。

3. 香槟酒的开瓶方法

（1）左手握住瓶颈下方，瓶口向外倾斜 15 度；右手将瓶口的包装纸揭去，并将铁丝网套锁扣处的扭缠部分松开。

（2）在右手除去网套的同时，左手拇指须适时按住即将冲出的瓶塞。然后，右手以餐巾布替换左手拇指，并用手掌捏住瓶塞。

（3）瓶塞冲出瞬间，右手迅速将瓶塞向右侧揭开。

（4）如果瓶内气压不够，瓶塞无力冲出，可用右手捏紧瓶塞不动，再以握瓶的左手将酒瓶左右旋转，直到瓶塞冲出为止。

4. 啤酒的开瓶方法

啤酒开瓶简单易懂，建议采用缓冲法开酒，即在开瓶器翘起瞬间留有余地，使瓶盖不完全离瓶，再稍微用力去除瓶盖。开瓶时，将瓶子举在身体侧面，眼睛不要正对瓶子，不要离客人太近。

二、酒水的保管

1. 基本程序

（1）入库的酒水要登记。每一类酒水应配以一张卡片，对酒的名称、产地、日期、标价等登记在册。

（2）酒水放置后，不要随意挪动。懂行的管理人员通常不会清扫酒瓶外面的灰尘，对高级的酒水尤其如此，其目的：一是防止酒瓶摇晃，沉淀物泛起；二是证明酒水的古老名贵（如拉菲等）。

（3）酒库切勿与其他仓库混用。不少酒水“呼吸”较强烈，外来异味极易透过瓶塞、瓶盖而进入酒内，以致酒液吸收异味而变味。因此，不可将其他货物存入酒库。

2. 酒类贮存要领

（1）各种酒水应放置于阴凉处。

（2）勿使阳光直接照射酒水。

（3）装酒密封箱勿常搬动。

（4）标签、瓶盖保持完好无缺。

（5）不可与有特殊气味的物品并存。

任务二：酒水服务

Task2: Beverage Service

案例导入

在舒缓的背景音乐下，丽莎忙着为碧云厅的10人桌的客人点菜和酒水。从客人的表情可以看出，他们对丽莎的服务很满意。在接下来的酒水服务中，丽莎动作规范，不滴不洒，斟酒量恰到好处。然而，在为第六位客人斟倒酒水时，丽莎将这位客人点的白葡萄酒和下一位客人点的红葡萄酒的顺序记反了。这两位客人看到自己面前的酒不是自己所点的，虽稍有不悦，但碍于丽莎之前的良好表现，没有指出其错误，而是自己将两个酒杯换过来了。

思考讨论：当客人比较多的时候，怎么才能准备记好每一位客人的酒水需求呢？

知识准备

一、酒水服务知识 Beverage service knowledge

（一）斟酒前的准备工作 Preparation work for pouring wine

在斟酒前，须将酒瓶擦干净，特别要将塞子屑和瓶口部位擦净；要检查酒水质量，如发现瓶子破裂或酒水有变质现象，如有悬浮物、浑浊沉淀物时，应及时调换；准备好的酒水要摆放整齐，这样既美观又便于取用。

Wipe the wine bottle before pouring, especially clean the cork and bottleneck before taking the wine to the dining table; Change the wine if you find the bottle has been broken or the wine has become degenerate with sediment inside. Make sure every wine has been put in right place to use easily.

（二）斟酒服务形式 The form of pouring wine

1. 徒手斟酒 Pouring without tray

徒手斟酒的服务形式是左手拿一块餐巾，右手握瓶为客人斟倒酒水。其基本要求如下：站在客人的身后右侧，面向客人，左手持一块洁净的餐巾随时擦拭瓶口，右手掌自然张开，握住酒瓶的中部偏下部位，拇指朝内，食指指向瓶口，与拇指成约60°，其余三指基本并在一起，与拇指配合握紧瓶身，商标朝向客人；右腿伸入两客座椅之间半步，身体微侧。斟酒时，瓶口对准杯口，斟倒一般酒水时，瓶口应距离杯口约 2cm，瓶口对准杯中心，缓缓地将酒水注入酒杯中。斟倒啤酒或起泡酒时，应将酒液沿杯壁注入杯中。

The form of pouring wine without tray is to use the left hand holding a service towel, hold the bottle in the right hand and pour the wine for the guest. The basic requirements are as follows: Stand behind the guest on the right side and face towards the guests; Hold a clean service towel with the left hand to wipe the bottle if necessary; Hold the bottom half of the bottle with the right hand which is naturally open, and the thumb of the right hand faces inside, the forefinger points to the top of the bottle with about 60 degrees from the thumb, the other three fingers draw close to each other to hold the bottle together with the thumb, and trademark faces to the guest. The right foot steps forward between two chairs with the body slightly leaning to one side. When pouring the wine, the mouth of the bottle should have about 2cm gap from the cup, and the rim of the bottle is aligned to the center of the glass. Pour the wine gently, and pour along the glass if it's beer or sparkling wine.

斟倒香槟时，用手握住瓶子中部，用食指撑住瓶颈，以求稳妥。初往杯子里斟倒时，气泡会喷起来，因此要先斟少量。等气泡减少时再继续斟至大半杯为止，然后将瓶向上方扶正，以防酒漏到外面。

When pouring champagne, use your hand to hold the middle of the wine bottle and the forefinger to support the bottleneck and make the bottle steady. At the beginning, pour a little bit wine into glass for avoiding bubble spouting. When the bubbles are reduced, continue to pour until more than half of the glass, then pull the bottle up in case the wine leak out.

2. 托盘斟酒 Pouring with tray

托盘斟酒适用于同时为同桌多位客人斟倒多种酒水的服务。托盘斟酒服务可提高服务的效率和方便服务工作，也有利于酒水饮料的推销。

Pouring with tray is a good way to serve more than one guest who sit at one table. It can improve the efficiency of the wine service and it is also a better way to do the promotion sales about wine.

其基本要求如下：左手托盘，右手斟酒，右脚在前并插入两椅之间，侧身站在客人的右侧斟倒。托盘斟酒包括托盘和斟酒两项技能。一是托盘的姿势。服务员在为客人斟倒时，左手的托盘应打开，并将托盘拉开至座椅椅背后，托盘要与客人保持一定的距离。二是斟酒的姿势。斟倒时上身略向前倾，掌握好自己身体的重心，切忌将自己的身体贴靠在客人身上或餐椅上进行服务，要掌握好距离。在换为下一位客人斟倒时，应先将重心从右脚脚尖移向左脚，抽出右脚，走向下一个餐位，进出餐位的时候必须侧身进行，动作幅度不能太大，应尽量避免影响客人。

The basic requirements are as follows: Use the left hand to hold the tray and use the right hand to pour the wine. The right foot steps forward between the two chairs, and stand on the right side of the guest to serve the wine. Pouring with tray includes two skills: hold the tray and pour the wine. For holding the tray, the server should open the tray and keep a distance from the guest while pouring the wine. For the gesture of pouring the wine, the server should control the center of gravity with upper body leaning forward. Do not lean your body against the guests or the dining chairs for service. When serving the wine to the next guest, you need to move your gravity from the right foot to the left first, and then walk to the next seat. The action should be gentle with the body slightly leaning to one side to avoid influencing the guests.

3. 捧斟 Pouring with glass in hand

此方式适用于酒会和酒吧服务，其方法是一只手握瓶，另一只手将酒杯捧在手中，站在客人的右侧，然后向杯内斟酒。斟酒动作应在台面以外的空间进行，然后将斟满的酒杯放置在客人右手处。捧斟适用于非冰镇处理的酒，捧斟的服务员要做到准确、优雅、大方。

This pouring method is suitable for wine party and bar service. This service method is that one hand takes the bottle, the other hand holds the glass. Then stand on the right side of guest and pour the wine into glass. The action of pouring should be finished outside of the desk and the glass with full wine should be put on the right hand of the guest. Pouring with glass in hand is suitable for wine unfrozen. The server should be accurate, agile and gentle.

（三）斟酒顺序 Sequence of pouring

（1）根据客人出席宴请的身份和座次高低决定斟酒顺序。一般是先从主宾位开始，再斟倒主人位，然后按顺时针方向依次进行。同桌人数比较多时，可有两名服务员同时进行服务。一名服务员从第一宾客开始，另一名服务员从第二宾客开始，按顺时针方向依次绕台进行斟酒服务。

Determine the sequence of wine pouring according to the guests' status and seating capacity. Usually it can be started from the main guest position, the host position next, and then goes clockwise in turn. There can be two servers at the same time if the guests are numerous. One waiter begins with the first guest, and the other one starts clockwise from the second guest to serve the wine.

（2）根据出席宴请宾客的国籍、地区、礼仪风俗决定斟酒顺序。例如：对来自欧美国家的客人，应按“先女主宾、后男主宾再一般来宾”的服务顺序。

Determine the sequence of wine pouring according to the guests' nationality, region and custom. For western countries' guests, it should start from the main female guest to the main male guest, and then serve the other guests.

（3）根据客人用酒不同决定酒水的斟倒顺序。在通常情况下，中餐斟酒是先斟酒、后斟饮料。如果客人在一餐中同时饮用白酒、红葡萄酒、啤酒，其顺序应是：先斟倒红葡萄酒，再斟倒白酒，最后啤酒。

Determine the sequence of wine pouring according to different wines. In general, the Chinese dinner will pour wine first and beverage next. The order of pouring wine for different wines is that pouring red wine first, then spirit, and beer at last.

（四）斟酒量 Volume of pouring wine

（1）八分满：白酒、黄酒、饮料。

Eighty percent full: spirit, yellow rice wine and beverage.

啤酒斟倒后最好呈“八成酒液、两成泡沫”状。

The beer should be twenty percent bubble with eighty percent full liquid.

（2）1/2 满：红葡萄酒。

Fifty percent full: red wine.

（3）3/4 满：不加冰块的冰水；加冰块的冰水先斟 1/2 水再加适量冰块。

Seventy five percent full: ice water with no ice cube; to serve the ice water with ice, you should add 1/2 water first, and then add ice cube.

（五）餐酒搭配小贴士 Tips to better wine matching

厨师往往讲求食物口味的平衡，这同样适用于葡萄酒。值得注意的是，食物不应使酒黯然失色（尤其是当酒很贵的时候）。用葡萄酒搭配食物时，请记住以下几点：

Chefs often stress the balance of food taste. The same rule applies to wine, but it’s also important to not overshadow the wine (especially when it’s expensive). Keep the following tips in mind when matching wine with food:

（1）搭配沙拉，酒应该有更高的酸度；

The wine should have higher acidity when matching with salad;

（2）葡萄酒应该和肉的颜色相配；

The wine should match the color of the meat;

（3）应将质朴的酒和质朴的食物搭配；

Match earthy wines with earthy foods;

（4）高单宁的葡萄酒可以中和丰富的肉类食物；

Neutralize high tannin wines with rich meaty foods;

（5）搭配甜点，葡萄酒应该稍甜一点。

For dessert, the wine should be sweeter.

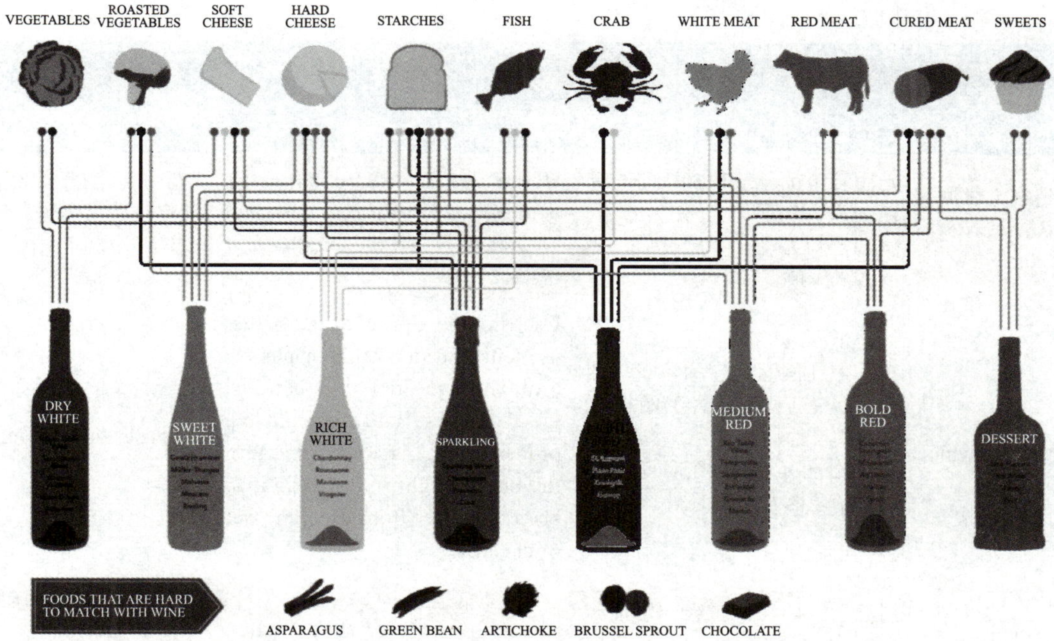

图 6.1　餐酒搭配图
Pairing Wine & Food

图片来源：http://winefolly.com.

二、斟酒服务操作流程 The service procedure of pouring wine

表 6.2　斟酒服务操作流程
The Service Procedure of Pouring Wine

操作流程 Service Procedure	服务标准 Service Standard		常用句式 Sentence Patterns
示酒 Show the wine to the guest	取来客人选定的酒，在客人桌边用左手托住瓶底，右手握住瓶口，使瓶口朝上呈 45° 角，酒牌对着客人向客人示酒。	Take the selected wine to the guest with left hand holding the bottom of wine bottle, and right hand holding the bottleneck with bottleneck up to 45°angle. Let the label of the wine face to the guest and show the wine.	“先生，这是您点的茅台酒。” “This is your Moutai, sir.”
开酒 Open the wine	用正确的开瓶方法开酒。	Using accurate method to open the wine.	“我可以打开吗？” “May I open it?”
请客人检查确认 Let the guest confirm the wine	开瓶后向客人简单示意，以便确认。	After opening the bottle, make a simple gesture to the guest to confirm.	

续前表

操作流程 Service Procedure	服务标准 Service Standard		常用句式 Sentence Patterns
请客人试酒 Guest tastes the wine	先用餐巾擦净瓶口和瓶身，并在主人杯中倒入 2cm 深的酒，帮助轻轻晃动一下酒杯后，先请客人试酒。	Using the napkin to wipe the bottleneck and pour 2cm wine into host's glass to let the guest taste it first.	"先生，请您试酒，您觉得还可以吗？" "Please taste it, sir. Is it all right?"
斟酒 Pour the wine	右手握住酒瓶，左手拿餐巾或托盘，右脚跨前踏在两椅之间，举瓶高低适当；倒完酒后，把瓶子向右稍微转动收起，防止酒水滴在杯外。	Use right hand to hold the bottle, use left hand to take the napkin or tray. The right foot steps between the two chairs. Hold the bottle to a proper height. After pouring, turn the bottle slightly to the right to keep the water from dropping out of the glass.	"请慢用。" "Please enjoy your wine."
斟添 Refill the wine	斟酒后，要注意观察，发现客人杯中的酒剩 1/3 时应及时斟添。	Refill the wine for guest when there is only 1/3 left in the glass.	"先生，您需要再添一点酒吗？" "Would you like more wine, sir?"

三、常用中英文标准用语 Common expressions in Chinese & English

（1）这是酒水单，先生。请问您想喝点什么？

Here is the wine list. What would you like to drink?

（2）您喜欢什么牌子的啤酒？我们有一些中国品牌，如青岛、雪花，还有一些外国品牌，如麒麟、喜力和百威。

Which brand of beer would you like? We have some Chinese brands such as Tsingtao, Snow, and some foreign brands such as Kirin, Heineken and Budweiser.

（3）请问加不加冰？

With or without ice, sir?

（4）请问需要给您的红酒里加一些苏打水吗？

Would you like to add some soda to your wine?

（5）鲍勃先生，请您品尝。味道可以吗？

Please taste it, Mr. Bob. Is it all right?

（6）有哪些酒或饮料是女士们喝的？

Any wine or soft drinks for the ladies?

（7）女士，需要我为您添一些酒吗？

Would you like me to pour some more wine for you, Madam?

（8）您的这瓶酒已经添完了，请问是否需要再加一瓶？

Your bottle of wine is finished. Would you like one more bottle?

（9）您要咖啡还是茶？

Would you like coffee or tea?

（10）我们有散装的雪花啤酒和瓶装的青岛啤酒。

We have Snow on tap and Tsingtao in bottles.

（11）樱桃酒很受客人的欢迎。

Kirsch is very popular with our guests.

（12）茅台是中国最著名的白酒之一。

Moutai is one of the most famous liquors in China.

（13）我们有各种不同的罐装和瓶装啤酒，也有生啤（扎啤）和黑啤。

We have different kinds of canned and bottled beers, as well as draft beer and black beer.

（14）青岛啤酒是我们本地的啤酒。它世界闻名，口味很好而且价格不贵。

Tsingtao is our local beer. It is well known around the world, inexpensive and tastes well.

（15）茅台的酒精含量有 56 度和 38 度的。

We have Moutai with 56% alcohol and 38% alcohol.

（16）广东米酒要比北方的酒淡一些。

Guangdong rice wine is milder than those from the north of China.

（17）罐装的可乐售价 7 元，瓶装的可乐售价 10 元。

The canned coke costs 7 yuan, the bottled coke costs 10 yuan.

（18）我们的鲜榨果汁有橙汁、苹果汁、西瓜汁、芒果汁、雪梨汁和胡萝卜汁。每杯 15 元。

We have fresh orange juice, apple juice, watermelon juice, mango juice, pear juice and carrot juice. It cost 15 yuan per glass.

（19）黄酒在中国很受欢迎。我们有绍兴饭酒、龙岩沉缸酒和即墨老酒。

Chinese yellow wine is very popular in China. We have Shaoxing Rice Wine, Longyan Chengang Wine and Jimo Wine.

（20）自带酒水会按照市场价格的 20% 收取服务费。

All liquors brought in will be subject to a 20% service charge based on the market price.

任务实施

第一步：教师导入本节情景设定：晚餐时间，餐厅服务生史密斯在为一桌客人（共 4 位）服务，客人表示喜欢喝红葡萄酒。史密斯应该如何进行酒水服务？

Step 1: The teacher introduces settings of this section: Smith is a waiter in a restaurant. He is serving a table of four at dinnertime. The guest expresses preference for red wine. How should Smith serve red wine?

第二步：教师列出酒水服务可能用到的相关英文词汇、短语，供学生参考。

Step 2: The teacher lists some phrases and vocabularies of the wine service for students' reference.

酒水单 Wine list
软木塞 Cork
赤霞珠 Cabernet Sauvignon
我能现在为您斟酒吗？ May I serve it now?

第三步：教师给出示范案例，并予以示范。

Step 3: The teacher gives cases and demonstrates it.

（S：史密斯，G：客人）
（S: Smith, G: Guest）
S：先生，请问您要喝些什么？这是我们的酒水单。
S: Would you like something to drink, sir? Here is the wine list.
G：请给我一瓶 2011 年的赤霞珠。
G: Em..., please gives me a bottle of Cabernet Sauvignon in 2011.
S：好的，先生。我很快为您取来。
S: Ok, I will be right back, sir.
（过了一会儿）
（Affter a while）
S：（示酒）先生，这是您要的酒，现在可以打开吗？
S: (Show the brand to the guest.) This is your wine, sir. May I serve it now?
G：好的，谢谢。
G: Yes, please.
S：我把软木塞放在这里。（斟酒）先生，您看先醒酒如何？
S: I'll put the cork here. (Pour wine) May I decant it now to allow it to breathe? How is it, sir?
G：太棒了！
G: Excellent!
S：（给客人一小杯酒）先生，请您试酒，您觉得还可以吗？
S: (Give a sip to the guest) Please taste it, sir. Is it all right?

G：很棒！

G: Wonderful!

S：谢谢您，先生。请慢用。

S: Thank you, sir. Please enjoy your meal.

第四步：将班级学生分组（5 人 1 组），其中，1 位学生扮演酒水服务生，另外 4 位学生扮演客人，进行情景模拟（5 位学生轮流进行）。

Step 4: Practice in groups (5 persons per group), one of the students acts as the waiter, and the other four students act as guests. Each student takes turns to carry out scenario simulation.

任务评价

表 6.3 葡萄酒服务评价表

Evaluation Form of Wine Service

评价内容 Evaluation Items	评价标准 Evaluation Standard	分值 Score	小组自评 Self-evaluation （20%）	小组互评 Peer-evaluation （30%）	教师评价 Teacher-evaluation （50%）	综合得分 Subtotal
准备工作 Preparation	斟酒所需的酒水和酒具准备齐全。 All the necessary wine and wine utensils are prepared.	30				
服务操作程序 Service Operation Procedure	操作规范，符合标准。 Standard Operation Procedure.	30				
语言能力 Language	中英文表述正确、清晰；发音标准、声音洪亮。 Correct and clear expression in both Chinese and English; Standard pronunciation and loud voice.	20				
模拟情景 Simulation Scenarios	模拟内容完整；能灵活应变。 Complete content;Flexibility to deal with situations.	10				
团队精神 Teamwork	分工明确，团队协作。 Clear division of labor and good teamwork.	10				
合计得分 Total						

评分标准（按 100 分制）：81～100 分为“优秀”；71～80 分为“良好”；60～70 分为“合格”；60 分以下为“不合格”。

Scoring Standards (On a scale of 100): 81–100 points as “Perfect”; 71–80 points as “Good”; 60–70 points as “Pass”; 60–below points as “Fail”.

拓展阅读

如何避免餐厅自带酒水的尴尬?

高档餐厅都有自己的酒单，但《葡萄酒观察家》（*Wine Spectator*）的吉姆·菲斯认为，因为餐厅需要根据大多数客人的喜好来决定餐厅的酒单，所以很少有餐厅能够提供一些个性较为独特的葡萄酒，这就意味着有时客人需要自带酒水到餐厅。但是，在自带酒水前，客人需要注意哪些方面以避免尴尬呢?

1. 自带酒水的主要原因

一般来说，自带酒水的主要原因有两个：一是想要在特殊的场合纪念；二是想要尝试一些更新的、更有个性的葡萄酒，而这些酒餐厅无法提供。客人千万不要为了省钱而自带酒水，因为有时候开瓶费比酒本身还要贵，美国一些高档餐厅的开瓶费高达150美元。在抱怨开瓶费高昂之前，客人千万也要站在餐厅的角度考虑，客人自带酒水对餐厅来说是一项很大的损失。客人在自带酒水之前，最好先了解餐厅现有的酒单，给予餐厅足够的尊重和理解。可以先尝试餐厅推荐的一些酒，如果都不满意的话，在下次光顾时再带上自己的酒。

2. 避免带去餐厅的酒水种类

如果客人带一瓶价格低廉的葡萄酒到高档餐厅，会被认为是对餐厅主人和侍酒师的侮辱，也会给其他客人留下不好的印象。这些葡萄酒可以在家里喝，但绝对不适合带去高档餐厅。客人可带一瓶和餐厅里中间价位的葡萄酒相当的酒。如果一家餐厅专注于提供赤霞珠，那么客人最好带马尔贝克。

3. 与侍酒师（工作人员）建立友谊

客人光顾某家餐厅的次数越多，与工作人员的沟通越多，餐厅的老板和侍酒师就越认同该客人对于葡萄酒的见解。侍酒师不会轻易聆听陌生客人对酒单的评价，但他们很乐意倾听那些常客的意见和想法。当客人表现出购买意愿并与工作人员交流时，他很有可能会省去一笔开瓶费。除此之外，他还可以了解餐厅酒品挑选的过程。客人可与侍酒师分享葡萄酒的饮用感受，从而获得专业建议。

Project 7

Table Service

项目七

席间服务

项目概述 PROJECT SUMMARY

餐饮服务讲求殷勤款待客人，以满足客人的需求从而产生满意的用餐体验。前面我们讲到的服务技能皆是优质服务提供的环节，这些环节影响客人对餐厅的整体评价。但是，与席间服务相比，这些环节对客服务的时间要短很多。因此，贯穿于客人整个用餐过程中的席间服务，可以说是影响客人服务体验的最重要环节。

简单的席间服务可能只是上菜撤盘，任何一个餐厅都很容易做到。但要突出餐厅的特色和优质服务，真正做好席间服务并不是一件容易的事情。席间服务是整个服务流程中的精华部分，高质量的席间服务可以赢得客人的信赖、满意。

从实践中我们得知，餐厅工作的各个环节、各项工作以及菜肴质量引起客人不满的事情偶尔会发生，但席间服务人员可以通过极强的应变能力、热情周到的用语及行动轻易化解这些小矛盾，从而密切客人与餐厅的关系。

席间服务是服务人员直接接触客人的服务，最能够了解、掌握客人的要求。服务人员在整个对客服务期间，可以根据客人的表情及细微的动作，观察客人对每道餐点、每个服务环节的反应，将客人无声的意见提供给餐厅的经营者，对于改进餐厅的经营活动、提高服务质量起着重要的作用。

项目目标 PROJECT OBJECTS

知识目标：熟悉席间服务的相关知识；掌握中、西餐席间服务的相关作业程序。

技能目标：掌握中、西餐席间服务所需要的相关技能。

素养目标：爱岗敬业、谦逊有礼，将“中国服务”精神贯彻到整个工作流程中；以人为本，具备勇于创新的意识。

任务一：中餐席间服务
Task 1: Chinese Restaurant Table Service

案例导入

某四星级酒店里，富有浓烈民族特色的牡丹厅热闹非凡。为庆祝某集团隆重成立，主办方包下这个可以容纳30张圆桌的宴会厅。由于来赴宴的都是商界名流，人多、品位高，餐厅自上而下早就忙坏了。从这天上午起，工作人员就已做好了一切准备。

宴会开始，一切正常进行。值台员送菜、报菜名、上菜、递毛巾、斟倒酒水、撤盘子，秩序井然。按预先的安排，在上完“京味片皮鸭”后，主人和主宾离开座位，走到台前，值台人员这时便给每位客人的杯子里倒满酒和饮料。主人和主宾的话筒旁，也有一名服务员托着一个装有两只斟满酒的杯子。等主人和主宾热情洋溢的讲话结束时，这名服务员会及时递上酒杯，接下来，就是全体来宾起立共同举杯祝酒。可此时，厨房里走出一列服务员，手中端着刚出炉的新菜，向各个不同的桌子走去。客人不约而同地把视线转投向这支移动的队伍，热烈欢快的场面就此给破坏了，主人不得不再一次提议全体干杯，但气氛已经大打折扣。

思考讨论：出菜秀是酒店的服务特色项目，应该在什么时机展示合适呢？

知识准备

中餐席间服务包括的呈递菜单、点菜、点叫酒水饮料这几个步骤前面已经提及过了，在此就不再多做赘述。

Delivering the menu and taking orders in the Chinese table service are already been mentioned before, we will not go into too much detail here.

一、茶水服务 Tea service

茶水服务是中餐服务中特别注重的一项内容。在中餐厅，当客人来到时，奉上一杯清香的茶是对客人的尊敬和礼貌，更是中华民族的待客之道。有些餐厅会提供免费茶供客人享用，一些高档餐厅会提供高品质的茶叶，所以会收取费用，一般有按位收费和按壶收费。

Tea service is an important part of Chinese food service. In a Chinese restaurant, serving a cup of fragrant tea is not only a courtesy to the guest, but also the hospitality of the Chinese nation. Some restaurants offer free tea for guests. Some high-end restaurants will provide high-quality tea, so they will charge a fee. Generally, some charge by seat, and some charge by pot.

茶水服务的步骤如下：

The procedures for tea service are as follows:

（1）按客人所点的茶的品种拿取适量茶叶。将茶叶放入茶壶内，加入 90～100 摄氏度的水沏至茶壶的八成满。

Take the proper amount of tea leaves according to the type of tea ordered by the guest. Place the tea leaves in the teapot and add 90–100 degrees Celsius water until the teapot is 80% full.

（2）注意水不要加得太满，否则服务员倒茶时容易漏洒。准备一个骨碟，在骨碟上垫上一块折叠成正方形的餐巾，将茶壶放在餐巾上。

Be careful not to add too much water, or the waiter may spill when pouring tea. Prepare a bone plate, place a folded square napkin on the plate, and place the teapot on the napkin.

（3）用托盘将茶水托至桌边，左手托骨碟的同时，用拇指扣住餐巾，右手握茶壶把，在客人的右手边斟茶。注意：斟茶时茶壶嘴不能碰倒茶杯，应距离茶杯口 1～2cm。

Place the tea on the table with a tray, place the plate on your left hand while clasping the napkin with your thumb, and pour the tea on the right side of the guest with the handle of the teapot in your right hand. Note that the spout of the teapot should not touch the teacup, and should be 1–2cm away from the mouth of the teacup.

（4）斟茶时动作应迅速，否则茶水很容易沿壶嘴滴漏出来。斟完茶后，将热水添至八分满，将茶壶放在垫有餐巾的骨碟上。

Pour tea quickly, or the water will easily drip out from the spout. After pouring out the tea, add the hot water to 80% full and place the teapot on the plate with a napkin.

> **小贴士：**
>
> 通常将茶壶把与客人呈 45° 角摆放，方便客人自己取用。有许多地方风俗很注重茶壶嘴的朝向，一些人不喜欢见到茶壶嘴对着自己，这一点服务员在斟茶时应特别注意。
>
> **Tips:**
>
> Usually the teapot handle at a 45° angle to the guest, which is convenient for guest to help themselves. There are many local customs which concern about the orientation of the teapot spout. Some people don’t like to see the spout facing them, so the server should pay attention when serving tea.

二、铺餐巾 Lay the napkin

为客人铺设餐巾，几乎是与呈递菜单同时进行的，一般会由呈递菜单的服务员（迎宾员）来完成。

Laying the napkins for guests is almost simultaneous with delivering the menu. It is usually done by the hostess.

铺餐巾的步骤如下：

The procedures for laying napkins are as follows:

（1）站在客人座位右后方，右脚在前，稍跨入客人位子的中间。

Stand at the right side behind the guest's seat with right foot in front, and a little step into the middle of the guest's seat.

（2）用右手从客人的右边拿起餐巾，用左手拿餐巾的一角，轻轻抖动使之展开。

Take the napkin from the right side of the guest with your right hand, take the corner of the napkin with your left hand, and shake it out gently.

（3）用右手拿餐巾的对角，将餐巾对折成三角形。然后，轻轻将餐巾铺在客人双膝上，餐巾三角形的边朝向客人，同时提醒客人："对不起，打扰一下……"

Take the opposite corner of napkin in your right hand and fold it in half into a triangle. Then gently place the napkin on the guest's knees, with the side of the napkin triangle facing the guest, and remind the guest with the expression "sorry to disturb you..."

小贴士：

注意铺餐巾时不要与客人发生不必要的接触。许多中餐服务中，客人不愿意将餐巾铺在膝盖上，而是把它压在餐碟或展示盘下面。主要原因是，在中国的就餐习惯中喜欢敬酒，因此将餐巾铺在膝盖上就不便于站立敬酒，而每次起身都要服务员重新整理餐巾也是很麻烦的工作。

Tips:

Be careful not to make unnecessary contact with the guests when laying the napkins. In many Chinese restaurants' services, guests do not want to put their napkins on their knees, but place it under the plate or display plate. The main reason is that Chinese people like toasting during dining, so the napkin on the knee is inconvenient for guests. Every time the guests get up, the waiter has to rearrange napkins, which is also a very troublesome work.

三、毛巾服务 Towel service

毛巾在中餐服务中又称"香巾"或"小毛巾"。一般在用餐过程中，至少需要提供两道毛巾服务。客人入座后，餐厅服务员将会提供第一次小毛巾服务。待客人用餐结束，再次提供小毛巾服务。

"Towel" in Chinese restaurants' service is also called "sweet towel" or "small towel". At least two times of towel service should be served during the meal. After guests are seated, the waiter will provide the first towel service. At the end of the meal, the server will provide another towel service for the guests.

毛巾服务的步骤如下：

The procedures of towel service are as follows:

（1）将保温箱内折好的小毛巾放入毛巾托内；

Place the small towel from the insulated box into the towel holder;

（2）手持托盘站在客人左侧，用毛巾夹从左边将毛巾递给客人；

Deliver the towel to the guest with the tray from the left side of the guest;

（3）递上毛巾时，应说"请用毛巾"；

小贴士：

一般来说，现在给客人递送毛巾更多的是表示敬意，毛巾已渐渐地失去其擦脸的用途。许多餐厅会在夏天为客人提供冰毛巾，在冬天提供热毛巾，这是非常温馨的做法。

Tips:

Towel services are now being delivered more as a sign of respect to guests, which have gradually lost its original use as face wipes. Many restaurants offer cold towels in summer and hot towels in winter, which is very sweet.

When handing over a towel, you should say, “Please use the towel”;

（4）在宴席进行中可随时提供毛巾服务，如客人食用点心、甜品时等，或客人主动要求提供时。

Towel service can be provided at any time during the banquet, such as when guests eat dessert or the guests demand initiatively.

四、调整餐具 Adjust the tableware

撤换或增加餐位、餐具的步骤如下：

The procedures for removing or adding seats and tableware are as follows:

（1）得到增加或减少用餐人数的信息后，首先增加或撤走餐椅，然后调整餐椅间距。

After getting the information of increasing or decreasing the number of diners, increase or remove the dining chairs first, and then adjust the spacing of the dining chairs.

（2）将餐椅均衡调整完毕后，立即撤走多余的餐具，或准备需要增加的餐具。

After the balanced adjustment of dining chairs, remove the excess or prepare additional tableware immediately.

（3）将需要增加的餐具放在最次要的餐位边，然后顺次挪移其他已经摆放的餐具，使其正对餐椅。如果是撤位，也从最次要的餐位开始撤走餐具。

Put the tableware that needs to be increased at the side of the least important place. Then move the rest of the table settings to make them face the dining chair. Remove the chair if necessary, and remember to remove the tableware from the least important place.

五、上餐前小食 Serve pre-meal snack

餐前小食是在中餐零点服务中常见的。提供餐前小食服务的主要目的，是让客人在用餐之前吃一些开胃食品，同时缓解等待上菜时的焦虑心情。

Pre-meal snack is common in Chinese restaurants’ service. The main purpose of the pre-meal snack service is to allow the guest to have some appetizers before the meal and relieve the anxiety of waiting.

餐前小食在口味上不能太重，否则会破坏味觉。通常由厨房准备好，交给备餐间打理。餐前小食制作好后，由备餐间员工分装在小碟中，在上茶的同时摆放到餐桌的正中央。服务餐前小食需要注意客人的就餐人数。通常，6～8 人、8～10 人的圆桌应上两份餐前小食，对称地摆放在转盘的两边，10 人以上的大圆桌应上 3 份。

Pre-meal snack should not be too heavy on taste. Otherwise, it will destroy the guests' gustation. It is usually prepared by the kitchen staffs whose responsibility is to divide the food into small plates, and then placed in the center of the table while serving tea. Attention should be paid to the number of guests before serving pre-meal snacks. Usually a round table for 6–8 people or 8–10 people should be served two pre-meal snacks, and placed symmetrically on both sides of the turntable. A round table for more than 10 people should be served three.

六、斟添酒水 Refill the beverage

客人进餐过程中，若客人点了酒水，应在第一次斟酒后，注意观察酒杯中的酒量，以便及时添加。一般情况下，当发现客人杯中的酒剩 1/3 时，应及时斟添。餐厅服务员也可视情况，先征求客人的同意再进行添酒服务。添酒时可说："先生 / 女士，需要我为您添一些酒吗？"

During the meal, if the guests ordered beverage, the waiter should pay attention to the amount of wine in the glass after the first pour in order to add beverage in time. Under normal circumstances, if the wine of guest only remains one third, the waiter should timely refill. The waiter can also do the refill service according to the situation and ask for the guest's permission with the expression "Would you like me to pour some more wine for you, sir/madam?"

七、上菜及分菜 Serve dishes and split the dishes

上菜、分菜是餐厅服务人员的基本功，掌握熟练的上菜、分菜技能，不仅能让客人品尝到美味佳肴，也能让客人领略到中国的饮食文化，同时，优雅娴熟的动作还能给客人带来赏心悦目的艺术享受。

Serving and splitting the dishes are basic skills of restaurant staff, which can not only let guests taste delicious food, but also let them appreciate the Chinese food culture, and especially bring the guests a feast for the eyes.

（一）上菜的顺序 Order of serving dishes

由于中国菜系品种很多，中餐上菜的顺序也会因各地风俗习惯而有所不同，因此，上菜顺序可根据用餐的类型、特点和需要而定。中餐上菜的大体顺序原则上是：先凉菜后热菜；先荤菜后素菜；先优质或风味菜后一般菜；先菜后汤；先点心后水果。

As there are many varieties of Chinese cuisine, the order of serving Chinese food is also different due to the local customs. Therefore, it can be determined according to the type, characteristics and needs of meals. The general order of serving Chinese food is as follows: Serve cold dishes first and then hot dishes; Serve meat or fish first and then vegetables; Serve typical or local dishes first and then daily cuisine; Serve dishes first and then the soup; Serve dessert first and then fruit.

（二）上菜的位置 The position of serving dishes

中餐厅以不打扰客人用餐为原则上菜，在位置方面比较灵活。中餐宴会的上菜位置一般选择在副主人的右侧，也可选择在陪同与翻译之间，这样有利于向客人介绍菜品。严禁在主人和主宾之间上菜；严禁在老人和儿童、行动不便的人中间上菜。

The serving position of the Chinese restaurant is flexible and on the principle of not disturbing the guests. At a Chinese banquet, the dishes are usually served on the right side of the deputy host. The waiters can also serve dishes between the escort and the translator, which is convenient to introduce the dishes to the guests. It is strictly forbidden to serve food between host and the guest of honor, or between the elderly, children, and disabled people.

（三）上菜服务注意事项 Matters need attention of serving dishes

（1）上菜服务人员不应是传菜员。

The pantry helper could not serve the dish to the guest.

（2）上菜前要找到上菜服务所站立的位置。

Find the position where the serving service will carry out.

（3）上菜前服务人员应先查看是否有放菜的位置，若没有，尽快挪出。

Check if there is a place for the dishes. If not, make room for the dishes as soon as possible.

（4）上菜时必须双手递送菜肴。

Dishes must be delivered with both hands.

（5）上菜时必须清楚菜品及准确报出菜名。

Name the dishes accurately.

（6）上菜时切忌发出较大声响。

Avoid making loud noises when serving dishes.

（7）菜品上齐后，应及时提醒客人所点菜肴已上齐。

When all the dishes are served, remind the guests of the completion in time.

（四）分菜的顺序 The sequence of splitting entrées

先主宾后主人，然后按照顺时针方向依次分送。

Generally, the sequence of splitting entrées is from the guest of honor to the host, and then serving other guests clockwise.

（五）分菜服务的方法 Different approaches of splitting entrées

中餐分菜分为餐台分菜、托盘分菜、分菜台分菜三种方法。

There are 3 approaches of splitting entres: splitting entrées on the table, splitting entrées on the tray and splitting entrées on the work station.

1. 餐台分菜 Splitting entrées on the table

餐台分菜适用于团体聚餐或普通酒席，不适用于高规格的宴会。这是因为操作时常常会干扰到客人的谈话，影响餐桌氛围，且对于餐厅服务人员的技术要求比较高，速度既要快、又要准，否则分菜不均匀，也容易弄脏转盘。

Splitting entrées on the table is suitable for group dinner or ordinary banquet. Because the operation often interferes with the customers' conversation which will influence the atmosphere of dining table, it's rarely used in high-end banquet. In addition, this approach has high skilled requirement for restaurant service personnel. If the server can't split the entrées quickly and correctly, it will result in the inequality of each dish or the pollution of the turntable.

2. 托盘分菜 Splitting entrées on the tray

操作时，餐厅服务员左手垫上餐巾布，端托菜盘，右手持服务叉和服务勺，站在客人左侧，从主宾开始分菜。站立要稳，微弯腰，身体不能靠在客人身上。菜盘应托至客人餐碟左侧边缘，在把菜肴分到客人菜碟后，右手的服务叉和服务勺须马上随着左手菜盘一起退出。

When splitting the dish, the waiter should hold the dish plate with napkin in the left hand, hold service fork and service spoon in the right hand, and stand at the left side of the guest to split the dish from the main guest. Stand straightly, bend slightly, and do not lean your body on the guests. After finishing splitting entrées, service fork and spoon of the right hand should be taken back immediately with the dish in left hand.

托盘分菜适用于 15 人以上的大圆桌或长条桌台，不适用于高规格的宴会。因为随着分菜的进行，最后两位客人看到的菜肴并不太雅观。

Splitting entrées on the tray is suitable for large round table or long table with more than 15 people. According to the clockwise serving sequence, the last two guests can't see the whole beautiful dish, so this approach is not suitable for the high-end banquet.

3. 分菜台分菜 Splitting entrées on the work station

首先，在客人餐桌旁准备好一辆服务车（或服务桌），准备好干净的餐盘，备好分菜用的叉、勺等餐具。当菜肴从厨房送到餐台后，餐厅服务人员应先把菜肴展示给客人，并介绍菜肴的名称、特色及烹饪方法。然后将菜撤到分菜台，由分菜服务人员把菜均匀、迅速地分到客人的餐碟中。菜分好后，将餐碟放在托盘里送到客人面前。

First, a service car (or service table) should be prepared beside the guests' table. Prepare a clean plate with a service fork, service spoon, etc. When the dishes are delivered from the kitchen to the dining table, the service staff should show the dishes to the guests first, introduce the name and the cooking method of the dish. And then, put the dish on the service cart or service table to split into each plate. Finally, put the dishes on the tray and bring them to the guests' table.

菜台分菜适用于规格较高的宴会。在分菜台分菜，对客人的干扰较少，能很好地照顾到客人，但是比较浪费服务时间和人力。

This approach is suitable for the high-end banquet, because it could help take good care of the guests by less interference with them. However, it will cost lots of time and need more service staff when serving the guests.

八、撤换骨碟、烟灰缸 Change the plates and ashtray

（一）撤换骨碟 Change the plates

撤换骨碟的正确方法是：撤换骨碟时要用左手托托盘，右手撤换，从第一主宾开始，按顺时针方向依次撤换。撤换时要待客人将盘中食物吃完后再进行，如客人盘中有未吃完的食物，只有征求客人同意后才能撤换。将干净的骨碟从客人的右侧摆放，然后从客人左侧将用过的骨碟撤下。

The correct method is: Use the right hand to change the plates with tray in left hand clockwise from the main guest. After the food is eaten up or getting the permission from guest, take the plate from the left hand of guest, and put a clean plate from the right hand of the guest.

> 小贴士：
>
> 遇到下列情况时应及时更换骨碟：
>
> - 客人吃过鱼腥味食物后，应更换骨碟；
> - 上风味特殊、调味特别的菜肴时，应更换骨碟；
> - 客人吃过甜味的菜或汤后，应更换骨碟；
> - 客人吃过带骨头的菜肴后（如螃蟹、虾），应更换骨碟；
> - 当骨碟内食物残渣超过1/3，影响美观时，应立即更换骨碟。
>
> Tips:
>
> In the following situation, it is necessary to change the plate in time:
>
> - If the guests order fishy smell food;
> - If the guests order special flavor dishes;
> - If the guests order soup or dish with sweet flavor;
> - If the guests order dishes with bones like crab or shrimp;
> - If the food residues left in the plate are more than 1/3, the server should change the plate immediately.

撤换骨碟时应注意，将用过的骨碟和新的骨碟严格区分开，以防交叉污染。应根据菜肴的品种更换骨碟，如果是一般宴席，应是2～3菜更换一碟；如果是高档宴席，应是一菜一碟。在一般情况下，餐厅服务员可视具体情况，灵活掌握。

Pay attention to separate the used plate from the new clean one to avoid pollution. The frequence of changing plates should depend on the varieties of the dishes. The service staff should change the guests' plates every two or three dishes in the ordinary banquet, and should change the guests' plates for every dish if it is a high-end banquet. Generally, the service staff could do the service flexibly due to the specific situation.

（二）撤换烟灰缸 Change the ashtray

在客人就餐过程中，服务员应注意观察烟灰缸的使用情况。一般高档宴席中，若烟灰缸内有 2 个及以上的烟蒂，就应撤换。常用的方法是以二换一法：

During the banquet, the waiter should observe the use of ashtray. In the high-end banquet, the requirement is to change the ashtray when there are two butts of cigarettes left. The most common-used method of changing ashtray is "Use two to change one":

（1）托盘内放两只干净的烟灰缸，用左手托托盘，从客人的右手边撤换烟灰缸；

Put two clean ashtrays on the tray. Use left hand taking the tray and start from right side of guest to change the ashtray;

（2）将一只干净的烟灰缸盖在需要撤换的烟灰缸上，并一起取出放回托盘里，再拿另一只新的烟灰缸放回餐桌上，这样做可避免烟灰飞扬。

Put clean ashtray cover the old one and take the two of them into the tray, and take another new one to the right position to avoid flying ash.

九、点主食 Order staple food

服务员按照客人点菜的要求上菜后，需要观察客人所点菜肴的搭配情况，询问客人是否需要相应的主食。

After serving the dishes according to the requirements of the guests, it is necessary for the server to observe the collocation of the dishes ordered by the guests and ask them whether they need the staple food.

（1）主食的搭配，可以根据客人所点的菜来决定。一般来说，菜式比较油腻的，可以推荐较清淡的主食。当然，这完全取决于客人的喜好。

The collocation of staple food can be decided according to the dishes ordered by the guests. In general, a light staple food can be recommended if the dish is oily. Of course, it all depends on the guest's preference.

（2）一般而言，有些客人会在用餐过半时才点主食。这时，服务员要特别注意向客人事先说明主食的烹饪时间。

Some guests won't order staple food until the middle of the meal, at this time, the waiter should pay special attention to explain to the guests about the cooking time of staple food in advance.

（3）白米饭上桌时，服务员不能碰到碗边。

The waiter must not touch the edge of the bowl when the white rice is served.

十、撤台、服务餐后甜品及水果 Clear the table, serve dessert and fruits

（一）撤台 Clear the table

客人用完餐后，服务员应及时上前清理餐桌上的空碟和碗筷。如遇客人点菜数量较多、菜肴上到餐桌上无法摆放，服务员应建议客人撤下吃剩的菜肴，换成小碟盛放。这样，餐桌（转盘）上就能有更多的空间摆放菜肴。

After the guests finish the meal, the waiter should clean up the dishes and chopsticks on the table in time. If the guests order too much dishes to place on the table, the waiter should advise the guests to remove the remaining dishes and replace them with smaller ones.

撤台的步骤如下：

The clean-up procedures are as follows:

（1）得到客人的同意，先将空的餐碟撤离餐桌。

Remove empty dishes from the table with the guest's permission.

（2）在撤下第一碟菜前，询问客人是否要将剩余的菜式先行打包。如果客人要打包剩菜，则先撤下需要打包的菜进行打包，然后逐步撤下其他菜肴。

Ask the guests if they want to pack the remaining dishes before removing the first dish plate. If the guests want to pack leftovers, remove the dishes that need to be packed for packing first, and then gradually remove other dishes.

（3）撤去客人的餐具。用左手托盘，从客人的右手边撤下骨碟，然后撤下酱油碟和翅碗。在此过程中应轻拿轻放，避免酱汁洒在客人身上。

Remove the guest's cutlery. Use the left hand holding the tray, remove the plate from the guest's right hand side, then remove the soy sauce dish and shark's fin bowls. Handle with care to avoid spreading sauce on the guest.

（4）将撤下的器具分类摆放在托盘上。依次撤去下一位客人的餐具。

Arrange the removed utensils on the tray. And remove the cutlery of the next guest in turn.

（5）撤台时不必撤走餐桌上的酒杯，除非客人示意或杯子已经空了。

Do not remove wine glasses from the table unless the guest indicates or the glass is empty.

（二）服务餐后甜品及水果 Serve dessert and fruits

服务餐后甜品及水果的步骤如下：

The procedures of serving dessert and fruits are as follows:

（1）当餐碟撤下之后，服务员可以向客人询问是否需要点叫甜品或水果。有些餐厅的甜品和水果是赠送的。

After the plates are removed, the waiter can ask if the guest would like to order dessert or fruit. Some restaurants serve free dessert and fruits.

（2）点甜品的步骤和点菜的步骤相同。由于中餐的甜品相对简单一些，如糕点类、糖水类、西点类等，上甜品时一般不需要先摆放餐具，视情况而准备。

The procedure for ordering dessert is the same as that for ordering dishes. Chinese desserts are relatively simple, such as pastry, sweet water, etc. Therefore, it is unnecessary to put tableware in advance when serving dessert, it depends on the conditions.

（3）在上蛋糕或水果时，应将筷子或叉子放在客人的右手边。

When serving a cake or fruit, place the chopsticks or fork on the guest's right hand side.

（4）餐后水果一般采用水果盘的形式呈递给客人。有些餐厅在上水果时会放一些牙签，但这并不卫生，建议吃水果使用甜品叉。

The after-dinner fruits are usually presented to the guests in the form of a fruit plate. Some restaurants will serve fruit with toothpicks, but it is not sanitary. Dessert forks are recommended for having fruits.

任务实施

第一步：教师导入本节情景设定：王小姐一行五人来到一家高档中餐厅就餐。服务员威廉为其服务。在王小姐和朋友落座之后，威廉为客人进行上茶、上毛巾、点餐、铺餐巾、上餐前小食、斟添酒水、上菜、分菜、席间撤换餐具、撤台以及服务餐后甜品水果等一系列席间服务。

Step 1: The teacher introduces the settings of this section: Miss Wang and her friends (party of five) came to a fancy Chinese restaurant for dinner. William was their waiter that evening. After Miss Wang and her friends took their seats, William served tea and small towels, ordered meals, laid napkins, served pre-meal snacks, refilled drinks, served main dishes and splitted dishes, removed tableware, and served dessert and fruits after meals.

第二步：教师讲解中餐席间服务的相关知识，列出席间服务可能用到的相关英文词汇、短语或句型，以供学生参考，并针对一些实际情况进行演示。

Step 2: The teacher explains the knowledge of Chinese table service and lists the English vocabularies, phrases and sentence patterns that may be used during the service for students' reference. And the teacher does the demonstration of some practical cases.

我点的菜还没有来，为什么要等这么久？

My order still hasn't come, why it takes so long?

你能为我们把鱼分一下吗？

Would you please separate the fish for us?

酱油 / 芥末酱 / 蒜和生姜

Soy sauce/mustard/garlic and ginger

还有一些汤，请问哪位客人需要添加？

There is still some soup left. Would anyone care for some?

第三步：教师给出示范案例，并予以示范。

Step 3: The teacher gives examples and demonstrates it.

■ **撤换菜肴**

（W：服务人员，G：客人）

（W: Waiter, G: Guest）

W：女士，这是您的蔬菜汤。

W: Here's your vegetable soup, madam.

G：我想我并没有点这道汤。

G: I don't think I ordered it.

W：我来确认一下……我想恐怕没错，女士。这是您点的汤。

W: Let me check... I'm afraid there is no mistake, madam. This is the soup you ordered.

G：好吧，我可以问一个问题吗？

G: All right. Can I ask a question?

W：当然，请说。

W: Sure. Please.

G：如果我不喜欢这道汤的口味，我可以换吗？

G: If I don't like the taste of this soup, can I change it?

W：恐怕不行。我们的菜品一经售出，概不退换。如果需要的话，您可以点其他的汤。

W: I'm afraid not. Once it's ordered and served, it can't be exchanged. But you can order another soup if you want.

G：好的。

G: That's all right.

W：实在抱歉。

W: I'm so sorry about that.

G：没关系的。谢谢你。

G: Don't worry. Thanks.

■ 不小心把茶洒在了客人身上

G：看看你都做了什么！

G：Look what you have done!

W：女士，实在不好意思。我立刻给您拿一块干净的布来。您是否被烫到了？

W: I'm so sorry, madam. I'll bring you a cloth right now. Have you been scalded?

G：没有，我还好。但是我的衣服脏了，而且我晚上有一个重要的约会。

G：No, I'm ok. But the suit is dirty, and I have an important appointment this evening.

W：我真的感到非常抱歉，请您相信我真的不是故意的。可以让我来给您整理一下吗？

W: I'm terribly sorry about it. Please believe me I didn't mean to do it. May I clean it up for you?

G：好的，大概需要多长时间？我如何取回我的衣服？

G: Ok, but how long will it take and how can I get my suit back?

W：女士，您不用担心，只需要30分钟。我们已经为您安排了一个房间，您可以在房间里等候直到您的衣服烘干。

W: Don't worry, madam. It only takes 30 minutes. We have arranged a room for you where you can wait until your suit is dry cleaned.

G：好的。

G: All right.

W：为您带来不便，我感到十分抱歉。

W: I'm very sorry for the inconvenience.

G：没关系的。

G: Never mind.

■ 询问客人是否需要服务

W：一切都满意吗？

W: Is everything all right here?

G：很好！谢谢。

G: Great! Thanks.

W：您需要再加些酒水吗？

W: Would you like me to refill your wine glass?

G：不用了，谢谢。这些已经够了。

G: No. Thank you. We're OK for now.

W：好的。如果您有任何需要的，尽管告诉我。

W: Good. If there is anything else needed just let me know.

第四步：以小组（5 人 1 组）为单位，其中，1 位学生扮演餐厅服务员威廉，另外 4 位学生扮演客人。根据情景设定，学生可进行不同突发情况的模拟练习（5 位学生轮流进行情景模拟）。

Step 4: In groups of 5, 1 student plays the role of the waiter William, and the other 4 students play the role of the guests. According to the scenario setting, students can carry out simulation exercises for different emergencies(5 students take turns to do the scenario simulation).

任务评价

表 7.1 中餐席间服务评价表

The Evaluation Form of Chinese Restaurant Table Service

评价内容 Evaluation Items	评价标准 Evaluation Standard	分值 Score	小组自评 Self-evaluation （20%）	小组互评 Peer-evaluation （30%）	教师评价 Teacher-evaluation （50%）	综合得分 Subtotal
上茶 Tea service	操作正确规范；仪态优雅。 Compliance with operational specifications; Elegant manners.	5				
毛巾服务 Small towel service	操作正确规范；仪态优雅。 Compliance with operational specifications; Elegant manners.	5				
点餐服务 Order service	操作正确规范；使用适当的服务语言。 Compliance with operational specifications; Use the appropriate service language.	5				
铺餐巾 Table napkin service	客人身后轻轻打开；正确放置到客人腿上。 Open behind the guest; Put on the right position.	5				

续前表

评价内容 Evaluation Items	评价标准 Evaluation Standard	分值 Score	小组自评 Self-evaluation (20%)	小组互评 Peer-evaluation (30%)	教师评价 Teacher-evaluation (50%)	综合得分 Subtotal
餐前小食和菜肴服务 Pre-meal snacks & food service	上餐前小食；上菜顺序明确；上菜动作正确；服务无噪音、不打扰客人；收撤餐具及时、准确；随时留意客人需求。Set up pre-meal snacks properly; The order of serving is clear; Serve correctly; No noise, do not disturb the guests; Timely and accurate collection and withdrawal of tableware; Keep an eye on guests' needs.	35				
酒水服务 Beverage service	斟倒酒水动作专业；斟添及时。Professional pouring action; Refill timely.	20				
撤台、服务餐后甜品和水果 Clear the table, serve dessert and fruits	操作正确规范；动作轻盈迅速。Compliance with operational specifications; Gentle and rapid action.	20				
团队精神 Teamwork	分工明确，团队协作。Clear division of labor and good teamwork.	5				
合计得分 Total						

评分标准（按 100 分制）：81～100 分为“优秀”；71～80 分为“良好”；60～70 分为“合格”；60 分以下为“不合格”。

Scoring Standards (On a scale of 100): 81–100 points as “Perfect”; 71–80 points as “Good”; 60–70 points as “Pass”; 60-below points as “Fail”.

拓展阅读

菜肴摆放原则

摆放菜肴是一门艺术，不宜随便乱放。服务员既可以根据宴会的性质、特点、目的来摆放菜肴，也可以根据客人的饮食习惯、爱好摆放菜肴，还可以根据菜肴的颜色、形状、菜种、盛盘及原材料等因素摆放。菜肴摆放原则如下：

1. 台面整齐美观

大型宴会或高档宴席中，在摆放大拼盘时，要注意其观赏面朝向主要宾客，其他围碟要注意颜色和荤素的搭配；要注意台面的造型美观，富有艺术性和观赏性。若餐桌上只有一盘菜，则应摆在餐桌的中间位置；两道菜可摆成“一”字形；三道菜应摆成“品”字状；四道菜应摆成菱形或四方形；五道菜应摆成梅花状；五道菜以上可摆成圆形。

2. 菜肴对称摆放法

菜肴还可根据其形状、颜色、种类等进行摆放。如鱼对虾、鸡对鸭等。同颜色、同形状、同菜种类应对称摆放在餐桌的上下或左右，一般不并排摆放在一起。同时，也应注意两盘之间的距离、口味、荤素等的搭配。

3. 便于观赏

菜肴的观赏面，也就是最适宜观赏的一面。通常，头菜的观赏面应对正主人位，其他菜的观赏面要朝向四周。同时，还应注意遵循“鸡不献头，鸭不献掌，鱼不献脊”的摆放规矩，即在上此类菜肴时，不要将鸡头、鸭掌、鱼脊朝向主宾，以示对主宾的尊重。

4. 尊重主宾

由于主宾是宴席的服务重点对象，因此应先考虑将每道菜肴摆放到主宾位置前，然后上下一道菜时再将其移到其他的位置。

5. 轻挪轻撤

摆放前应把宾客食用完的盘子撤走，或当菜盘中剩余 1/3 时，将大盘撤下换成小盘，再放回餐桌上。注意轻挪轻撤，不推盘、不拖盘。

任务二：西餐席间服务
Task 2: Western Restaurant Table Service

案例导入

某天早上，到餐厅用餐的客人特别多，服务员都在紧张地忙碌着。这时，餐厅走来了一对年老的夫妻，领位员将客人带到一张还没来得及收拾的餐桌前，跟客人说完“稍等一下，马上叫人收拾”后就离开了。客人等了半天，也不见有人过来收拾，老先生环视一周都找不到服务员，顿时非常恼火。

终于等来了服务员边致歉边收拾了餐桌，可是自始至终都没有人过来问这对夫妻是否需要茶或咖啡。老先生感觉这完全不符合高级酒店的餐厅服务水平，一气之下回到房间，打了酒店的投诉电话。

酒店收到投诉后，第一时间找到餐饮部核查相关情况，并带着果篮到客人房间表示了歉意，对客人给餐厅提出的意见表示感谢，并一再表示，餐厅会提升服务质量管理水平，避免此类情况再次发生。

你认为该餐厅应在哪些方面做出改进？

知识准备

西餐席间服务应包括的递送菜单、点叫酒水及菜品前面已经提及过了，在此就不再赘述。

Delivering the menu, ordering the beverage and the dishes which are included in western restaurant table service have been mentioned before, we will not repeat them again.

一、展口布 Opening napkin

（1）取下展示盘或餐桌上的口布，在客人右后方轻轻打开。

Remove the table napkin from the display plate or dining table and gently open it at the right rear of the guest.

（2）将展开的口布由外往内轻轻铺在客人腿上，注意手不要碰到客人的身体。

Spread the table napkin from the outside to the inside on the guest’s leg, avoiding touching the guest’s body.

（3）为客人展口布时，注意女士优先的原则。

Pay attention to the principle of “ladies first”.

二、供应冰水 Ice water service

（1）右手持水壶，左手拿一块折成方形的干净口布垫在壶下，从客人右侧斟倒，冰水一般斟至水杯 3/4 处即可。注意保持所有餐位水杯水位一致。

Hold the pot in the right hand, take a square towel pad with left hand and put it under the pot. Pour the ice water from the right side of the guest and fill the water to 3/4 of the glass. Pay attention to keep the water level of all table glasses consistent.

（2）倒水时不可拿起水杯。

Do not pick up the glass when pouring water.

（3）每服务完一位客人，应用干净的口布擦拭壶口，然后为下一位斟倒。

Wipe the spout with a clean cloth every time after using, then pour the water for the next guest.

（4）及时为客人添加冰水，一般看到客人水杯只剩 1/3 时需要添加。

Add ice water for guests in time. Generally, the water glass can not below 1/3 of the cup.

三、服务餐前饮品（开胃饮品）Pre-meal beverage (aperitifs)

（1）服务餐前饮品时，应使用托盘服务。

Tray service should be used during the pre-meal beverage service.

（2）服务顺序遵守女士优先原则，然后依顺时针依次服务即可。

The service order should follow the principle of “ladies first”, and then serve clockwise.

（3）当客人饮用完毕没有追加意愿时，应及时撤回酒杯。

When the guest has no additional intention to refill, the server should take the glass back in time.

四、调整餐具 Adjust the tableware

当客人完成点餐后，服务人员要根据客人所点餐食来调整餐桌上的餐酒具，看是否需要增加或撤换，并调整其排列情况，依照上菜的顺序，由内而外排列餐具。注意增减餐具时，动作要专业、语气要轻柔，避免打扰到客人。

When the guests have done with the order, the server should add or remove the tableware for the ordered wine and food, and adjust their arrangement according to the order of serving from inside to outside. Attention to present professional service with polite tone, and avoid disturbing the guests.

五、派送面包 Bread service

在服务开胃菜前，可先行为客人提供面包。为客人提供的面包要盛放在面包篮内，并保持相应的热度。

Bread can be served before appetizers. The bread provided to the guest should be placed in the bread basket with corresponding heat.

（1）派送面包时站在客人左侧服务，熟练使用服务叉、匙。

When doing the bread service, the server should stand on the left side of the guest and use the serving fork and spoon expertly.

（2）与面包搭配的黄油、果酱等也要一并上桌，共用的放在餐桌中央。

The butter, jam and those which are used with bread should be served together. The sharing items should be put on the middle of the table.

（3）面包是无限量供应，要依照客人意愿为客人不断补充。

Bread is unlimited and should be replenished according to the guest's wishes.

六、上开胃菜 Appetizers Service

开胃菜是西餐的第一道菜，也叫"头盘"，一般多是冷盘，以海鲜或者加工肉类为主，美式餐厅多以沙拉为主。

Appetizer is the first western dish which is also known as "the first dish". Generally, appetizers are cold dishes which are seafood or processed meat, but American restaurants prefer salad more.

（1）开胃菜可直接放置到展示盘上，若客人未点开胃菜，则可直接为客人上汤。

Appetizers can be placed directly on the display plate. If the guests haven't ordered appetizers, the server can serve guests soup directly.

（2）大盘开胃菜可直接用手端送，服务时站在客人右侧服务。

Appetizers which are placed in a large plate can be delivered directly by hand. The server should stand on the right side of the guest to do the service.

（3）若餐盘有标识，则应注意标识正面对准客人。

If the plate has a logo on the edge, the server should turn the logo to face the guest.

七、酒水服务 Beverage service

（1）酒水服务包括示酒、开瓶、试酒、倒酒等一系列服务，客人点完酒水后就可以进行酒水服务了。

Wine service includes bottle showing, opening, taste-testing, pouring and so on. Drinks can be served after the guests have done with the order.

（2）服务酒水时通常是先白酒再红酒；先淡酒再浓酒；先新酒再老酒；先喝不甜的酒再喝甜的酒。

Wine service should follow this rule: white wine first, then red wine; light wine first, then strong wine; new wine first, then old wine; dry-sweet wine first, then sweet wine.

（3）注意餐酒的搭配。

Pay attention to the collocation of wine and food.

酒水知识本书前面章节已经详细介绍，在这里不再赘述。

The previous parts of this book have described the knowledge of wine in detail, and it will not be repeated again in this section.

八、上汤 Soup service

（1）上汤时必须使用底盘，且底盘应与汤碗一起上桌，不允许出现分开服务的情况。

The soup bowl must be used with the chassis. Separating service will not been allowed.

（2）汤的温度一般很高，服务时务必小心，提醒客人"先生/女士，帮您上汤"，然后由客人右侧服务。

The temperature of soup is usually very high. The server needs to be careful and remind the guests that the soup is coming and serve it from the right side.

九、上主菜 The main course service

（1）服务人员上主菜之前，要先检查餐桌上的餐具是否齐全，随时为客人增补餐具。

Before serving the main course, the server needs to check if the tableware on the table is complete and prepare to add the tableware for the guest at any time.

（2）服务主菜时注意主菜、配菜摆放的位置及佐料添加的方式。

Put all the main course and side dishes on the right position.

（3）若此主菜允许客人用手拿取，注意为客人提供洗手盅，并向客人口头说明，以免客人误用。

If the main course needs the guest to take by hand, pay attention to provide the guest with a hand-washing cup and explain to the guest to avoid misusing.

（4）上完主菜后，立即进行佐餐酒服务。若是葡萄酒，则应按照葡萄酒的服务步骤进行服务。

After serving the main course, the server needs to do the wine service immediately. If the guest ordered wine, the server should serve in accordance with the wine service procedures.

十、清理桌面，服务餐后甜品、饮料 Clear up, serve the dessert and beverage

（1）主菜用完之后，收走餐桌上的餐具及酒杯。

After the guest is done with the main course, the server needs to take away the tableware on the table.

（2）将甜品叉放置到客人左手边，甜品匙放到客人右手边。

Place the dessert fork on the left hand side of the guest and the dessert spoon on the right hand side of the guest.

（3）根据客人所点甜品及时撤换相应餐具。例如：如果客人所叫甜品为冰激凌，不要把甜品叉放在桌上。

According to the desserts ordered by guests, the server needs to change the appropriate tableware timely. For example, if guests called ice cream for desserts, do not put dessert fork on the table.

（4）甜品送上后，询问客人何时上饮料。餐后饮料以红茶和咖啡为主。

After the dessert is served, the server needs to ask the guest when to serve the drink. The drinks after meal are mainly black tea and coffee.

（5）使用托盘服务咖啡和红茶。注意服务咖啡时，应先放置糖盅和奶盅，再端送热咖啡。

Use the tray to serve coffee and black tea. The server needs to put sugar cup and milk cup first and then serve the hot coffee.

（6）咖啡和茶的放置位置视客人情况而定。若客人已经享用完甜品，则可直接放置在餐位中间；若客人还在食用甜品，则可放置在客人的右手边。

The position of tea and coffee depends on the different guest's situation. If the guest has finished the dessert, the server can put the drink in front of the guest; if the guest is still eating the dessert, the server needs to put the drinks on the right hand side of the guest.

十一、服务餐后酒和雪茄 After-dinner wine and cigars

正式的西餐厅中，在服务完咖啡或红茶后，还会有餐后酒及雪茄服务。

A formal western restaurant will have after-dinner wine and cigar service after coffee or black tea.

（1）展示餐后酒车，询问主人是否餐后用些利口酒、白兰地或雪茄烟。

Show the wine truck and ask the host if he wants to taste liqueur, brandy or cigar.

（2）为客人斟倒利口酒或白兰地，并随后开列订单。

Pour liqueur or brandy for the guest and remind to make an order.

（3）如果客人点了雪茄烟，则要帮助客人点燃。

If the guest orders a cigar, the server needs to help the guest to light it.

在服务过程中，若客人吸烟，服务人员还应注意随时为客人更换烟灰缸，更换烟灰缸原则如下：

In the course of service, if the guest smokes, the server should also pay attention to replacing the ashtray for the guest at any time. The principles are as follows:

（1）左手托托盘，托盘上放置干净的烟灰缸。

Hold the tray with the left hand and place a clean ashtray on the tray.

（2）站于客人右边，用右手将干净的烟灰缸放在脏的烟灰缸上面。

Stand on the right side of the guest and place the clean ashtray on the dirty ashtray with right hand.

（3）同时拿起两个烟灰缸到托盘上，将干净的烟灰缸放回到台面上。

Take two ashtrays to the tray at the same time and put the clean ashtray back on the table.

任务实施

第一步：教师讲解西餐席间服务的相关知识，并做出演示。

Step 1: The teacher explains the relevant knowledge of the western table service and makes the demonstration.

第二步：教师导入本节情景设定：李先生打电话预订了一家高档西餐厅四人位（3 男 1 女）。随后李先生一行四人来到该餐厅用餐，服务人员为客人开口布、斟倒冰水，依次询问每位客人所需的开胃菜、汤、主菜、甜品及饮品，并做好记录，依据客人所点内容，进行西餐席间服务。

Step 2: The teacher introduces the settings of this section: Mr. Li reserved a table for four people (3 men and 1 woman) in an upscale western restaurant by phone. Then Mr. Li and his friends came to the restaurant to have dinner. The server opened the table napkin for the guests, prepared ice water, and asked each guest in turn what appetizers, soups, main courses, desserts and drinks were needed, which were all recorded. According to the contents ordered by the guests, the server provided perfect table service.

第三步：以小组（5 人 1 组）为单位，其中，1 位学生扮演餐厅服务员，另外 4 位学生扮演客人，分别模拟进行西餐席间服务（5 位学生轮流进行情景模拟）。

Step 3: Make the group (5 people per group) as the unit, in which 1 student acts as the waiter of the restaurant, the other 4 students play the role of the guest, and all of them simulates the service process (5 students should simulate the server in turn).

任务评价

表 7.2　西餐席间服务评价表

Evaluation Form of Western Restaurant Table Service

评价内容 Evaluation Items	评价标准 Evaluation Standard	分值 Score	小组自评 Self-evaluation（20%）	小组互评 Peer-evaluation（30%）	教师评价 Teacher-evaluation（50%）	综合得分 Subtotal
点餐服务 Order service	操作正确规范；用语标准。Correct operation and standard language.	5				
展口布 Table napkin service	在客人身后轻轻打开；正确放置到客人腿上。Open behind the guest; Put on the right position.	5				
菜肴服务 Food service	上菜顺序明确；上菜动作正确；服务无噪音、不打扰客人；收撤餐具及时、准确；随时留意客人需求。Clear serving order; Correct serving action; No noise, do not disturb the guests; Timely and accurate collection and withdrawal of tableware; Keep an eye on guests' needs.	35				
酒水服务 Beverage service	斟倒酒水动作专业；酒水斟倒量一致；酒水斟倒时机把握准确；及时补充客人杯中不足的水。Professional action; Equal pouring; Accurate timing; Refill guest's glass with water in time.	35				
餐后饮料 After-dinner wine	正确服务餐后饮料。Correct service of after-dinner wine.	15				
团队精神 Teamwork	分工明确，团队协作。Clear division of labor and good teamwork.	5				
合计得分 total						

评分标准（按 100 分制）：81～100 分为“优秀”；71～80 分为“良好”；60～70 分为“合格”；60 分以下为“不合格”。

Scoring Standards (On a scale of 100): 81–100 points as “Perfect”; 71–80 points as “Good”; 60–70 points as “Pass”; 60–below points as “Fail”.

拓展阅读

西餐服饰礼仪

吃西餐的时候，服饰也是一件十分重要的事情。正规的西餐厅中，如果客人衣衫不整，是不允许进入的。

西餐宴会的正式着装需要领结。这是西方社交场合在晚宴最正式的着装守则，也称为“full dress”“evening dress”或“full evening dress”。这种全套礼服一般在国宴、正式宴会等场合穿着。

男士着装：男士要穿黑色燕尾服、与燕尾服面料相同的长裤、纯白色衬衫、白色可折卸翼形领、白色领结、白色低领口马甲、黑色短袜、黑色宫廷鞋。

女士着装：女士要穿下摆及地的长裙。在最正式的初次社交舞会上，裙装常被要求为白色。

在半正式场合的着装要求如下：

男士着装：男士要穿晚礼服，即黑缎面前襟领子、白色衬衣、黑领结、黑腰带、黑袜子和黑色鞋子。

女士着装：女士要穿晚礼服，即长至脚踝或及膝的晚礼服、相配的小包和高跟鞋。

鸡尾酒会一般在下午4点到7点举行，要求半正式着装。

男士着装：男士要穿深色西装。

女士着装：女士穿短裙或套装，可搭配闪亮的首饰，也可搭配围巾。要穿高跟鞋，适当化浓妆。

Project 8

Handling Payment and Seeing off Guests

项目八

结账和送客服务

项目概述 PROJECT SUMMARY

结账是客人在餐厅用餐的最后环节，优质流畅的服务往往会给客人留下深刻的印象。在服务过程中，应有意识地通过观察、倾听等技巧了解客人的需求，与客人建立良好的关系。结账时，要规范、流畅地完成结账。客人离开时，与其道别。用寒暄礼仪向客人表示自己的敬意，以及乐于为对方提供服务。

项目目标 PROJECT OBJECTS

知识目标： 掌握结账和送客服务的基本流程；掌握结账和送客服务的基本表达。

技能目标： 掌握各种结账方式的操作流程；熟悉结账时突发事件的应急处理方式；提供超预期的服务品质。

素养目标： 具备服务意识、诚信意识与安全意识；爱岗敬业、具备团结合作、勇于创新的意识；遵纪守法、严守职业道德与职业规范；具有强烈的职业责任感。

任务一：结账服务概述
Task 1: Check-out Service Overview

案例导入

某天，张先生夫妇来到餐厅用餐。结账时，张先生发现账单上的菜名和他们吃的菜完全对不上，于是就问服务员是怎么回事，经过查实后，得知是服务员拿错了账单。虽然事情最后得到了妥善处理，但是客人再也没有来光顾这家餐厅。

思考讨论：该服务员的做法有哪些不妥之处？

知识准备

通常而言，上菜完毕后即可做结账准备。结账分为三个步骤，分别为结账准备、递送账单和处理付款。

Usually, the bill has to be prepared for the guests when all the dishes are set on the table. The procedures of handling payment consist of three parts: prepare the bill, deliver the bill and handling payment.

图 8.1　结账工作流程
The Procedures of Check-out Service

一、结账工作流程与服务标准 Procedures and standards of handling payment

（一）结账准备 Preparing the bill

（1）给客人上完菜后，餐厅服务员要到收银台核对账单。当客人要求结账时，请客人稍后，立即去收银台取账单。

After serving all the dishes, the waiter should check the bill at the cashier's desk and wait for the guests to check out.

（2）将账单放入账单夹内，并确保账单夹打开时，账单正面朝向客人，准备好结账用笔。

Put the bill into the check book (bill folder) with a pen, and make sure the front of the bill facing to the guest when it's opened up.

（二）递送账单 Deliver the bill

走到客人右侧，打开账单夹，右手持账单夹上端、左手托账单夹下端，递送至客人面前，请客人看账单。注意不要让其他客人看到，并说："先生 / 女士，这是您的账单，请您过目。"

Walk to the right side of the guest, open the bill folder, hold the bill with the right hand, hold the bottom of the bill with the left hand, and deliver it to the guest and say,"Excuse me, sir/madam. This is your bill, please." Pay attention not to show the bill to other guests.

（三）处理付款 Handling payment

从客人处接过现金或信用卡送至收银台，找零或还卡后礼貌致谢。

Receive cash or credit card from the guest and send it to the cashier. Give the changes or credit card back to the guest with polite thanks.

二、实用场景对话 Practical conversation

分开结账 Go Dutch

（W：服务人员，G：客人）

（W: Waiter, G: Guest）

G：打扰一下，我们已经吃完了。请把账单拿过来好吗？

G: Excuse me, we are finished here. Could you bring us the bill, please?

W：请稍等，我现在去拿。（过了一会儿）好的，这是您的账单。

W: Please wait a moment. (After a while) Here you are.

G：一共多少钱？

G: How much is it in all?

W：一共是 280 元，其中包含 10% 的服务费。

W: 280 yuan in all. It includes a 10% service charge.

G：好的。但是我们想要分开付账。你可以帮我们弄吗？

G: Fine. But we would like to pay separately. Would you take care of that?

W：没问题。嗯，我待会儿会把你们每个人的账单送过来。

W: No problem. Well, I'll bring separate bills in a minute.

G：好的。顺便说一下，我们把小费留在桌上就可以了吗？

G: Ok. By the way, should we just leave the tips on the table?

W：感谢您的关照，不过我们不收小费。

W：Thank you for your kindness, but we don't receive tips.

任务实施

第一步：教师设置场景，学生以小组为单位进行模拟练习。

Step 1：The teacher sets the scenario and the students practice in groups.

第二步：课堂展示成果，小组互评。

Step 2：The students simulate the situation on class and finish the peer-evaluation.

第三步：教师总结服务过程中的要点。

Step 3：The teacher sums up the key points in service.

任务评价

表 8.1　结账服务课堂展示评价表

The Evaluation Form of Check-out Service Presentation

模块 Module	内容 Content	达标情况（是 / 否） Achieved (Yes/No)
结账准备 Preparing the bill	给客人上完菜后，餐厅服务员要到收银台核对账单。 After serving all the dishes, the waiter should check the bill at the cashier's desk and wait for guest to check out.	
	将账单放入账单夹内，并确保账单夹打开时，账单正面朝向客人，准备好结账用笔。 Put the bill into the check book (bill folder) with a pen, and make sure the front of the bill facing to the guest.	
递送账单 Delivering the bill	走到客人右侧，打开账单夹，右手持账单夹上端、左手托账单夹下端，递送至客人面前。 Walk to the right side of the guest, open the bill folder, hold the bill with the right hand and hold the bottom of the bill with the left hand.	
	将账单呈送给客人并说："先生 / 女士，这是您的账单，请您过目。" Deliver the bill to the guest and say,"Excuse me, sir/madam. This is your bill, please."	
处理付款 Handling payment	从客人处双手接过收现金或信用卡送至收银台。 Receive cash or credit card from the guest with both hands and send it to the cashier.	
	找零或还卡后向客人礼貌致谢。 Give the changes or credit card back to the guest.	

评价标准：完成内容 90% 及以上为"优秀"，80% 以上为"良好"，70% 以上为"中等"，60% 以上为"合格"。

Scoring Standards: Mark "Perfect" when 90% of the contents are completed; Mark "Good" when 80% of the contents are completed; Mark "Medium" when 70% of the contents are completed; Mark "Pass" when 60% of the contents are completed.

任务二：结账方式

Task 2: Payment Methods

案例导入

小李是一家本地中档酒店中餐厅的服务员，今天晚餐时他服务了一桌来自美国的游客。两位客人非常有礼貌，小李为他们推荐了好几样特色菜，客人非常满意。但在结账环节出现了一点小问题：客人来自美国，他们习惯用刷卡的方式结账，但当客人拿出美国运通卡时，由于这个酒店不接纳此卡，且小李也未见过此卡，因此小李很抱歉地告知客人酒店不接受此卡，并请客人换其他的卡付款。客人同意，并给了他一张维萨卡。但小李在刷卡的时候，POS 机又出现了故障，导致一直刷不出来。10 分钟过去了，客人还是未等到小李回来，便有些不耐烦了，走到前台去询问，得知本餐厅的 POS 机故障，小李只能去酒店其他餐厅刷卡，所以耽误了这么长时间。当小李着急地跑回来，将刷好的卡和单据交到客人手上，并解释自己为什么耽误这么长的时间时，客人却依然带着不悦的心情离开了餐厅。小李这时也露出很无奈的表情。

思考讨论：当结账出现问题时，如何与客人沟通解释？

知识准备

一、常见的付款方式 Common methods of payment

目前，常见的付款方式主要有现金结账、信用卡结账、签单结账、手机 App 结账和支票结账等。

Currently, cash, credit card, bill, mobile payment Apps and check are popular payment methods among customers.

（一）现金结账 By cash

（1）客人付现金时，服务员要礼貌地在餐桌旁当面点清钱款，请客人稍候；将账单及现金送给收银员后，核对找回的零钱及账单上联是否正确。

The waiter should check the cash in front of the guest before sending it to the cashier. Ask the guest to wait a moment. Double check whether the number of change and the bill are correct.

（2）服务员将账单上联和所找零钱、发票夹在账单夹内，返回客人右侧，打开账单夹，递送给客人。

The waiter should attach the bill with the changes and the invoice. When returning to the guest, open the bill folder and present it from the right side of the guest.

（3）如果客人要求去收银台结账，应礼貌地引领客人到收银台。

If the guest insists to check out at the front desk in person, lead the guest to the cashier politely.

（二）信用卡结账 By credit card

（1）首先确认是否是本餐厅接纳的信用卡，然后请客人稍候，并将信用卡和账单送至收银处。

First of all, confirm whether the restaurant accepts the category of the credit card. If yes, send it with the bill to the cashier and ask the guest to wait for a moment politely.

（2）服务员检查无误后将收据、账单及信用卡夹在账单夹内，交还给客人，请客人在账单和信用卡收据上签字，并检查签字是否与信用卡上一致。

Double check the amount and make sure it is correct on the receipt and bill. Put them into the bill folder with the credit card and present them to the guest. Remind the guest to check and sign the name on the bill and credit card receipt. Check if the signature is consistent with the credit card.

（3）将账单第一页、信用卡收据、客人联及信用卡递还给客人，并将其余票据及存根送回收银台。

Return the first page of the bill, the guest stub of the credit card receipt and the credit card. Send the remaining bills and stubs back to the cashier.

（三）签单结账 Charged the bill to the room account

这一方式适用于：住店客人、与酒店签订合同的单位、酒店高层管理人员及酒店的VIP客人等。

This method is appropriate for the guests who live in the hotel, have contract with the restaurant, or the senior managers and the VIPs of the restaurant.

（1）如果是住店客人，礼貌地要求客人出示房卡。

For hotel guests, ask them to show their room cards politely.

（2）递上笔，示意客人写清房号。

Deliver the pen, and ask the guests to write down the room number.

（3）与前台确认房间是否有余额，如有，呈上账单请客人签账；如余额不足或用尽，向客人说明情况并请客人更改付款方式。

Check with the hostess to make sure the account balance is enough to cover the bill. If yes, present the bill to the guests and ask them to sign. Otherwise, tactically state the fact and ask them to change the way of payment.

（4）客人签好账单后，将账单放入账单夹内，迅速将账单送交至收银处，查询客人的名字与房号是否相符。

After the bill is signed, put it into folder, send it to the cashier quickly and check if the guest's name is the same as the registered.

（5）确认信息准确无误后，真诚地感谢客人光临。

After the information is confirmed, sincerely thank the guests' presence.

（四）手机 App 结账 By mobile App

指导客人用手机打开支付宝或微信等 App，扫描本店的二维码进行付款。

Guide the guests to use Alipay or WeChat with scaning the QR code to process payment.

（五）支票结账 By check

这一方式适用于：大企业、大公司的订餐或大型宴会、旅游团队用餐。

This methed is appropriate for big companies, grand banquets or tourist groups.

（1）如客人使用支票结账，应礼貌地请客人出示身份证或工作证及支票，然后将账单及支票、证件同时交给收银员。

If guests would like to pay the bill by check, ask them to show their ID card or employee's card with the check politely, and send them together with the bill to the cashier.

（2）收款员办理结账手续，填写支票，记录证件号及联系电话。

The cashier goes through the procedures including filling the check, recording the certificate number (ID or employee's card) and their telephone number.

（3）服务员核对后，将账单第一联、支票存根、证件、发票一齐送还给客人，并真诚地感谢客人。

Double check the item and the amount, send the first page of the bill, the check stub, the certificate and the invoice back to the guest. Sincerely thank him/her for his/her presence.

二、实用表达 Useful expression

（一）询问结账方式 Enquiry of payment

（1）请把账单给我。/ 请结账。

Can I have the bill, please?/Let me have the bill, please./Bring me the bill, please./May I have the bill, please?/The bill, please./Bring me the check, please.

（2）请问您打算用什么方式结账？

How would you like to pay the meal?/How would you like to make the payment?/How would you like to settle the bill?

（3）用现金、信用卡、旅行支票、计入房账。

Pay in cash./By credit card./By traveler's checks./Charge it to my room.

（4）请问是分开结账还是一起结账？

Would you like to pay together or separately?/Separate bills or one for all?/A check for each or a check for all?/Will these be on a separate check?/One bill or separate bills?

（5）AA 制。

A Dutch treat./Go Dutch.

（6）您的账目要细分吗？

Would you like a breakdown of the bill?

（7）您可以付现金，或者用信用卡、支票支付，或者计入房账。

You may either pay in cash, with credit card, check or charge it to your room.

（8）我想用信用卡代替现金付款。

I'd like to pay by credit card instead of in cash.

（9）您接受外币吗？

Do you accept foreign currency?

（二）找零 The change

（1）这是找回的零钱，先生。感谢您的光临。

Here is your change, sir. Thank you for coming.

（2）这是您的收据和找回的零钱。

Here is your receipt and change.

（3）这些零钱给你了。

Keep the change, please.

（4）我们很乐意为您服务，但我们不能接受小费。

We are happy to serve you, but we do not accept tips.

任务实施

第一步：教师导入本节情景设定：王先生和朋友在酒店用完餐，用信用卡结账，刷卡时服务员发现信用卡额度不足，此时他该怎么处理？请考虑多种结果，并使用英文为王先生提供结账服务。

Step 1: The teacher introduces the settings of this section: Mr. Wang finished his meal with his friends and was ready to pay the bill with credit card. In handling the payment, the waiter found it's not enough to balance the account. What would you do if you were the waiter? Think of more than one solution and use proper language to perform the service.

第二步：教师列出结账用到的相关英文词汇、短语或句型，以供学生参考。

Step 2: The teacher lists related vocabularies, phrases or sentence patterns in English for students' reference.

- 请问用什么方式结账？
- How would you like to settle the bill?
- 用现金 / 信用卡 / 旅行支票 / 计入房账。
- Pay in cash./By credit card./By traveler's checks./Charge it to my room.
- 这是您的收据。谢谢光临。
- Here is your receipt. Thank you for coming.

第三步：教师给出示范案例，并予以示范。

Step 3: The teacher gives cases and demonstrates it.

（W：服务人员，G：客人）

（W: Waiter, G: Guest）

G：服务员！

G: Excuse me, please!

W：是的，先生。您还有别的需要吗？

W: Yes, sir. Do you want something else?

G：没有了，请帮我结账。

G: No. Bring me the check, please.

W：好的，请稍等。先生，这是您的账单。您想用什么方式结账？

W: Ok, please wait for a moment. Here is your bill, sir. How would you like to make the payment?

G：刷卡。（拿出信用卡）

G: By credit card.(Take out the card)

W：（接过信用卡）好的，先生，请稍等。（离开到收银台）

W: (Accept the card) Yes, sir. Just a minute. (Leave to the cashier)

W：（送回卡片，走到客人身边轻声说）不好意思先生，卡里余额不足，您要换一张卡片还是改成其他方式结账？

W: (Return the credit card and go back to the guest, speak gently) Excuse me, sir. The balance is not enough. Would you like to change another card or pay by other methods?

G：（拿出另一张卡片）换这张试试。

G: (Take out another card) Try this one, please.

W：好的，谢谢。（折回座位）先生，办好了。这是您的收据，请收好。

W: Ok, thank you.(Walk back to the seat) It's all done, sir Here is your receipt, please keep it well.

第四步：以小组（3 人 1 组）为单位，其中 1 位学生扮演服务员，另外 2 位学生扮演结账客人，模拟结账环节的情景。

Step 4: Three students form a group, in which one student plays the waiter, the other two act as the guests. Simulate the situation with proper English.

任务评价

表 8.2 结账方式演示评价表

The Evaluation Form of Payment Service Presentation

评价内容 Evaluation Items	评价标准 Evaluation Standard	分值 Score	小组自评 Self-evaluation (20%)	小组互评 Peer-evaluation (30%)	教师评价 Teacher-evaluation (50%)	综合得分 Subtotal
服务流程 Service procedures	内容真实还原，情节完整。The content conforms to the reality; The plots are complete with details.	30				
服务礼仪 Service courtesy	服务礼仪符合情景，用语规范、表述正确。Meet the requirement of the service courtesy with standard language and correct expression.	40				
团队精神 Team spirit	分工明确，团队协作。Clear division with cooperation.	30				
合计得分 Total						

评分标准（按 100 分制）：81～100 分为“优秀”；71～80 分为“良好”；60～70 分为“合格”；60 分以下为“不合格”。

Scoring Standards (On a scale of 100): 81–100 points as “Perfect”; 71–80 points as “Good”; 60–70 points as “Pass”; 60–below points as “Fail”.

任务三：突发事件处理

Task 3: Dealing with Accidents

案例导入

一次，某公司需要宴请几位客户吃饭，秘书小王陪同老板和客户一同到一家高档餐厅就餐。老板是个美食家，也是那家餐厅的常客，因此无须服务员多作介绍，餐厅便很快安排了一桌丰盛的菜品和酒水。

席间，服务员态度热情，菜色丰盛可口，加上老板频频劝酒，客人非常尽兴，一笔不小的订单马上确定下来。即将结束时，小王准备结账，并把优惠卡交给服务员。不一会儿，餐厅经理拿着账单进来。"各位先生小姐菜品还好吗？"经理笑着向大家打招呼。"好，好！"客人高兴地回答。寒暄之后，经理退到小王身边，指着账单金额并轻声说："王小姐您好，请付这个数。"小王快速地查看了账单，核对无误后按照账单上的金额刷卡结账，并提醒经理开具发票。

这时，客户突然问小王："这顿饭花了多少钱？"小王一下子不知道该怎么回答才好，便看向老板。此时老板的脸色也沉了下来，气氛一下子凝重起来。经理一见马上将话题引开："各位，我是餐厅的经理，这是我的名片，请各位多指教，欢迎以后多来。"经理一边说着一边将名片递给各位客人。气氛渐渐好转，经理才礼貌地出去。事后，小王忙向餐厅经理表示感谢，并将以后的商务宴请都定在了这家酒店。

案例中的经理如何巧妙地化险为夷，并将常客转化成了酒店的忠实顾客？

知识准备

一、突发事件处理 Dealing with accidents

酒店员工可能碰到的问题会因客人而异。不管是什么样的情况，服务是首要任务。许多情况没有现成或明确的解决方法，此时酒店员工便要利用判断、专业和创造力。如果不确定如何处理，应该果断寻求同事的协助。

The problems that hotel staff may encounter will vary from guest to guest. Whatever the situation is, the quality service should be the priority. As accidents may occur without existing reference, a well-trained staff will try to solve the problem with wisdom, professional tactics and creativity. If you are not sure about the situation, do not hesitate to ask your colleague for help.

（一）客人对账单持有疑义 Enquiries on the bill

客人在点单时，有时会看错价格，在结账时对金额有疑义。此时，服务员应拿来菜单请客人核对，并认真、耐心地向客人解释菜单。

Misunderstanding of the bill may occur because the guests slip the line when making the order. Check the menu and bill, and patiently explain the items to the guests.

若责任在服务员，则应立即调整，向客人道歉并说明情况，做出适当优惠或补偿，获得客人谅解后再结账。

In some cases, the waiter is responsible for the mistake. Apologize to the guests and make certain concessions on the account or compensate the guests with something else such as coupons. Offer the guests with a satisfied solution.

（二）留意跑单情形 Watch out for the guests leaving without paying

餐厅中的逃账现象偶有发生，须格外注意以下几种情况，预防此类事件发生：

Occasionally, guests may leave without paying the bill. Watch out for the following situations to prevent it from happening:

（1）单独就餐的初访客人借口上厕所或接电话趁机溜走。

Single dinner who comes to the restaurant for the first time may leave with an excuse of going to the toilet or answering the phone.

（2）挑选最贵的菜点的客人需要引起重视。一般来说，公司宴请有一定经费限额，点菜时会注意均衡点几个名贵菜肴配以普通菜肴较为常见。

Pay special attention to the table with expensive orderings. Normally, as there is a budget for cooperate entertaining, the host may order dishes with treasurable cuisines along with common dishes to balance the expense.

（3）一桌客人席间分别以各种理由离席且未再返回。

Watch out for the table where the guests leave successively with different reasons and never come back.

二、常见中英文表达 Common expressions in Chinese and English

（一）核实及解释账单 Check and explain the bill

（1）让您久等了，布朗先生。这是您的账单。您需要核对一下吗？

Thank you for waiting, Mr. Brown. Here is your bill. Would you like to check it?

（2）那比我预料中的要超出许多呢。

That's much more than I expected.

（3）需要我解释一些项目吗？

Shall I explain some items for you?

（4）总共多少钱？

How much is the total?

（5）你能给我一个折扣吗？

Can you give me a discount?

（6）服务费怎么算呢？

How about the service charge?

（7）可以给我开张发票吗？

May I have an invoice?

（8）当然可以，先生。请问贵公司名称是什么？

Certainly, sir. May I know the name of your company?

（9）请问所有的费用都包含在里面了吗？

Does it include all the expenses?

（10）您的账单包含 10% 的税和 10% 的服务费。

Your bill includes a 10% tax and a 10% service charge.

（11）很抱歉，折扣卡和赠券不能同时使用。

I'm sorry, discount cards and coupons cannot be used at the same time.

（12）我们有一些赠券送给您，下次您在我们餐厅用餐时可以使用。请留意使用说明和有效期。

Here are some coupons for you. You can pay with them next time if you have dinner in our restaurant. Please pay attention to the instructions and expiry date.

（二）其他 Others

（1）100 元 4 份饮料，包括 8% 的服务费。

100 yuan for four drinks which includes 8% service charge.

（2）酒吧里不收座位费。

There is no cover charge for seats at the bar.

（3）这是我们的最低消费。

That's our minimum charge.

（4）我能复印一下您的卡吗？

May I make a copy of your card?

（5）对不起，根据酒店政策我们不接受个人支票。

I'm sorry, but we don't accept personal checks according to the hotel policy.

（6）我们接受美元，但只能用人民币找零。

We accept US dollars, but we only have RMB for change.

（7）我很遗憾地告诉您这张钱是假币。

I regret to tell you that this bill is a forged one.

（8）5 岁以下的儿童有折扣。

There is a discount for children under 5 years old.

（9）真对不起，收银员把您邻桌的账记到您的账单上了。

I'm awfully sorry. The cashier miscalculated the bill by adding the bill of other table to yours.

（10）劳驾到收银台付账。

Please pay at the cashier on your way out.

（11）其中一份啤酒应该从您的账单中扣除。

One of the beers should have been deducted from your bill.

任务实施

第一步：教师导入本节情景设定，安娜和朋友在酒店用完餐准备结账。检查账单时，发现一条鱼的价格和菜单上标得不一致。服务员向其解释，安娜确认没有问题之后，拿出折扣卡和赠券以及现金结账，并要求开具发票。服务员向其解释，折扣卡和赠券不能同时使用。最后安娜用折扣卡和现金结了账。

Step 1: The teacher introduces the settings of this section: Anna and her friend finished their meal and were ready to pay. When they checked the bill, Anna found the price of the fish was different from that on the menu. After the waiter explained the menu, Anna took out her discount card and coupons and wanted to pay in cash. She also asked for the receipt. Because the hotel claimed that discount card and coupons couldnot be used at the same time, Anna chose the discount card and settled the bill with cash.

第二步：教师列出突发事件及其解决方法的相关英文词汇、短语或句型，以供学生参考。

Step 2: The teacher lists related vocabularies, phrases or sentence patterns in English for students' reference.

- 需要我解释一些项目吗？
- Shall I explain some items for you?
- 很抱歉，折扣卡和赠券不能同时使用。
- I'm sorry, discount cards and coupons cannot be used at the same time.
- 加上 8% 的服务费，一共是 1 200 元。
- It's 1,200 yuan in total with a 8% service charge.

● 我们有一些券送给您，下次您在我们餐厅用餐时可以使用。请留意使用说明和有效期。

● Here are some coupons for you. You can pay with them next time if you have dinner in our restaurant. Please pay attention to the instructions and expiry date.

第三步：教师给出示范案例，并予以示范。

Step 3: The teacher gives cases and demonstrates it.

（W：服务人员，A：安娜）

（W: Waiter，A：Anna）

A：你好，请帮我结账。

A: Excuse me, how much is the total?

W：好的，一共是 1 200 元。

W: Yes. It's 1,200 yuan in total.

A：咦，菜单上鱼是 100 元，怎么在这里是 280 元？

A: Really? It's 100 yuan for the fish on the menu, why it turns to 280 yuan on the bill?

W：（拿来菜单）女士，菜单上的鱼是论斤标价，100 元是一斤的价格，这条鱼的重量是两斤八两。

W: (Bring the menu) Madam, the fish is priced by weight on the menu, and 100 yuan is for 0.5kg. The fish you ordered is 1.4kg.

A：哦，是这样。你们应该标注得清楚一些。

A: I see. You should highlight it to make it more clear.

W：好的，我们会把您的意见反馈给部门的，谢谢您。您怎么结账呢？

W: Ok, we will give your comments back to the department. Thank you very much. How would you like to pay the bill?

A：现金吧，还有折扣卡和赠券，一起用了。

A: In cash with the discount card and coupons.

W：不好意思，女士，折扣卡和赠券不能同时使用。建议您用折扣卡，优惠力度更大一些。

W: I'm so sorry that the discount card and the coupons cannot be used at the same time. I suggest you use the card which has more discount.

A：好的，麻烦了，再帮我开一张发票。

A: Yes, please. And please give me an invoice.

W：好的，请问贵公司的名称和税号是什么？

W: No problem. May I have the name and VAT number of your company, please?

A: ××公司，税号 123456789。

A: It's ×× Company, and the VAT number is 123456789.

W:（拿笔记录）好的，请稍后。（结账回来）女士，您好，这是您的找零和发票，请收好。您需要停车票吗？

W: (Record) Please wait for a moment. (Come back after the payment.) Madam, this is your receipt and change. Please keep it well. Do you need the parking coupons?

A: 两张，谢谢。（起身准备离开）

A: Two, please.(Ready to leave)

W:（递上停车票）请慢走，欢迎下次光临。

W: (Deliver the parking coupons) Please watch your step, hope to see you again.

第四步：以小组（3 人 1 组）为单位，其中 1 位学生扮演服务员，另外 2 位学生扮演结账客人，模拟结账环节的情景。

Step 4: Three students form a group, in which one student plays the waiter, the other two act as the customers. Simulate the situation.

任务评价

表 8.3　突发事件处理模拟演示评价表

The Evaluation Form of "Dealing with Accidents" Presentation

评价内容 Evaluation Items	评价标准 Evaluation Standard	分值 Score	小组自评 Self-evaluation (20%)	小组互评 Peer-evaluation (30%)	教师评价 Teacher-evaluation (50%)	综合得分 Subtotal
服务流程 Service procedures	内容真实还原，情节完整。The content conforms to the reality; The plots are complete with details.	35				
服务礼仪 Service courtesy	服务礼仪符合情景，用语规范、表述正确。Meet the requirement of the service courtesy with standard language and correct expression.	35				
团队精神 Team spirit	分工明确，团队协作。Clear division with cooperation.	30				
合计得分 Total						

评分标准（按 100 分制）：81～100 分为"优秀"；71～80 分为"良好"；60～70 分为"合格"；60 分以下为"不合格"。

Scoring Standards (On a scale of 100): 81–100 points as "Perfect"; 71–80 points as "Good"; 60–70 points as "Pass"; 60-below points as "Fail".

任务四：送客致意

Task 4: See off guests

案例导入

朱先生一家来餐厅用餐。朱先生的奶奶因为年事已高，所以需要坐在轮椅上以方便行动。一家人用餐完毕结账后，服务员小王主动提供停车券。一行人准备离开时，小王将一家人引至电梯口，替他们按好电梯，向他们问候、告别并目送他们离开。朱先生一家满意而归。

思考讨论：是哪些服务细节感动了客人？

知识准备

当客人离开时，感谢至关重要。送客致意往往容易被忽视，却是客人对餐厅最后印象的总结。餐厅工作人员留心观察客人的需要，在恰当的时间提供恰当的服务，为客人提供超出预期的服务，会给客人带来惊喜。

It's crucial to show our appreciation when the guests leave the restaurant, which is usually ignored, but will leave a full stop for the journey and the impression may last. An experienced waiter will observe guests' need to offer service in a proper time which will surprise their guests.

一、送客人离开餐厅服务流程及规范 Procedures and standard of seeing off guests

（一）送别客人 See off guests

（1）客人起身时，服务员须主动为客人搬开座椅，并按先宾后主、女士优先的原则。

When the guests finish their meal and are ready to leave, move the chairs for them under the principle of "guests first" and "ladies first".

（2）提醒客人带好随身物品，环顾四周再次确认。

Remind the guests to take their belongings. Look around to make sure no private stuff is left.

（3）礼貌地向客人道别，感谢客人的光临，送客人至餐厅门口。

Bid farewell to guests with courtesy and see them off to the doorstep of the restaurant.

（4）如客人乘坐电梯，服务员应为客人叫梯，送客人进入电梯后，目送客人离开。

Call the lift for the guests if the restaurant is on the upper floor. See them off until the door is closed.

（二）整理台面 Clean the table

（1）客人离开餐厅后，服务员须检查台面上下有无客人遗忘的物品。

After the guests have gone, check if they leave their belongings behind.

（2）撤下台面上的餐具等用品。

Change used tableware and replace them with the new ones.

（3）铺换新台布，重新摆台并调整座椅。

Change the tablecloth, set the table, and adjust the setting of chairs.

二、实用表达 Useful expressions

（1）请带好您的随身物品。Please don't leave anything behind.

（2）请注意脚下。Please mind/watch your step.

（3）请当心。Please be careful.

（4）再见，谢谢您的光临。Thank you for coming, goodbye.

（5）再见，期待再次见到您。Goodbye, hope to see you again.

（6）一路平安！ Have a nice trip!

（7）祝您旅途愉快！ Wish you a pleasant journey!

任务实施

第一步：教师导入本节情景设定：张先生一家在餐厅用完餐后，服务员小王向其道别并送其离开。

Step 1: The teacher introduces the settings of this section: After Mr. Zhang's families finished their dinner, the waiter Xiaowang saw them off.

第二步：教师列出相关英文词汇、短语或句型，以供学生参考。

Step 2: The teacher lists related vocabularies, phrases or sentence patterns in English for students' reference.

- 请带好您的随身物品。
- Please take care of your belongings.
- 请注意脚下。
- Please mind/watch your step.
- 再见，欢迎您再次光临。
- Goodbye and welcome again./Thank you for coming, and hope to see you again.

第三步：教师给出示范案例，并予以示范。

Step 3: The teacher gives cases and demonstrates it.

（张先生一家起身准备离开）

(Mr. Zhang and his families were ready to leave.)

小王：请带好您的随身物品（环视一周查看是否有遗漏物品）。

Xiaowang: Please take care of your belongings (Look arount to check if there is anything left).

小王：（引客人至餐厅出口电梯处）请注意脚下。

Xiaowang: (Lead the guests to the lift) Please watch your step.

小王：（替客人按好电梯，客人进入后站在门口）欢迎您再次光临（目送客人离开）。

Xiaowang: (Help the guest press the button of the lift, stand at the door after the guests walk into the lift) Thank you for coming, hope to see you again (See them off).

第四步：以小组（3 人 1 组）为单位，其中 1 位学生扮演服务员，另外 2 位学生扮演结账客人，模拟结账环节的情景。

Step 4: Three students form a group, in which one student plays the waiter, the other two act as the. Simulate the situation.

任务评价

表 8.4　送客致意模拟演示评价表

The Evaluation Form of "See off guests" Presentation

评价内容 Evaluation Items	评价标准 Evaluation Standard	分值 Score	小组自评 Self-evaluation（20%）	小组互评 Peer-evaluation（30%）	教师评价 Teacher-evaluation（50%）	综合得分 Subtotal
服务流程 Service procedures	内容真实还原，情节完整。The content conforms to the reality; The plots are complete with details.	30				
服务礼仪 Service courtesy	服务礼仪符合情景，用语规范、表述正确。Meet the requirement of the service courtesy with standard language and correct expression.	40				
团队精神 Team spirit	分工明确，团队协作。Clear division with cooperation.	30				
合计得分 Total						

评分标准（按 100 分制）：81～100 分为"优秀"；71～80 分为"良好"；60～70 分为"合格"；60 分以下为"不合格"。

Scoring Standards (On a scale of 100): 81–100 points as "Perfect"; 71–80 points as "Good"; 60–70 points as "Pass"; 60-below points as "Fail".

知识拓展

结账时的注意事项

（1）凡有涂改或不洁的结账单，不可呈递给客人。

（2）结账单送上后，若未付款，千万留意防止客人逃账。

（3）付款时零钱当面给客人点清，对于外籍客人，不妨用加法算账找钱。

（4）钞票上附有细菌，取拿后，手指不可接触眼睛、口及食物。

（5）结账付款方式：有现金支付、签单、使用支票或信用卡支付等方式，由于手续的不同，其风险性需要注意。

（6）付外币时，应将兑换率、消费金额详列，并使用兑换水单填写后，请客人签名并填写护照号码。

（7）酒店餐厅对住店客人的签账，需请其出示房卡证明，登记房号并核对住客名单后，将账单递送给住客签字，然后转入酒店前台结账。

（8）服务费与小费在性质上是不同的：服务费是按照固定的百分比计算，通常在账单内列入；而小费是客人对服务员提供的劳务而随意给予的报酬。

参考文献
References

［1］魏晓楠，陈丽宇．中餐服务与管理［M］．杭州：浙江大学出版社，2016.

［2］殷安全，刘容．中餐服务［M］．重庆：重庆大学出版社，2014.

［3］孟森．中餐服务（双语）［M］．北京：北京师范大学出版社，2014.

［4］滕悦然．餐饮服务常用英语口语大全［M］．北京：化学工业出版社，2017.

［5］童霞，丁峰，王慧勤．中餐服务职业能力综合实训［M］．北京：机械工业出版社，2015.

［6］张波．中餐服务与督导培训全攻略［M］．北京：化学工业出版社，2015.

［7］吴澎．中国饮食文化［M］．北京：化学工业出版社，2014.

［8］李勇平．餐饮服务与管理［M］．大连：东北财经大学出版社，2018.

［9］李晓红．酒店英语综合教程［M］．北京：中国人民大学出版社，2017.

［10］浩瀚，钟乐平．酒店饭店英语口语［M］．大连：大连理工大学出版社，2011.

［11］李洪涛．酒店英语口语［M］．大连：大连理工大学出版社，2012.

［12］钱嘉颖，吴云．酒店英语口译［M］．上海：上海交通大学出版社，2016.

［13］余超．饭店英语［M］．杭州：浙江大学出版社，2016.

［14］袁露，阮蓓，李飞．酒店英语［M］．天津：天津大学出版社，2010.

［15］杨六兰．酒店英语实训指南［M］．武汉：武汉大学出版社，2016.

［16］陈蔚．旅游与酒店英语口语［M］．大连：大连理工大学出版社，2011.

［17］王淑媛、夏文媛．餐饮服务技术［M］．台北：龙腾文化事业公司，1998.

［18］郑佳欣，林香君等．餐饮服务理论与技巧［M］．台中：华格那出版有限公司，2011.

［19］陈尧帝．餐饮服务培训教材［M］．沈阳：辽宁科学技术出版社，2001.

［20］郭敏文，樊平．餐饮服务与管理［M］．北京：高等教育出版社，2001.

［21］广东省中等职业学校教材编写委员会．餐饮服务［M］．广州：广东科技出版社，2008.

［22］姜文宏，王焕宁．餐饮服务技能综合实训［M］．北京：高等教育出版社，2004.

［23］劳动和社会保障部中国就业培训技术指导中心．餐厅服务员［M］．北京：中国劳动社会保障出版社，2002.

［24］牛志文．中、西餐厅服务员职业技能培训［M］．北京：电子工业出版社，2008.

［25］毛慎琦．餐饮服务技能实训［M］．北京：机械工业出版社，2008.

［26］单慧芳，李艳．餐饮服务与管理［M］．北京：电子工业出版社，2009.

［27］姜玲，贺湘辉．中餐服务员工作手册［M］．广州：广东经济出版社，2007.

［28］郭剑英．餐饮服务［M］．长沙：湖南科学技术出版社，2005.

［29］Graham Brown，Karon Hepner，Alan Deegan. Introduction to food and beverage service［M］.London：Blackwell Scientific Publications,1994.